ALIEN HORRORS

TIM CURRAN

WEIRD
HOUSE

Text © 2022 by Tim Curran

"Flypaper," "The Killing Jar," and "Stowaway," are original to this collection.
"The Black Ocean" originally appeared in *Burning Sky* #5,
Thievin' Kitty Publications, 2000
"Heatseeker" originally appeared in *Weirdbook* #44, Wildside Press, 2021
"Dead Planet" originally appeared in *Burning Sky* #6, Thievin' Kitty Publications, 2000
"Migration" originally appeared in *Dead Planets, Unhallowed Stars,* Dark Tree Press, 2003
"The City of Frozen Shadows" originally appeared in *Burning Sky* #10,
Thievin' Kitty Publications, 2001
"Ghost Ship" originally appeared in *Burning Sky* #7, Thievin' Kitty Publications, 2000
"Graveyard" originally appeared in *Allen K's Inhuman Magazine* #2,
A Die, Monster, Die Publication, 2004
"No Life on Mars" originally appeared in *Outer Darkness* #30, Dennis Kirk, 2004
"Charnel World" originally appeared in *Black Satellite* #5, Dark Tree Press, 2003

ISBN: 978-1-957121-13-0
Interior and cover design by Cyrusfiction Productions

Cover art (c) 2022 by K. L. Turner

Editor and Publisher, Joe Morey

Weird House Press
Central Point, OR 97502
www.weirdhousepress.com

TABLE OF CONTENTS

THE BLACK OCEAN

I t was a warm, wet world known as Q-23. The Aldebaran sun shone down hotly on its steaming seas, turning its hothouse air into mist and cloying dampness. After the asteroid knocked out the star drive and seized up the magnetic core, the Polaris was looking for a place to set down. It chose Q-23.

That was a mistake.

"No land," Cameron said. "Not so much as a fucking rock to stand on."

And there wasn't.

Q-23 was also called Manny's Planet for Robert Manny, the astrophysicist and celestial cartographer who'd originally mapped it out during a brief flyover twenty years before. Manny's charts revealed that Q-23 was dotted by numerous landmasses ranging from mere metric inches to thousands of square kilometers in surface area.

But Manny was wrong.

There was no land on Q-23. Just huge floating masses of yellow-green seaweed that must've confused or misled his probes and sensory instrumentation. Things like that had happened before. The Polaris came in fast on a quick computer trajectory. The computer, of course, had only selected a suitable landing zone based on Manny's charts. It scanned the area, found the landmass indicated by Manny's coordinates and set the ship down.

One minute, the crew of the *Polaris* were all groggy from six weeks in hyperspace, the next they were down on Q-23.

Where the ship sank like a brick.

There were three of them, besides the captain, three facing a big, brave new world.

"I can't believe," said Sandersen, the engineer, "that there's no land here. I mean, there's gotta be something, don't you think? This place is made of rock like every other and somewhere there's gotta be a piece of it sticking up out of this...this soup."

"You would think so, wouldn't you?" Spivey said.

Captain Warwick was silent. He'd been silent since they'd clamored up from the stagnant depths, everyone crying out and splashing around in circles until they found the life raft bobbing gently in the waves. He wasn't a man given to strong emotion. He calmly accepted things as they came.

"What do you think, Skipper?" Spivey said. "You think there's land here?"

Warwick sucked in air through his teeth. "Plenty of it under the water. But above it? I don't know. If it's here, we'll find it sooner or later."

"Sure, sooner or later," Cameron said. "I like that. In the meantime, we drift around while our food and water runs out, dozens of light years from home."

"Maybe they'll come for us," Spivey said, always brimming with youthful hope and enthusiasm. When you hadn't yet seen twenty-one, you just couldn't accept death.

"Sure they will, kid," Cameron said, wiping beads of sweat from his face. "Sure they will."

But they all knew better.

There was a war on and a Class-C freighter with a belly of iridium and silver ore wasn't of primary concern to the Agency. Not when you had crippled warships screaming out distress calls from every quadrant. Merchant vessels were not a high priority.

Still, they went through the motions. The raft was equipped with survival gear, food and water for sixteen days. It also had a high-frequency subspace light transmitter. They were sending distress pulses every fifteen minutes. But even if they were received, the chances of rescue were slim.

"It'll take a week for the SOS to get through," Cameron said dismally. "And even if it does and they mount a rescue the same day they get it, they won't make it out this far for six weeks. Six fucking weeks, gentlemen. And by then...by then we'll all be—"

"That'll do," Warwick said. "I think we're all aware of the straits we're in here."

"Yeah, knock it off," Sandersen said.

He was clenching his hands into fists just to keep them from shaking. He didn't like shit like this. The natural world was too full of unknowns, imponderables, crazy random events. You couldn't count on anything, expect nothing but the unexpected. This was why he liked machines. They always did what they were told to do, acted within a controllable framework. And when they didn't, they could be fixed. But out here in nature, on this godforsaken hellhole, things just happened and they were beyond control. By the time you saw what was wrong, you were usually dead or damn close to it.

He would've killed for some good whiskey. Or bad, for that matter.

"There's lots of water, anyway," Spivey said, sheepishly, never knowing if he was saying the right thing or not. You never could tell with Cameron. He lived to insult people.

And this time was no exception. "Water?" he said, laughing dryly. "You call this water, you dumb pup?" He reached out and scooped up a handful of it. It was pale green in color, full of sediment and runny slime.

"Maybe it can be purified," Spivey said. "Maybe."

Cameron laughed again. "Fucking soup, that's what it is."

No one argued with that.

No doubt the ocean of Q-23 was water-based (they didn't know yet, it hadn't been tested with the EnviroKit), but it was like no water they'd seen before. Thick, swampy, more liquid than solid but not much more. A foul steam rose off it, filling the damp air with an awful, decayed stink. It created a hazy, cloistral yellow mist that engulfed everything. Visibility was down to less than ten yards at best.

The raft drifted slowly, very slowly. The sluggish, plasma-like content of the sea was brushed by very few currents and no wind whatsoever. Waves were minimal and nearly nonexistent. The surface was veined with rotting creepers and scraggly floating plants, clots of red algae, jellied clumps of seaweed. It looked almost like you could walk across it.

"Our choices are few," Warwick said. "We're stuck here and we're going to have to make the best of it. We'll keep sending out distress calls, but we're to proceed as if they haven't been heard. We have to find some dry land or die trying. Sandersen, get out the scope and start scanning. Cameron get out the kit and test the water. Spivey, you and me will start unpacking some of this gear."

Finally, everyone had something to do.

Sandersen went about happily setting up the scope and checking relays. Cameron got out the EnviroKit and sucked up some water. Warwick and Spivey unpacked tarps, sleeping bags, food, water, medical supplies and survival gear. It was good for everyone to have a purpose. Better than brooding about death. Even Cameron wasn't grumbling too much.

An hour later, everyone was reclined on their sleeping bags. It was far too hot to actually slip into the bags which were good to sixty below. The heat was suffocating. It seemed like the air was made of the same stuff as the water. It was so moist it made your lips wet just breathing.

Sandersen was not resting. His eyes were fixed on the blue screen of the scope. By making numerous adjustments and readings he was able to distinguish between water and floating islands of weeds. He even discovered a shelf of rock only three feet below the surface. But that dropped away into the abyss quickly enough. He was in his element with electronic devices.

"Skipper," he said breathlessly, "I got something."

"Land?"

Everyone was breathless now.

"Yes. Yes, I think so. Not big. About a hundred and fifty meters long, thirty in diameter."

Everyone was watching the screen. They could see it. A long, lozenge-shaped streak of dark blue. And as they watched, it suddenly disappeared.

"What the hell?" Sandersen said.

It was gone...just gone.

"Must be the machine," Spivey said.

"There's nothing wrong with it," Sandersen contended, checking meters and connections. "It's working."

"Can't be," Warwick said. "Land does not appear, and then disappear."

Cameron laughed with a high, unpleasant tittering sound. "Must've been a mirage. Probably was never there to begin with. That thing's just a piece of junk; goddamn toys."

Sandersen clenched his teeth. "Bullshit. This scope's fine. I recalibrated it myself."

Warwick raised a bushy eyebrow. "Explanation?"

All eyes were on him now. Sandersen licked his lips, choosing his words carefully. "Some sort of strange atmospheric anomaly maybe. Either that or the landmass just sank. Take your pick."

"Maybe it was a whale," Cameron said. "Maybe it dove beneath the surface."

Although it was meant as a stupid joke, the possibility of what he was saying hit them all. A living thing. A huge living thing out there, somewhere, rising and diving at will. It was not a comforting thought when you were in a life raft.

"That big," Spivey said. "Something that big?"

"Is that possible?" Warwick asked.

Sandersen wiped rivers of sweat from his face. He gobbled a few salt tablets to regulate his water. "Yeah, sure. This thing isn't made to differentiate between organic and non-organic like the one on the ship."

Spivey looked suddenly very pale, very old. He crawled away and laid on his bag, closing his eyes very tightly. He did not want to hear anymore.

"Maybe it's a shark," Cameron said. "Some big hungry shark swimming through the murk."

Warwick narrowed his eyes. "That'll do, mister."

Suddenly, the blip appeared again, then disappeared. It kept doing so at random intervals. But each time, it was closer.

No one was speaking now. The idea that it was a landmass had been forgotten. Land masses did not dive in and out of the water.

Sandersen's fingers were trembling at the controls of the scope. Spivey was still laid out on his bag, curled up now in a fetal position. His lips were moving silently. The others watched the screen. Illuminated by the soft blue glow of the scope, their faces were sweaty and strained. The world was silent as if it was holding its breath.

"One kilometer and closing," Sandersen said. "It's bearing down on us, Skipper. It's coming *right* at us."

"We've got to get out of here," Spivey said in an awful, screeching voice. It was a voice of mental strain, prolonged hardship. A voice that should not belong to a twenty-year old. The mind that directed it was cracking around the edges, coming apart. "WE'VE GOT TO GET THE FUCK OUT OF HERE!"

"All right, Spivey," Warwick said, trying to sound fatherly and comforting, though he had no children and had never even held a baby. "Take it easy. There's nothing to get excited about here."

That met with a sarcastic chuckle from Cameron.

"Five-hundred meters," Sandersen droned, more machine than human now.

"Well, Skipper?" Cameron said. "What are we gonna do? Are we gonna just fucking sit here while that thing gets closer and closer or are we gonna do something? I don't know about you, but I sure as hell didn't join the service to be a hot lunch."

Warwick said nothing. He was still vainly clinging to the idea that this was no beast, no alien predator stalking them. But, deep down, he knew better. He'd been with the Agency for twenty years. And if that experience had impressed nothing else upon him it was the fact that life existed just about anywhere, under any circumstances. And life survived by consuming other life.

"Well?" Cameron screamed. "You're the fucking captain here, Warwick! Give us a command! Do something for chrissake! IT'S GETTING CLOSER AND WE HAVE TO GET THE FUCK OUT OF HERE!"

"Shut up, you fool, or I swear to God I'll feed you to that thing personally," Warwick said, showing about as much emotion as anyone had ever seen from him. He duck-walked over to the survival gear. He took out a flare gun and a blue pistol with a short, blunt barrel. A pulser.

"You gonna blast it, Captain? You gonna blast it?" Spivey asked.

"Two-hundred meters," Sandersen mumbled.

"All right, let's get this thing out of here," Warwick said.

The raft canopy was unzipped, oars passed out. There was a small electric outboard, but it was of no use—the props would get clogged in the muck before they got a dozen yards. Cameron and Spivey sunk their oars into the water and started paddling. It went much easier than anyone imagined. Though the water was a semi-fluidic slush clogged with rotting organic matter, its very composition gave the oars easy purchase. Rather than rowing through the mire, they were actually pushing the raft through it, the rubberized bottom sliding easily over the colloidal surface.

"Seventy-five meters," Sandersen said. "It...it's changing course. It's compensating. It's turning as we move. It's seeking us out."

"Shit," Cameron said, rowing madly now, his breath coming in ragged gasps, sweat rolling down his face.

Warwick put a cartridge in the Pulser and got ready. He took up the flare gun with his other hand. The planet wasn't exactly dark nor exactly light. The heavy, congealing mists made it murky, stygian almost. Very little sunlight penetrated the cloudy atmosphere and what did was filtered by the mist.

"Thirty meters," Sandersen said. "Should be visual soon. Should be able to—"

And then they all heard it. *Slop, slop, slop.* An awful sloshing, squishing sound like an elephant stumbling through a swamp. Warwick clenched his teeth and fired a flare in the direction of the noise. There was a blinding, yellow-white explosion of phosphorus and the mists flared with flickering, eerie light. They heard the splashing sounds and glimpsed something shiny and wet like gray neoprene slithering down into the water.

"Oh my Christ," Sandersen said.

They rowed with renewed frenzy, but it was no good. The oozing waters were alive now as some huge, nightmarish body moved around and beneath them sending fingers of undulating currents in every direction.

"Come on you bastard," Warwick growled. "Show yourself."

Sandersen was crouched before the Scope, his jaw sprung, a trickle of drool on his chin. Cameron was rowing and rowing and they were beginning to spin in circles now as Spivy had simply given up. He was rolled up in a ball, whimpering.

"Coward!" Cameron wailed. *"Fucking baby pussy sissy mama's boy faggot you're gonna get us all fucking killed!"*

At that particular moment, there was movement beneath the raft. A horrible, sluicing eruption of primal force and the raft was lifted from the slime and dropped back down again. Someone screamed. Someone else yelled. A voice begged God for mercy.

There was a colossal explosion of viscid water and the beast showed itself. It came up from the marshy depths like a rocket, a surge of gray, quivering flesh in the shape of a gigantic worm. It exuded a cloudburst of pink slime that rained down in globs.

And as quickly as it had shown itself, it dove back down, leaving a stink of carrion and decaying mud behind. The raft heaved and rolled in its wake. Everyone was tossed asunder.

Warwick never even got off a shot.

He steadied himself as it came again, tried to get a clear shot as bodies scrambled about him and voices screamed and cried and shouted. It shot out of the muck again and this time everyone got a good look at the business end of the thing. Its snout was eyeless and conical, a mouth opening wider and wider like a train tunnel.

Warwick shouted something unintelligible and squeezed off a shot with the pulser. A burning column of red slit through a segment of the beast with a hissing squeal, vaporizing flesh and black blood in an acrid smoke.

"Got to get out of here!" Spivey bawled mindlessly. "I've got to get out of here! OUT OF HERE!"

Before anyone could stop him, he threw himself overboard and into the black, seething ocean. For one crazy moment, he looked utterly ridiculous as he floated on the muck on his back, his legs and arms bicycling madly. Then he broke through the film and went down. He came back up, gagging, his face black with sludge.

Warwick reached out to him. "Give me your hand! Spivey! Your hand!"

But there was no time.

The worm came again and grabbed Spivey, diving into the abyss.

There was another massive splash and the remaining crewmen were inundated with rotting muck and weeds. Then there was silence. For maybe five, ten seconds, the amount of time it takes the human mind to reorient itself to a fresh slate of horrors. About twenty yards distant, Spivey came back, bobbing up and down as if something was tugging at him from below, his face dead and yellow. He bobbed up a final time and tipped over.

There was nothing beneath his waist but red confetti.

The beast came up again, from beneath the raft. Everything and everyone in it was sent airborne and then into the rippling miasma. The remaining crewmen came up, clawing weeds and silt from their faces. The worm circled them with great fluidic speed, creating a whirlpool that spun them around and around. Then it went for the raft, engulfing it and disappearing.

The whirlpool dissipated, the three survivors left treading water.

"Maybe it just wanted the raft," Sandersen panted.

Warwick shook water from his face. "Could be. When I shot it, maybe it thought the raft had attacked it."

Cameron laughed with a short, sharp bark. "We fucked with it, so it fucked back." He laughed again. "Imagine that, will ya? I guess there's only one question left now."

Sandersen and Warwick looked at him.

"How long do you think we can tread water?"

But they never put it to the acid test because the sea around them began to move and thrash with rippling currents, conflicting waves lifted them up and dropped them into the troughs between.

"Oh Christ," Warwick said as the whirlpool rose up again, whirling them around, making them bob up and down. And then the yawning gargantuan mouth of the worm opened beneath them like a black, fathomless gulf, sucking them into darkness.

After a time, the sea settled down. And much later, a single boot floated to the surface. But nothing else.

HEATSEEKER

1

The screaming brought them.

They came running through the narrow passages in their green terrain suits—Wells, Sarrasin, and Gill—kicking up clouds of pink Martian dust. Screaming wasn't something you heard much in the immense, dead desolation of Mars, but once you heard it, you would never forget it.

Bouncing through winding corridors in low gravity, trying to stay on their feet, they climbed over hoses and bumped their helmets on pipes and tripped over heaps of rubble. This was the reality of subsurface mining on an alien world: weird gravity and crowding.

The screaming echoed through their headsets, shrill and deranged, the agonized sound of an animal being tortured to death. By the time they reached #4 Compressor Shack, it had stopped.

And the silence that followed was somehow worse.

Like hearing footsteps coming at you in a dark, empty house, then hearing nothing.

They stopped running once they entered the high cavern where the shack and maintenance sheds were housed.

Sarrasin was the first one into the shack. "Dientz!" he cried out, his voice modulated through both internal and external speakers. "Dientz! Royer! Jesus Christ, where the hell are you guys?"

"Out here," Gill said. "Out here."

Dientz was over near the entrance to an intake shaft, crouching there, rocking back and forth on his heels, gloved fists pressed to the bubble of his helmet. His face looked yellow and slack. His shiny green insulated jumpsuit was spattered with something dark as if he'd been sprayed with ink.

"Dientz!" Sarrasin said as he raced over there. "Where's Royer? What the hell gives—"

But then he saw the same thing that made Gill and Wells turn away.

Royer was right there by Dientz.

Sarrasin could see fragments of his terrain suit, except now it was shredded and torn, dipped in red.

"Oh, Jesus," he said.

That about covered it. Royer looked like about 200 pounds of red, well-marbled meat that had been caught in an ice auger, sucked in and spit out the other end. He was splashed over the walls of the cavern and down the intake shaft a good ten feet. Bits of him hung like stalactites from the roof overhead, fifteen feet up. Like some kind of sick joke, one of his boots was dangling from a lip of rock above...a knob of bone spilling a red icicle.

Sarrasin wanted to be sick, but he didn't dare.

He just kept looking at the remains, amazed at how most of Royer's anatomy was still connected, spread out maybe twenty feet, but still connected. Some of him was in the shaft, some of him was hanging from the cavern wall, and some of him was spilled underfoot, yet linked by muscle and tendon and nerve ganglia as if he'd been full of springs and had exploded. One of his hands, still in its glove, twitched once or twice and went still. His blood was everywhere, crystallized in the subzero temperatures like rubies.

Deintz got to his feet and nearly fell over. "I heard him scream...I came running out...then he hit me, Royer fucking hit me..."

Gill grabbed him by the arm. "Hit you with what? What the hell do you mean?"

Deintz kept shaking his head inside his helmet. "I was hit *with* him. I saw a big shadow...something huge, something fast jumping around...and then Royer...oh Christ, Royer...he...what was left of him...*slammed into me...*"

They got it then, all of them, though they didn't understand a thing.

Deintz stumbled about in a tight little circle, moving from Sarrasin to Gill to Wells and they each in turn backed away from him. Maybe it was what he was splattered with and maybe it was something else. He began to sob, then to gasp. He went down to his knees and frantically tried to pop the plastic bubble of his helmet, which would expose him to the frigid, poisonous atmosphere.

Sarrasin and Gill took hold of him so he couldn't break the seal. The atmospheric pressure of the red planet would have boiled away the moisture in his sinuses, eyes, mouth, and lungs...if the massive decompression didn't kill him first.

His lunch came out in a steaming gush, splattering the inside of his face bubble with vomit. He gagged and coughed, making choking sounds.

"Goddamn idiot," Gill said, her mouth pulled into a scowl.

They took him back into the shack and sealed the airlock, decompressed. Then they all took their helmets off, helped Dientz clean up.

It took some time for him to come out of it and when he did, he just kept looking at them with wide, glazed eyes like he was drunk. But he wasn't drunk.

Wells kept shaking his head. He looked over at Sarrasin. "What was he trying to do, boss? You puke in your helmet for chrissake, you never take that bubble off. Was he trying to kill himself or what?"

Gill said, "Maybe you saw what he saw, you'd wanna kill yourself, too."

2

Fifteen minutes later, sipping a mug of hot coffee, Dientz started to talk. "It was like I said...just a blur, a big shadow or something. Whatever it was, it was already finished with Royer by the time I got there. It wasn't my fault. It wasn't any of it my fault. There wasn't anything I could do."

"Course not," Gill told him, but it almost sounded like she didn't mean it.

"What did you see?" Sarrasin asked. "Just take your time. You were in the shack, you heard that screaming on your set, you got suited up and went through the airlock...what then?"

"Just like I said," Dientz told them. "Just that blur, a shadow or something sliding around and then he slammed into me, Royer slammed into me, knocked me flat. Next thing I know, he's...well, he was all like you saw. Then you guys were there."

Wells and Gill looked at each other.

"That's it?" Sarrasin said.

"That's it."

Sarrasin didn't like it. He believed every word Dientz told him. Something had happened, something terrible, but as to what that really was, who could say? Royer had been slaughtered. But how and by what?

"You quit looking at me like that, Wells," Dientz said.

"Like what?"

"Like what, he says. You been looking at me like that ever since we got into the shack, since I came around. I know what you're thinking, I know what's going on in that mind of yours, but you listen to me, you sonofabitch, there wasn't anything I could do. It wasn't my fault."

"Never said it was."

"You telling me you're not thinking it?" Dientz set his coffee down. There was something in his eyes. Before it had been fear, shock, and revulsion. Now it was murder. "Royer was my friend. Not like you. He was good, he was decent. He cared about people. He wasn't an asshole like you, always saying shit behind peoples' backs."

Wells turned away. "Oh, shut the hell up."

"All right," Sarrasin said. "Everyone just settle down."

Gill wasn't saying anything; she was just watching.

Dientz pounded a fist on the table. "It's not me, boss, it's Wells. That dirty sonofabitch. He's acting like I killed Royer. Like I'd do something like that."

"Well, did you?" Wells put to him, then shook his head. "No, I'm figuring something came out of the tunnels and went after Royer. And you just pissed your pants and let it happen, scared shitless."

"Fuck you!"

Dientz was small, but wiry, and he launched himself right at Wells. And Wells was grinning, waiting for it. But Sarrasin and Gill got in between them, breaking them apart like a couple mouthy drunks ready to go at it over a football game.

"Knock it off! Both of you!" Sarrasin shouted. "We can't afford this candyass shit! There's too much on the line here! Now both of you act your fucking ages because I'm not in the mood for this crap. We got a dead man out there and I wanna find out how he died. They'll be back to pick us up in two days and I want some answers by then. You people with me on that? Good. Because you start in again and I'll crack both your heads together."

He meant what he was saying and they all knew it. Nobody said anything for a time.

"Get suited up," Sarrasin told them. "We're going back out there."

He figured it was the best thing for all considered. In here, in the normal gravity, those two could make mincemeat of each other, but out in the low gravity, they couldn't do much but dance around. The terrain suits they all wore were weighted to compensate for the low Martian gravity. You could move around fine in them, do anything you could on Earth, but if you tried running or fighting, anything really physical, you'd just bounce around comically. You could grab a 200-pound man and toss him fifteen feet, but he'd just bounce. You couldn't really hurt him. There was no impact, just a lot of silly bouncing and hopping.

Suits and helmets on, they moved into the airlock, crowded shoulder to shoulder.

"You can wait in here if you want," Sarrasin told Dientz.

"No way," he said. "I'm going with you."

"Well, try not to piss yourself," Wells said.

"What did I tell you?" Sarrasin said to him.

The atmosphere in the airlock decompressed with a hiss and they stepped out into the cavern. Though nobody really wanted to, they went over to the body. They were all glad they couldn't smell through the helmets, because they'd gotten a good whiff of Dientz's suit in the shack and all that blood had smelled raw and savage. Just plain bad.

"You sure you saw something?" Sarrasin said. "A shape?"

Dientz shrugged. "I think so…I don't know. It happened too fast."

Sarrasin just sighed. "Could have been just about anything. Maybe Royer hit some kind of weird gas, maybe there was an explosion."

It sounded weak and nobody was buying it, not even Sarrasin himself. But he was in charge here, he had to keep everyone's head level. He had to feed them bullshit even if he knew it was an out and out lie. Because the idea of a monster running around down in the shafts, well, that wouldn't do at all.

"Explosion," Wells said, laughing dryly in his throat. "I like that. That's good. Take a long look at Royce, boss, weren't no explosion that did this. Look at that trauma, will ya? Look at those wounds...looks like somebody took a goddamn scythe after him."

Everybody was thinking it, but nobody was saying it, so Gill did. She said it in a whisper, but they all heard her. "Heatseeker," she said.

Sarrasin just shook his head. "C'mon, Gill, that's an urban legend. There is no such thing. Just talk."

"What about that crew they found in Sarvis Valley?" Wells pointed out. "They were gutted like this."

"Stop that," Sarrasin said.

But Wells shook his head. "Not about to, boss. Not now. Something got those men. You know it, I know it. The Company knows it. Only no one wants to talk about it."

Sarvis Valley was three klicks over the next rise, topside, and everyone there knew it.

"That business was all eighteen years ago. There was no evidence then and there's none now. Use your head." Sarrasin had been waiting for this. Oh yes. It was only a matter of time. "Just drop it. Last thing we need here, people, are ghost stories."

Mars was full of them.

You hung around the edges of the colonies or the far-flung outposts, you could hear stories that would turn your hair white, make you afraid to step outside at night. There were tales of Martian ghosts prowling the deserts, dead intelligences that could possess a man and make him kill himself. Crazy shit about dead Martian cities full of monsters and entire colonies that had vanished, things that scratched at your door in the dead of night and ancient voices that would call you to your death like sirens. The Heatseeker was just another one, a story passed around from the early days of exploration. The favorite Martian boogeyman. Anytime somebody went missing, the Heatseeker was resurrected.

But Wells was not pacified. "I'm thinking the Heatseeker ain't a ghost, boss. But something else. Something...something with big goddamned claws. And it's hunting us."

"Knock it off. You're acting like a kid afraid of the dark."

"I am afraid, boss."

And what could Sarrasin say to that?

"That's all bullshit, right?" Dientz said like he needed to believe it.

"Sure it is. No evidence whatsoever."

Gill motioned them towards a down of pink sand across the way. It was illuminated by her exterior LEDs. "How's this for evidence? It fit the bill?"

Pressed down in the soft sand was a grotesque print. Several of them, in fact. They were diamond-shaped, about five inches from tip to tip, with four smaller indentations spaced evenly around them. Like some sort of weird alien foot had been set down, one with spurs coming off it.

Gill said, "What leaves a track like that?"

"I know," Wells said. "It's some of that weird gas."

Sarrasin ignored him, studying the print. He was thinking maybe something had been set down there—a lot of somethings, because there were quite a few prints—but deep in the barren wastes of his soul, he knew better.

This was it.

This was the spoor of the beast.

The Heatseeker.

3

The real crazy thing was, it should have been a milk run.

The sort of thing they could have done with their eyes closed. Sarrasin and the others formed part of a large maintenance crew that bopped around the extensive, endless canyon system of the Tharsis Bulge performing general upkeep on a string of propellant factories and subsurface ore refineries, all completely automated. These installations were vital to man's existence on the Red Planet. The factories processed propellant from the raw carbon dioxide of the Martian atmosphere which was used to power the outgoing spacecraft for the long flights back to Earth. The refineries refined iron ore on-site to be used in composite metals for building, construction, just about anything. Everything was metal on Mars. With the lack of free oxygen in the atmosphere, nothing corroded.

So that was the deal. Sarrasin's team had been dropped off at the Rift Valley Refinery for a few days' work. The hovercraft would pick them up in 48 hours. All they had to do was make their checks, charge the batteries, blow out the lines, the usual.

And now this.

Royer was dead, slaughtered, and everyone was getting panicky. The four survivors were alone, hopelessly alone. The nearest colony was New Providence, some 500 kilometers to the east. Sarrasin could have called for an early pick-up, but that would've been a big deal. The hovercraft ran on tight, inflexible schedules like everything on Mars. If one of them had to divert a few hundred miles, it would mean some outpost wouldn't get their supplies or their relief team. There would be hell to pay and the bureaucracy would see to it that Sarrasin was never in charge of anything more challenging than a broom until he went back home in sixteen months.

But either way there was going to be hell to pay.

For there was something down in the mines with them.

Something that liked to kill.

4

"I can't stand this place," Dientz said as they stood watch just outside the maintenance conduit to Level #3 Substation. "I hate it here. I hate this whole goddamn place."

Gill just sighed. "Settle down, will ya? They'll be back to pick us up tomorrow afternoon. Just hang tight."

"I don't mean these mines, Gill. I mean this whole fucking planet. I hate it here. I just hate it. I hate the cold and these goddamned helmets. I hate the dust storms and the emptiness…I hate it all." He stood there in his terrain suit, peering around in his helmet with beady, watching eyes. "I grew up in Bayonne, you know? Goddamned New Jersey. I thought Bayonne was a shithole. But you know what? Bayonne's like fucking Palm Beach compared to this place."

Gill just shrugged, didn't bother arguing the point.

Sure, Mars was a hellhole. It was barren and desolate and goddamn spooky. But people kept making the trip same way they'd once kept making the trip to the Old West back on Earth. Why? Space, freedom, a new start…and money. Yeah, there was big money to be made on Mars. The mining companies were making a fortune and they needed everyone they could get. So in the last three decades since the early manned expeditions, colonies had sprouted up quicker than mushrooms after a rain—New Philadelphia and New Chicago, New Atlanta and New Baltimore, New London and New Hamburg. Dozens and dozens of colonies, manned mining camps and automated installations, research outposts and you name it.

People came to Mars because they could make as much money in a year or two as they could make in a lifetime back home.

That's why Gill was there.

That's why they were all there, except for the labcoat johnnies and bugheads who actually liked Mars.

It had been nearly twelve hours now since Royer's death. Sarrasin didn't want to call for an early pick-up and Wells was riding him hard about that. Sarrasin had called it all into the Company and they agreed with him—wait it out. Not good. On the other hand, Sarrasin *had* issued particle blasters to everyone so at least they could defend themselves. That and a lot of amphetamines, enough to keep them all wired until pick-up came.

Dientz kept pacing around, kicking up dust. Now and then he'd stop dead, listen, then shake his head. "No, nothing. I thought I heard… never mind," he'd say, driving Gill nuts with the repetition of it all.

Gill was with him because Sarrasin didn't like the idea of Dientz and Wells being around each other, especially when they were carrying blasters. So they were down here on #3 at the substation which powered most of the levels and Sarrasin was with Wells up on #2, going through the motions of maintaining ore crunchers. When that was done with, Sarrasin said, they could all hide out in the shack until the hovercraft got there.

Dientz said, "You think the Heatseeker is real, Gill? You think there is such a thing?"

"You tell me," she said. "You saw what took Royce. Not me."

"I…I don't know what I saw."

Gill aimed her blaster down the conduit shaft, the halogen light fixed to it lighting up the tunnel for forty feet. "Maybe there's a Heatseeker and maybe not. I don't know. Something got Royer, though."

"No life on Mars," Dientz said.

That's what they always said before man got there. No life on Mars. Of course, that was bullshit. There weren't any little green men stalking around, of course, but there was life. In the early days of exploration, hydrobot ice corers had drilled through the ice caps and found huge lakes beneath them, lakes warmed by geothermal energy. The water was full of microbes and protozoa, things like primitive sponges, echinoderms, and bryozoa, not much else. Down deep in the natural limestone caves, lots of weird toadstools and fungi were found growing, colonial organisms like jellyfish living in streams polluted by methane and sulfur dioxides.

So there was life, just not any large terrestrial forms.

But the fossil record of the red planet was very rich. At one time, the surface had been teeming with life. There had been extensive river systems and floodplains that fed lush plant life, supported a variety of Martian invertebrates—flatworms and gastropods, mollusks and bizarre moss animals. An incredible variety of arthropods: creatures like crabs and spiders, beetles and pillbugs, locusts almost as large as dogs.

But they were all long gone.

And none of them had been as large as what Dientz had claimed to have seen...or glimpsed. There were ruined cities in the desert, but no remains or evidence of who or what had built them. The most recent had been abandoned at least 30,000 years, if not much longer. The general consensus was that they were built by some great extraterrestrial civilization that had seeded much of this part of the galaxy during Earth's prehistory and then died off.

So, no Martians.

No intelligent Martians.

Nothing smart and nothing large enough to tear a man apart. So what then? What had gotten Royer? Was it the mythical Heatseeker that was rumored to be a surviving Martian predator from a long-dead race? Or was it something else? A remnant of what built those cities? Some nightmare still defending its turf?

It was really hard to say.

Mars was a place of secrets and it would take centuries of looking before every spook from every moldering casket was dragged out and every skeleton was shaken out of every closet.

"You believe any of that stuff about those colonies that vanished?" Dientz asked. "You hear lots of things about that. Down south they were, I heard."

"Who knows?" Gill said.

She knew about them, of course, as did everyone. The one you heard most about was a place called New Salem—appropriately named—where some 200 members of an early research team just up and vanished. New Salem carried the same connotation in Mars folklore as the *Mary Celeste* or the Roanoke Colony in Virginia did back on Earth. Twenty-seven years ago, it was. Back then, it took almost six months to make the hop out to Mars and this with a gravity assist. When New Salem hadn't been heard from in three months, a rescue mission was sent and they found nothing, just a lot of empty domes and buildings, but no people. Whatever had happened, legend said, it happened fast because it looked like everyone had just stepped out… food on tables, beds slept in, nothing missing or moved. Through the years New Salem had become the focus of ghost stories and conspiracy theories. It was located down in the Southern Highlands, but there wasn't anything within a thousand miles of it these days. And maybe that said something about the truth of that matter.

"Yeah, those mining companies, they own everything and everyone," Dientz said. "Anytime something weird happens, they cover it up. Hey, you ever hear about that wrecked ship they found in the ice up north? Well, it wasn't one of ours. About as close to a flying saucer as you could—"

"Shut up," Gill told him.

"What?"

She grabbed his shoulder. "*Listen.*"

They stood there shivering in their suits, trying not to breathe or make a sound, just listening over their external mics. For a moment there was nothing and Dientz was all set to get back to his tales of flying saucers and frost ghosts, but then…well, then they both heard it.

Singing.

At least, that's what it kind of sounded like…a high, melodic singing or humming, very shrill, rising and falling and echoing. It was weird and unearthly. It made something pull tight in Gill's stomach, made gooseflesh ride up her spine and settle at her throat. It stopped, then started again. It had a strange, almost feminine caliber to it, like some morbid Irish funeral dirge as sung by keening locusts.

"Let's get out of here," Dientz breathed. "Man, I don't...I don't like the sound of that."

"Quiet," Gill told him.

The singing—if that's what it was—was getting neither closer nor farther away. Whatever it was coming from seemed stationary. They waited there, trembling, listening to it and thinking that it sounded like the Sirens of Greek Mythology calling them to their deaths or the high and evil-sweet voice of a wraith echoing from a haunted house. They did not know what it could be, only that it was alien and macabre. To Gill it sounded almost melancholy and deranged, like the voice of that woman from Poe who'd been buried alive and escaped, her mind shattered.

"C'mon," she said. "It's coming from down that tunnel. We got our blasters."

Dientz pulled away from her. "No! I'm not going down there! Are you out of your fucking mind? Can't you hear it? Can't you *feel* it? It's not right, it's horrible...Jesus, Gill, it sounds like a voice from a grave..."

Gill stood there. Dientz was right. Completely right. Nothing that could sing like that was remotely human or remotely sane. Yet, she was compelled to follow that voice, to seek it out, to see what could possibly be making it. "Then wait here because I'm going."

"No! No! You can't...you can't go in there! You can't leave me alone!"

"Then come with me," Gill said.

The tunnel led up to a pump house. There was nothing else up there but a lot of rudimentary tunnels the engineers had never finished, some old and unsafe cave networks.

Dientz was shaking so badly he thought he might fall out of his suit. "I'm calling Sarrasin! You're out of your fucking head! I'm calling him! You hear me? I'm calling him!"

"So call him," Gill said and slipped into the tunnel.

5

Dientz was alone.

He could see the retreating glow of Gill's helmet LEDs bobbing away into the darkness. The singing had stopped, but now it had started again, shriller, more rhythmic, more insistent than ever it seemed.

Dientz stood there unsurely. Funny, but that voice made him want to go into the tunnel, too. You listened and kept listening, it sort of wrapped something warm and fuzzy around your brain and you stopped thinking about how terrible it sounded, how morose and off-key and eldritch. You started thinking it sounded kind of nice. Like a lullaby your mother might have sung you to sleep with in your crib. Sweet and loving and—

Oh, Christ, oh my God.

Dientz nearly cried out, because he'd been walking towards the tunnel just as Gill had. He'd actually been letting that voice get into his head where it had settled warm and comforting, spinning webs through his mind.

He stepped back and away.

There was a ping at his headset which meant he was about to receive a communication.

"Gill!" he said. "Gill! Listen to me! You gotta come back, you gotta come back right now."

"Dientz, come into the tunnel," Gill said, very calmly. "You have to see this! This is incredible, this is really incredible…"

She said something else, but Dientz couldn't pick it up because the singing was blaring, blotting out everything else. He kept trying to get a hold of her, but it was useless. He shut the channel off and kept his exterior mic open.

The singing was very loud, echoing and shrilling.

And then there was a ping again and Gill came on, screaming and shouting in pure terror.

Dientz made a frantic call to Sarrasin.

He could hear things echoing from the tunnel now…wet, meaty sounds like a carcass being cut apart. Splashing sounds, but no more screaming. Then it all ended with a piercing roaring noise that echoed away and died.

Then there was nothing but silence.

Silence.

Dientz went down on his knees, sobbing and praying and waiting for death to find him, too.

But it didn't.

Sarrasin and Wells found him.

"Where's Gill?" Sarrasin said, yanking him to his feet and shaking him. "Where the fuck is Gill?"

"She went up that tunnel," Dientz said in a shallow, scratchy voice. "Went up that tunnel, following that singing, that beautiful singing."

"What the hell is he talking about?" Wells wanted to know.

But Dientz just nodded, like he was hearing something they couldn't. "That Heatseeker, boss…she's a female…she's a female…and she likes to sing…"

6

They were tracking her now.

They were going to bring her to ground or die trying. Sarrasin himself led the way up the tunnel after Gill. Dientz was right behind him. Wells was taking up the back door. Wells didn't care about Mars or the Company or any of that high happy shit, he just wanted to bag what was killing people. He saw nothing beyond that.

"Funny," he said to Dientz, "how every time we leave you alone with somebody, they get killed."

Dientz stopped. "What you mean by that?"

"Just curious, is all."

"Listen, you sonofabitch—"

"Shut up," Sarrasin told them. "I'm sick of both of you. Just plain sick of the bickering. Yeah, every time Dientz gets alone with somebody, they die. What of it? Could have been you or me that bitch went after, too. She tries to get us alone, Wells. She found Royer by himself and then she got Gill away from Dientz. That's how she operates and that's why we're not separating anymore."

"You're the boss," Wells said.

"Damn right I am."

Dientz said, "We should just make for the surface, wait for pick-up."

"It's pitch-black up there, dumbass," Wells said. "You think she couldn't take us up there, too?"

"The habitat. The emergency habitat. If we can get there…"

Wells laughed with derision. "*If, if if*...she'll never let us get that far."

Dientz didn't argue and Sarrasin was glad of that. One more pussy-ass suggestion from him and Sarrasin figured he'd cold-cock him and stake him out as bait for what they hunted...and what hunted them.

"No more talking," he told them. "We're getting up to the fork now."

They could all see it in the lights strung from the tunnel roof. One passage led to the pump house, the other wound off into the mountain itself into a labyrinth of ancient caves and half-finished tunnels that had been abandoned years before. Sarrasin knew why they'd been abandoned. He would have never admitted it to the others, but he knew, all right. Ten years before, the engineers were going to put in a new boiler system. The diggers cut about a quarter mile of new passages and broke into an ancient system of limestone caves. And that was like some kind of catalyst, because in the next two days, six men were killed, ripped apart like Royer. Two others just went missing. None of this was common knowledge. The truth of the matter was sealed up tightly in the Company's files and there it would stay.

Anyway, that's why the new tunnels were only half-finished. Word had it a few had even been collapsed on purpose. So the digger crew had been attacked by this creature ten years ago, same way the surveying team had been gutted in the Sarvis Valley eight years before that. And now this.

The bitch definitely liked to kill, but it wasn't like you could set your watch by her. She just came and went without rhyme or reason every now and then like a bad storm.

Sarrasin cut off into the right tunnel at the fork. The signs said it was dangerous past this point, unsafe, but they kept on. No lights now either. Only their helmet lamps to guide them.

They followed Gill's tracks.

Her boot prints were easy to see in the undisturbed sand which was very fine like that of a beach, red and pink and sparkling with mica. The helmet LEDs were splashing light onto the rough-hewn walls, creating wild leaping shadows.

"I don't like this," Dientz said.

"Shut the hell up," Wells told him.

Ten minutes into the passage, it broke off into three separate runs. The one to the far left, Sarrasin knew, just circled back into itself and the middle one was a dead end. He led them into the right channel, following Gill's footprints. The passage was getting narrow now like a spider hole, so tight in some places his shoulders brushed rock on either side.

Gill's footprints stopped.

The sand was disturbed like a whirlwind had blown through there. Blood was everywhere, a great splatter marking the spot where she had been attacked. It was frozen into crystals.

"Where's her body?" Wells wanted to know.

But that was obvious. There was a crystallized blood path before them, drag ruts. The bitch had dragged her off. Swallowing, Sarrasin led them on. Nobody was saying a thing, not even Dientz. They kept moving, the shadows jumping and the tunnel turning this way and then that. To a man, they couldn't shake the idea that they were being watched.

The tunnel began to break into the old caves. Offshoots ran to the left and right, some of them big enough to drive a sand rover through and others you would have had to navigate on your belly.

Sarrasin was still following the drag marks. The blood was very spotty now, a few drops here and there and he figured Gill was dead before she reached this point.

There was a sudden arc of light like one of the helmets had spun in a crazy circle. Sarrasin heard what he thought was a grunting sound. He stopped and swung around.

There was nobody behind Dientz.

No Wells.

Dientz started losing it right away. "Pick us off one by one, that's what she's going to do, Sarrasin! You played right into her hands! Oh, that's great, that's just fucking great!"

"Stop it!" Sarrasin told him. "You want out? You had your fill? Then take a fucking hike or just shut up!"

Dientz said nothing.

Sarrasin backtracked, but it was hard to say where Wells had disappeared to. There was some blood on one of the walls, but he could have been yanked into any of a half-dozen passages.

This was it then, he knew. They either hunted that bitch down and killed her or she killed them. Regardless, it would have been just as dangerous to turn back now as to go forward. Like slipping a noose around your throat and kicking out the stool, there was just no turning back.

The passage split again and this made Sarrasin stop.

"What?" Dientz said. "My God, what now?"

Sarrasin didn't answer at first, he had to be sure. Then he was. "Look, Dientz. That tunnel to the right…it's new. It didn't used to be there, I'm sure of it."

It was tall and narrow, more of a cleft through the rock than anything else. The floor was littered with detritus, lots of loose rocks and scattered pebbles. The walls looked as if they'd been cut with axes and picks. Sarrasin went in there, not caring now if Deintz was behind him or not. The drag marks were still evident and now they led into a low grotto that he had to crouch to get into. It was maybe thirty-feet wide in there. Once you got inside, the roof opened up into a wide cylindrical shaft that disappeared up into the blackness. Sarrasin put the lights of his helmet and blaster up there, but it just went up and up. He crouched, waiting for the Heatseeker to drop down on him like a spider.

But nothing happened.

Swallowing down something thick in his throat, he looked back once and Dientz was still with him.

First thing they saw were lots of odd-shaped boulders that looked as if they'd fallen from the roof overhead. Next thing was what was left of Gill. They could only see her legs—she'd been driven into the ground like a post. You couldn't say where her suit began and her flesh left off.

But that wasn't all.

Ancient elliptical depressions were carved into the walls, dozens of them. They led right up the shaft as far as their lights would reach. They were half-filled with sand and debris now, but they looked oddly like the honeycombed cells of a beehive. Most were still occupied.

Occupied by dead things.

They went over to them, not afraid really, because there was no possible way the things were alive. They were curled-up and horribly withered, leathery brown creatures about four-feet in length that reminded Sarrasin of katydids. Maybe they weren't insects exactly, but something like insects. Arthropods. Their thoraxes were ribbed, short and shriveled limbs branching out into triple-pronged appendages. Something like a narrow stalk rose from the thorax, looked like it was made of vertebrae, with a teardrop shaped pod at the end, gigantic hollows where no less than three eyes might have once been. They had too many limbs to count, bundles of whip-like things that might have been feelers.

Looking at them, desiccated and mummified, it was hard to say whether the creatures stood or crawled.

"I can't stand looking at them," Dientz said.

And for once, Sarrasin agreed with him. Rawboned and wiry and multi-limbed with horny, chitinous shells and too many anatomical adaptations you couldn't begin to guess at, they were about as alien as anything he could imagine. Seeing them alive, seeing them moving, it would have been almost too much for the human mind. They were repulsive and hideous; you wanted to step on them.

Yet, his curiosity got the better of him—he panned his light up and found more of the creatures interred above. These were larger, maybe adult forms, but just as withered and brown and crumbling. They looked somewhat like Earth mantises.

Dientz began to giggle, then he began to laugh...a dry and wizened laughter that was perfectly insane. The sound of a human mind emptying itself. "You know what this is, don't you?" he said. "Don't you, Sarrasin?"

"How could I?" Sarrasin said.

"This place," Dientz said, motioning around with his light and then jabbing one of the insects with his blaster so that a limb fell off, "this place is a burial chamber. These hills we've been tunneling into are probably part of some huge cemetery, some sacred burial ground. All these years we've been desecrating it."

He was out of his head.

He had to be out of his head.

But that didn't make him wrong. Rift and Sarvis Valleys were probably part of some sort of great Martian necropolis and men had been violating it ever since they arrived on Mars like dogs searching for bones. And the Heatseeker? A caretaker, a survival that should have died out eons ago, but kept living, probably demented even by

Martian standards, doing the only thing she could do…grieving her race. Probably hibernating for long periods of time, then waking up, pissed-off, and taking invading humans as sacrifice to the memory of her species.

His skin crawling, Sarrasin thought: *I'm in command here. I can't crack up. I can't let myself crack up.*

Dientz was out of his mind now and Sarrasin was close at his heels. He led him back out into the tunnel, nearly dragging him.

"Get a hold of yourself," he told him.

"I'm okay," Dientz said, but his eyes were wide and glassy and mad through his helmet bubble.

"C'mon," Sarrasin said. "Let's get the fuck out of this crypt."

7

The idea of escape, of making for the surface, slapped Dientz out of it. Whatever had been holding him, squeezing his mind flat, it let go now. He could do this. He could make the run with Sarrasin. He wouldn't lock up. He'd keep going.

Down the tunnel they went.

Death waited in any of the passages and spider holes arching off to either side. Dientz was sweating rivers in his terrain suit. He held his blaster tightly and anything so much as breathed, he was wasting it. If that was a man, so be it.

"We're going to make it," he told Sarrasin because he had the oddest sense that Sarrasin was beginning to unravel. He wasn't saying a thing; he was just waiting for the shit to fly. "We're going to get out of here and that bitch can't stop us."

"Sure," Sarrasin said.

No hope, no optimism left. Sarrasin, who was always so confident and sure of himself, always standing on sure ground, he had died now. What was left was a man that was sure of nothing, that dared hope for nothing He saw his death coming and did not shrink from it. Fatalistic.

Dientz didn't like this new Sarrasin. He was not in charge, he was not leading from the front. He had folded-up psychologically and there was nothing left but flesh and blood, nothing at all.

Dientz knew what he was feeling, what had taken possession of him. It had gotten him, too, but he'd managed to shrug it off. Had to. Because when you started thinking that way, your luck ran out and you wore a target on your back and fate was already to stuff an apple in your mouth and roast your ass over the hottest fire in hell.

"When we get back," he heard himself say, "when they pick us up, Sarrasin…what's the first thing you want to do?"

"Shut up," Sarrasin snapped.

"What?"

"Shhh!"

They were stopped now and Dientz didn't like it. Forward momentum was what he needed. Hesitation like this made all the bad things start crawling through him again. The paranoia and dread, the absolute fear. Sarrasin seemed to be listening, but Dientz heard nothing. Saw nothing. But he was feeling *everything*. There was simply no getting around what his nerve ganglia was telegraphing right up his spine…the sense that they were in incredible danger, that something was following them, shadowing them like a leopard in the jungle. Something patient and malevolent and deadly as poison. He could feel it watching them, studying them, deciding which of them it would bring down first. And when it did, it would be to maximize the utmost terror in the other. Because that's how the Heatseeker worked—it could smell fear, it could taste fear, and it knew exactly how to use fear.

It was so close, Dientz was certain he could smell it, as impossible as that was…gray, moldering, the stink of shrouds and bones.

Closer and closer still.

We're going to die, he thought then. *We won't make it out of here.*

And they wouldn't; he was certain of it. Just as certain as he had been that they would make it five minutes before. The mind was funny, wasn't it? It was like a green tree limb: you put too much pressure on it and it either snapped or it sprang back, swinging and swinging. That was what had happened to his mind.

The only reason we're not dead yet is because that bitch isn't ready to take us. She wants us more afraid, she wants to push us to the brink of madness. She'll be satisfied with nothing less.

Dientz was shaking badly now and Sarrasin was frozen into place. They did not speak and they did not move. Dientz knew they had to and right now. He opened his mouth to say so and then a shrill, insane screaming began to echo around them, coming from behind them or ahead of them, maybe from the mouths of all those other passages. It rose and fell, fragmented, and then started again.

He felt something like a sucking wind rush through him at the sound of it. He wanted to giggle, he wanted to cry, he wanted to scream along with it. He was going mad and he didn't see what he could possibly do to stop it.

The screaming came again, filling the tunnels and bouncing around until it was not a single scream, but a dozen. And then it rose to a strident, inhuman pitch and became the hysterical voice of Gill: "*Help me! Somebody help me! Please dear God don't let her touch me don't let her touch me!*"

Sarrasin tensed, turning in circles, trying to find where it was coming from. "We've…we've got to help her. That's what we've got to do."

"Are you crazy?" Dientz said. "That's not Gill! It can't be Gill!"

But it sure sounded like her. And about five seconds after it ended, it started again…only this time it wasn't just Gill, it was Royer, too, and Wells. They were screaming and screeching, begging for help, begging for Dientz and Sarrasin to help them before *she* hurt them anymore.

Dientz just stood there, breathing so fast he was hyperventilating. The sound of those screaming voices had locked him up inside—dear God, the suffering, the torture, the absolute pain. It sounded like they were being skinned. And Sarrasin? He was completely unhinged. Moving first this way, then that. Stopping, starting, aiming his blaster here, then there.

Finally he grabbed hold of Dientz's arm. "We've got to help them! We've got to go to them!"

Dientz yanked his arm away. "They're dead, Sarrasin! They're all dead! You know they're dead!"

"Then who? Who's calling us, dammit! Who in the fuck is calling for us?"

"She is," Dientz said.

But that wasn't good enough for Sarrasin. He shoved Dientz and Dientz went airborne in the low gravity, bouncing off a wall and thudding gently to the ground. By the time he was on his feet, Sarrasin was already gone. He caught a brief glimpse of his helmet lights bobbing up a passage and then disappearing.

"Sarrasin!" Dientz called through his mic, but it was pointless.

She wanted to separate them and now she had.

Dientz went after him, entering the darkened tunnel. It was cramped and close in there, the floor rising along a gentle incline. He had to find Sarrasin before she did, but he knew he wouldn't. And it was about that time that Sarrasin screamed. It was loud and piercing and short. There was a wet ripping sound, a thudding and cleaving noise like Sarrasin had been split lengthwise by an axe.

And then something came bumping down the tunnel from above.

Sarrasin's helmet.

It was crushed and battered, sprayed with frozen blood. And his head was still in it.

Dientz ran.

8

He could not remember much of his flight, only that he kept going until he was at the power substation. It was shut down and all the lights were off. And Dientz had been a maintenance tech long enough to know it wasn't a mechanical or electrical failure.

It was the Heatseeker.

She'd doubled back and did something.

She didn't need the light—she hunted by body heat, hence her name.

He began running, trying stay on his feet. The turbolift was just ahead. If he could get in there, it would shoot him up to the surface and there wasn't shit she could do to stop it.

He ran maybe twenty feet, felt something big pass by him. He went down in a crouch and fired random shots with his blaster. Bolts of blue light vaporized rocks with explosions of smoke and sparks.

He got to his feet, started running again and something hit him in the back, put him face down in the sparkling orange sand. Screaming, he got back up and then something grabbed his left ankle and flung him. He bounced from one wall to the next, spun head over heels and rolled to a stop.

His helmet LEDs threw grotesque shadows of him in every

direction. He sensed movement and brought up his blaster and something whipped into him like a tree branch and the blaster was snatched from his hands. He caught a glimpse of a black, spurred foreleg thick around as a fencepost.

Then he was crawling, whimpering and mumbling, but crawling, making for the turbolift.

Something grabbed his ankle again and threw him back down the tunnel.

Hopeless, it was completely hopeless. She was toying with him like a cat with a mouse.

Sobbing, his mind torn open in a bleeding gash, he fell onto his back, gasping for air.

And there she was.

The Heatseeker.

She was clinging to the roof of the passage like some immense and glistening insect, a mantis set with serrated, irregular plates that moved independently of each other. She was not an insect exactly, but a surreal version of one, too long and too thin, spindly and spidery, limbs jointed by spiked balls, body segments joined by what looked like threaded screws. She was a bug welded together out of odds and ends from a metal scrapyard…pistons and pipes, iron frames and corrugated steel.

Dientz didn't bother being afraid. He was beyond that now. He just looked at her and felt an almost surly sense of calm. "Got me, have you?" he said to her.

She just clung there, making a sort of trilling sound that his mic picked up, watching him with three huge liquid green eyes that were slit yellow like a cat's pupils. She was composed of an elongated, narrow body with dozens and dozens of wiry, hooked limbs. They were all moving like knitting needles and threshers and scythes. Glacial eyes studied him with grim, malefic amusement from atop a curling stalk shaped almost like a question mark, but longer than a man's leg.

So this was the Heatseeker, eh?

Every bit as awful as anything Dientz could have imagined. Maybe worse.

Just beneath the globular eyes, there was something like a proboscis, long and black and oily. As he watched, it split open, revealing a wicked, saw-toothed mouth, more jelly dripping from it, gouts of steam blowing from the throat channel.

Dientz sat up slowly, waiting for her claws and her teeth. He felt something rising inside him. Something sure and immovable. "No, you silly bitch," he said, popping the seal on his helmet bubble and feeling the bitter cold. "I won't make it that easy on you."

Then he let Mars have him.

And was dead almost before she got to him.

FLYPAPER

s they passed over the barren sand dunes, Rigler shook his head. "I tell you we did a flyover two months ago and that thing was not here. We'd have seen it. Whatever it is, it's recent."

Captain Noori nodded, staring down at the strange structure gleaming beneath the blazing sun of 18 Scorpii. Obviously, it was not natural in origin. Whatever it was, there was intelligence behind it. The question was: *whose?* The Agency had had people on the 4th planet, 18 Scorpii D, known colloquially as Turnbull's World, for nearly fifteen years now. No signs of intelligent life had ever been found.

"Pang," she said. "Take us down closer. I want a good look at it."

"Coming around," Pang said.

The shuttle flew to the east, banked, and came back, this time much lower and much slower. Everyone was at the viewport by then, shoulder to shoulder save Pang who kept an eye on his instrumentation. Rigler stood with Noori, Slade with Mlyca. They all knew what this meant: if it was indeed an alien edifice, then they were about to make history. The Agency outpost on D (New Horizon) was the farthest man had reached, being some 45 light years from Earth. It was remote from the other colonies, desolate and maybe even unsettling in its isolation.

The structure in question was black, and rectangular. It was glossy and impossibly large—Pang's readings told them it was nearly two kilometers in length, half that in width. It looked, if anything, like a giant shoebox lying in the sand.

"Is it possible," Mlyca said, "that it was buried in the sand for a long time and has just blown clean recently?"

"Possible," Noori said.

For many, many miles in every direction, there was nothing but sand dunes. Waves of them sculpted by the wind. They were constantly shifting, moving, crashing into one another, dissolving. The only constants were the rugged outcroppings of onyx-black rock.

"I think that's a good point," Rigler said. "It would explain things. Who knows what might be buried out there? And if you look at it, you can see how the sand is banked up around it."

Mlyca's idea made sense. If nothing else, it cut the rising tension. A relic, not a recent addition. That was much easier to take and it kept runaway human imagination in check.

As they passed over it yet again, Slade studied it with a wary eye. "Could be, I guess. The sand is like a sea, forever changing…"

"But…?" Noori said.

Slade sighed. "Could be that whoever put it there, wants us to *think* that."

"Quit with the conspiracies," Rigler told him. "You're always trying to get under everyone's skin with that stuff."

"Not my intention, I assure you," Slade said, unfazed. "It's just that we're a very long way from home and we need to be suspicious of all things. We need to practice caution."

"We will, have no fear," Noori said.

Slade nodded. "I refer to the crew of New Horizon Two, of course."

Which was a sore spot with all of them. New Horizon #2 was the second outpost on the planet. Two months before, all twenty of the crew had completely disappeared. They took no gear with them. No shuttles. No rovers. When they were not heard from in nearly twelve hours, a team from #1 went to investigate. Their findings were that, yes, they were all gone. But as to where and why nobody knew.

It wasn't discussed these days…except by Slade, who saw mathematical patterns in everything.

He was legendary for his skepticism. He had faith in absolutely nothing. When someone helped him, he questioned their motivation.

When a fair wind blew, he saw an oncoming storm behind it. And when providence favored the crew, he suspected an agenda.

"In chaos," he told them, "there is anything but chaos. Nothing in this world or out of it happens by accident. You can be sure of that. Take any arbitrary phenomena or occurrence, dissect it, expose its inner workings, and you will always find a deterministic set of equations. There is no such thing as a random incident. Particularly when a higher intelligence is at work behind the scenes."

"Or it just could be a relic that the wind blew clean," Rigler said.

Slade smiled. "And that sun blazing up there…it looks very much like an egg, but I assure you it isn't an egg nor is it a shiny coin or the corona of a wayward angel. Look beyond appearance and suspect motive."

Mlyca began to look uneasy, as she always did when he talked that way. There was something close to fear in her eyes, Noori saw. Slade was very intelligent, but he was also blatantly paranoid.

"Pang," she said, "take us down. We'd better log this, random or not."

The shuttle descended and Mlyca looked from the confident, sure eyes of Noori to the shifty eyes of Rigler. Finally, she looked over at Slade. And what she saw scared her.

On the ground, the box was even more perplexing. There seemed to be no purpose to it: it just was. There was no way in. No openings or seams, no external mechanisms or protrusions of any sort. It was smooth and perfectly quadrilateral. That was it. It seemed to be made of metal, but the scanner had no idea what kind.

They hiked around it in the heat, sipping water from their flasks, creating a meticulous video record of it which would be sent to the Agency for further study. It took them nearly ninety minutes under the blazing sun.

"It's nothing," Rigler said. "It serves no purpose. It might as well be a doorstop or a paperweight."

"But even those have purpose," Slade pointed out.

"So you think it's something?" Pang said.

Slade laughed. "Of course it's something. It has a purpose even if we can't divine it traditionally. It was obviously manufactured and those who did so were aware of its use. Something like this was not made and placed in this location for no reason."

"Maybe the reason is abstract," Mlyca suggested. "You know, maybe it has some ritualistic or religious purpose. One you could never figure out without understanding the culture that built it."

Rigler mopped sweat from his brow. "Oh Christ. Now you sound like Slade."

"Ignore him," Slade said. "You have a fine working brain, don't let him taint it with his inherent simian simplicity."

"Yeah, fuck you," Rigler said.

"All right, all right," Noori told them. "It's hot and dry out here. We're uncomfortable and getting testy. Let's get back to the shuttle. We'll let the Agency heads sort it out."

"I'm for that," Pang said. His khaki shirt was plastered to his back with sweat. Beads of perspiration rolled down his face. They looked like raindrops.

Noori said, "Sorry, Slade. I'm going to have to go with Rigler on this. This structure has no purpose."

"But it does."

"Do tell."

"Well, look at us. We're here, aren't we? We landed because we were intrigued. We walked around it because we were curious. It drew us in like a moth to flame."

"Guy's a headcase," Rigler said. "Don't even listen to him."

Noori led them on until they were back in the front of the box and the shuttle was thirty yards away, heat waves shimmering around it. She figured that a shower and a good meal back at New Horizon would straighten them all out. It was too damn hot out here at midday. The heat had a way of making brains boil in skulls.

They started off to the shuttle, but Mlyca was not with them. She was staring at the box with almost mystical reverence as if it was a holy relic.

"Come on," Noori told her.

She looked back. "It's…it's open. There's an opening here."

They moved toward her at a hurried clip. Maybe she was

hallucinating in the heat. That's what Noori wanted to believe. But when she got there, she saw it, too. There was a perfectly circular opening in the side of the box.

"It wasn't there before. We looked." Rigler kept shaking his head. "It makes no sense. This thing wasn't here before and then it is. There was no opening and suddenly there is."

"Maybe it makes all the sense in the world," Slade said.

"How so?" Noori asked.

Slade was down on his knees with Mlyca. They were peering into the opening. Using a light, they saw a tunnel that led away into the guts of the thing.

He cleared his throat. "You're asking me to make a judgement on an unpredictable system. I can't. What we want to know is inside there. We have to explore it to find our answer."

"Well, I'm not going in there," Rigler announced.

Noori nodded. She got on the channel with New Horizon and called in the discovery and its location. That she had intentions of exploring it.

"Slade? Mlyca? You come with me," she said. "Pang? You stay out here with Rigler. Let's get some lights from the ship and have a look."

The tunnel inside was not large: they had to crawl into it on their hands and knees. It moved in a straight line for maybe thirty or forty feet, then it diverged to the left, to the right, up a slight incline and down again. And there it opened into a large rectangular room.

"Empty. Not a damn thing," Noori said. She was getting frustrated with it all. "I'm not paid to crawl around in alien relics. This is a complete waste of time."

"How so?" Slade asked her.

She kept shining her light around. The walls, floor, and ceiling were made of that same glassy black material that might have been metal or plastic or composite, who the hell knew? Shiny, smooth, and like the box itself, the room seemed to serve no purpose.

"There's nothing here," she told him. "No remains, no aliens, no sign that any have ever been here. A room without any observable purpose."

"But, again, it drew us in, didn't it?"

"Yes, and for that we discovered an empty room in this relic."

"Not, relic, Captain. *Machine.* This must be a machine."

She just stared at him. "Machines have a purpose, Slade. This place has no purpose."

"But it does. It intrigued us, it interested us. It made us come in here so we could impress a practical use upon it. Don't you see? It *drew* us in."

"For what?"

"That's what I'm trying to determine."

Mlyca stayed out of it. She'd only been with the Agency for three years. She didn't figure she was in a position yet where she could get involved with what the old hands argued over. The only reason she'd gotten the posting to 18 Scorpii D was that no one with more seniority wanted it. It was too far out. It was a shit world at the shit outer edge of known space. Beyond was the blackness of the great unknown.

And the further you go out, the less support there is and the more dangerous things become, she thought, playing her light over the ceiling.

If there was an emergency, it would take an Earth ship ten months to get out here from the nearest colony. There was nothing remotely interesting on D. No alien culture to study. No artifacts. Nothing but rocks and sand, bugs and thorny scrub and more rocks.

In the southern hemisphere, there were mountains and thick forests and swamplands bigger than Texas. It was also a greenhouse of poisonous plants and deadly pathogens. There were corrosive rains and huge predators, venom-spitting needle spiders and a parasitic worm that considered the human brain a delicacy. New Horizon sent drones down there to study and collect, but never people. The Agency had lost too many already.

Still, she wished that just once she could—

Shit!

"Another opening," she cried to the others. "Look! I was just standing here and…and it opened like an eye."

Noori and Slade studied the room on the other side. It was much like the one they were in, save for one thing: there was sort of a wire frame rising from the floor and on it was a yellow hardhat.

"There's a New Horizon logo on it," Mlyca said, putting her light on it.

Slade nodded. "Yes, New Horizon Two to be exact."

Noori sighed. "Oh hell. This isn't good. What would it be doing in here? Did the crew already explore this thing?"

"You want me to go get it?" Mlyca asked.

Noori hesitated. "Yes…no…I'm not sure. I don't like the idea that this room opened and might close up again with you in it."

"But I don't think it will," Slade said. "We were drawn in here to find this item. Still, proceed with caution. The machine is active. It ticks away like clockwork."

Mlyca slipped in there without hesitation. She cast her light about. "Doesn't seem to be anything else in here. Just the hat. The ceiling is lower, though. Wait." She put her light on the wall. "Some sort of uprights there like part of a cage."

"Just get the hat," Noori told her.

She took hold of it. She had to pull very hard to get it loose. It was almost like it was magnetized. "There. Got it." She held it up and there was an instantaneous groaning sound like metal fatigue. The uprights she saw on the wall slammed down with a great booming noise, trapping her. There was an instantaneous crunching, a liquid sound, and a grunting from her. That was it. Everything seemed to happen simultaneously.

"MLYCA!" Noori shrieked, jumping through the opening and going to her. When she saw her up close, she turned away, made it two or three feet and vomited.

By then, Slade was in there.

He studied the mechanism and what it had done to Mlyca in some detail, though it was obvious he was no less repulsed than Noori. The uprights Mlyca spoke of were actually a U-shaped bracket, spring loaded. When she pulled the hat free, the spring was activated. A geyser of blood and tissue had been expelled from her mouth. It glistened wetly on the wall. The bracket had come down with incredible snapping force, crushing her midsection, forcing not only blood from her mouth but her insides as well.

"A mousetrap," Slade said, impervious to Noori's condition or the crushed carcass before him. "It's a goddamned mousetrap."

It was at that moment, as revelation settled in, that the circular opening leading to the other room closed with a whooshing sound.

They were trapped.

Outside, Rigler and Pang broiled in the heat. It was stagnant, oppressive. They were crouched in the shadow of the box. It gave them protection from the direct rays of the sun, but not much more.

"What we should do," Rigler finally said, "is take turns. One of us stays here while the other waits it out in the air conditioning of the shuttle. Least we both wouldn't be frying then."

"Noori told us to stay here," Pang told him. "We better not abandon our post."

"Listen to you."

Pang shrugged. He kept sticking his head and shoulders into the doorway. It was much cooler in there. Inviting.

"We could wait it out in there." He checked it with the scanner. "It's twenty C in there. Comfortable."

Rigler ignored him. He tried to contact Noori again. There was no reply. "Either they're in trouble or our signal is not carrying."

"Could be. Who knows what this thing is made of? Might be dampening our signal."

"What are you doing?"

Pang was inside now. "Oh, man. Come in here. It's so nice."

"Bullshit. I'm not going in there."

"It's cooler."

Rigler shook his head, but not with much conviction. He could feel the cool air blowing out. It was like standing before an open freezer. It felt wonderful. He suddenly couldn't think of a single good reason to stay outside...in fact, he felt an overriding compulsion to go inside. He could not make sense of it, so he didn't try.

He slipped in there with Pang.

"Oh, boy, now that's better."

"Isn't it, though?" Pang said. "I bet the further we go in, the cooler it will be."

Rigler was going to tell him he was crazy, but it made sense. Good sense.

"Lead on," he said.

Twenty feet in, they didn't even hear the door close behind them.

They had been in the room with Mlyca's corpse for two hours. There was no way in and no way out.

Slade had watched Noori go from being disgusted and horrified to angry. She raged. She kicked the walls. She pulled the pulser off her belt and fired at where the door was. It did no good. A pulser bolt could burn through six inches of tempered steel, but whatever this contraption was made of, it barely even warmed it. After that, she went hysterical, screaming and shouting, draining her pulser with a sustained burst. Then she tossed it against the wall. When her communicator couldn't reach the others outside, she threw that at the wall, too.

Finally, she collapsed against the wall and wrapped her arms around her knees.

"My fault," she mumbled. "It's all my fault. I knew it was a bad idea to come in here. I *felt* it. Yet, I allowed it. I ignored my common sense and listened to you. I should have known better. Now Mlyca's dead and it's my fault."

Slade was not insulted by what she said. She was blaming him, but that was fine. She needed to blame something or someone, so it was him. That's because she did not understand the inevitability of the situation. If he hadn't been there, she would have led Mlyca in there all the same. A metal filing cannot ignore the pull of a magnet anymore than she could ignore the attraction of the box.

Yes, yes, he thought. *Whoever designed this machine fully understood that. They factored in the attraction of the unknown to the human animal.*

"We came in here because we wanted to," he said to her. "And because *it* wanted us to. There is nothing random in what has happened. A small change at the beginning leads to a radical outcome at the end."

"What the hell are you talking about?"

"We entered this machine. That was the change we made. The radical outcome was Mlyca's death. From this point, we will be drawn to a certain place and time within this mechanism. There is an attractor out there, influencing us."

"Attractor?"

"Yes. If you throw a ball into a valley, it will settle in the lowest spot that gravity and mass will allow. That is the attractor," he explained. "The attractor in this machine will bring us to a particular point in time and space."

"Now you're talking destiny."

He laughed with a dry sound. "Hardly. It's mathematics that solve the equation of chaos."

She was holding back and he knew it. She wanted to tear him and his theories to shreds. Her professionalism stayed her hand from the former and her ignorance halted the latter.

"So if you can predict all this with your great mathematical mind, and tell me the outcome then will we be stuck in here forever or will we escape?"

He shook his head. "Too many variables. I would need to know the exact initial conditions of this system we are in. Without it, there is no predicative power."

What he failed to tell her was that the outcome most certainly would be similar to Mlyca's. It was an inevitability. That was, if the machine was designed to exterminate them. If it was simply to test their intelligence like rats in a maze, then the outcome would be potentially different.

"In other words you have no idea," Noori said with more than a little contempt. "You're tossing around theories as usual with no practical application."

He allowed himself to smile. "If you say so. Orderly effect will emerge from chaos. That's a given. In time, we'll see the pattern emerge."

Noori looked like she was ready to jump him...then, a doorway opened. This one was not circular, but triangular. Beyond was a corridor lit by a soft yellow glow.

"Our destiny awaits," Slade said.

"And if I refuse it? If I refuse to be part of this little experiment?"

"Then we'll die in here. We'll dehydrate, starve to death. Probably go mad."

"So we become part of the system whether we want to be or not?"

"Captain, we were part of the system the moment you decided to touch down. The rest is inevitability."

Feeling oddly like a whipped dog, she stepped through the doorway and Slade followed.

According to the chronometer on the scanner, they'd been inside the structure for six hours. Pang found it hard to believe, yet, in some way it was easy. They'd spent the first hour crawling through the passage that led into the box, calling out for Noori and Slade, only to discover that there was no way out.

The passage did not lead back. In fact, it led nowhere...except into itself. There was no end to it and no beginning. Forward, backward, it was all the same. When it did finally open, it was into this room which was roughly ovoid in shape. It beat being in the passage, but not by much.

They were trapped.

And there was no reason for us to enter at all, Pang thought, *except that we were too warm out there.*

But as he sat there, Rigler across from him, he didn't think that was the reason at all. Sure, they'd entered because of the heat but that didn't make them go off exploring the passage. Something else had. Only he did not know what it was. At the time, it had been a compulsion—he just *had* to. But now it was all murky.

What had Slade said?

We landed because we were intrigued. We walked around it because we were curious.

"And we entered it because we had to," Pang said out loud.

"What are you talking about?" Rigler asked him.

"Just thinking out loud."

"Well, stop it. I get enough of that intellectual slop from Slade. We need to think how we're going to get out of here."

"I'm open to suggestions."

The doorway leading in had closed the moment they turned their back on it. If this was where the box wanted them to go, then it had achieved that end effortlessly.

Rigler panned his light around. "Nothing, nothing, nothing. Not a seam, a crack, a vent, not even a fucking pinhole. How does somebody make something like this?"

"I don't know."

"And how long before our air runs out," he said, wiping sweat from his face. "Because it's going to. Sooner or later we won't be able to breathe."

"Maybe. If that's the point of this room."

"What other point could there possibly be? If the air doesn't run out, we'll starve to death. I haven't eaten in over twelve hours. I'm starving."

"It'll take weeks to starve."

"You know what I mean." Rigler kept pounding his fist against his knee. "You ever watched an animal starve to death? It's not pleasant."

Pang shook his head. He didn't want to know if Rigler had actually ever seen such a thing, why and under what conditions. He figured he was better off not knowing.

Rigler went silent for maybe ten minutes, then he said, "I keep thinking about food. Not the slop back at the outpost, not that dehydrated, processed, reconstituted shit, but *real* food. Good food. The kind of stuff we had in Chicago when I was a kid. You should've tasted the pan pizza. Oh, my Christ, was it good. They'd toss the dough right in front of you. Homemade sauce. Imported mozzarella. Wood-fired."

"Maybe we ought to talk about something else," Pang said, feeling his stomach growling.

"Like what? Hell, I've been working on this shithole planet for over a year with you and I know nothing about you. I mean, are you married? You got kids? Why the hell did you volunteer for this? D is way out here. I did it for money."

"I did it for the science."

Rigler made a grunting sound like that was the stupidest thing he'd ever heard. "Tell me about your family. What about your mom? Was she a good cook? My ma sure was. My old man, too."

Pang sighed. "How does this keep coming back to food?"

Rigler laughed. "I...I don't know. I'm trying not to think about it, but the more I shove it aside, the more I think about it. Hey...*wait*. You smell that? Tell me you smell that." He was on his feet, sniffing the air. "Roast chicken! By God, I can smell the sage and lemon. And... and potatoes with butter. *Real* butter the way my ma made 'em. And... damn...fresh-baked bread! Apple pie and vanilla ice cream!"

Pang was concerned. He kept thinking about all the things Slade had talked about, that which he put into words and that which he inferred. *Think!* he told himself, knowing it had never been so important. *There's a pattern here. It was blazing hot outside. The box offered you a cool place. You were going crazy in the maze of tunnels, so it gave you this room. Now Rigler is famished and it's tempting him with the odors of an old-fashioned Sunday dinner.*

"I don't smell anything," he admitted. "It's all in your head."

"You're nuts."

Pang was starting to believe he was, too. Rigler was convinced of the aroma of food. He tracked it around the room, stopping at the opposite wall.

"Here!" he said. "It's strongest right here! Man, my mouth is watering!"

He had barely finished saying that when a circular door slid open not five feet from him. Before Pang could even think of stopping him, he went through it.

"Hurry!" he cried.

"Rigler, goddammit! Wait! It's toying with us! It's drawing us deeper into the maze! It's giving you what you want! It's baiting you!"

But, by then, he had passed through the doorway, too. He had no choice. He had to keep an eye on Rigler who was running full out down a rectangular passage that opened into a large room with a vaulted ceiling. It was lit up in there. In the center, there was a dining table set with candelabra, serving dishes, plates and spoons and forks. Crystal glasses.

"See? See? Just like I told you!" Rigler said, excitedly opening the serving dishes. "It's all here!"

And it was.

The roast chicken was plump and browned, juices trickling from it.

The potatoes seeping with a golden nectar of butter. The loaves of bread steaming. The apple pie was hot from the oven, a crust of brown sugar and cinnamon atop it. There were pitchers of ice tea and lemonade and ice-cold water.

Pang took hold of Rigler before he touched any of it. "Think now," he said. "This is a trap. No, wait. Just stop and think for a moment. You have to see how weirdly coincidental this all is."

Rigler glared at him as if he wanted to punch him right in the face. For a moment, it was in his eyes, the knowledge that something was *very* wrong about all this, then it was gone. He shoved Pang away. It wasn't that he didn't believe what Pang said, he just didn't *want* to believe it.

"C'mon, Rigler...please, just use your head. You're being baited and you're going for it. Can't you see that?"

"Shut up," he said.

Almost defiantly, he poured a glass of lemonade. The ice cubes clinked together. He held it up to eye level. "Smells fine, looks fine." He raised it to his lips and took half the glass in a single pull. "Ah, delicious."

And it did look delicious with the condensation running down the glass. Pang became aware of just how dry his throat was. As he watched, Rigler poured a glass of ice tea, nearly swallowing the entire thing.

"Perfectly fine."

Yes, Pang wanted to tell him, *but the lemonade, the ice tea...it's window dressing. It accentuates the feast you dreamed of. But it's not the feast, it's not the rat bait itself...*

He didn't say any of it, of course, because what was going to happen was inevitable. How many times had Slade said that? That you cannot interfere with a fixed inevitability? Two plus two must make four and, in the end, regardless of your feeble interference, it still would.

Rigler studied him with distaste. He was a large, determined man and he would brook no interference. Like an animal, he tore off a hunk of chicken breast and shoved into his mouth. The skin was crispy, the meat juicy and tender. "Wonderful," he said. He swallowed it, smiled. There were no complications. He used the serving spoon and scooped up a generous pile of buttery potatoes. "Marvelous. Just like ma's."

While he was still savoring them in his mouth, he dipped a thick slab of bread into the buttery juices and crammed it into his mouth as well, chewing, enjoying immensely the amazing tastes and textures on his tongue.

That's when it happened.

Whatever sort of poison was in the food, it was of the trinity variety—the chicken and the potatoes and the bread had to mix together to activate it. A look of horror passed over his face and he spit out what food he hadn't swallowed. He fell forward to the table, going wild, gasping and choking, knocking plates and glasses to the floor with violent convulsions. He went to his knees, folding up, and struck the floor.

But it didn't end there.

He underwent a series of spiking clonic seizures, legs bicycling, arms whipsawing, body drumming against the floor. As Pang watched, his body swelled up as if it were pumped with helium. It expanded like a balloon, the zipper of his coveralls splitting open, buttons popping. His face went a livid purple-green, his bulging eyes the color of ripe beefsteak tomatoes. As he spasmed, copious amounts of slimy yellow foam vomited from his mouth, gurgling and slopping. His body ripped open and more of it spilled from him like fish roe in gushing pools. He lifted his head up an inch or two and a great bubble of blood expanded at his mouth, then popped.

He settled down in his own anatomical waste, shuddered and went still.

That was it. That was how he died.

Pang was right out of his mind by then. He would have screamed if his voice wasn't constricted deep in his throat. He ran toward the other end of the room and magically—but, of course, not so magically at all—a door opened and he fell through.

Because that's how the machine operated.

"You fail to see the patterns, Captain, taking shape around us. You fail to realize that free will, so cherished by you, is not part of the larger agenda," Slade said. "You believe you are determining your fate with conscious decisions on your part, but you're not. You are following a pre-set attractor which leads you to this ultimate inevitability. The equation will arrive at a fixed sum because even though this all appears chaotic, it is not chaos, but perfectly logical mathematics, clean and pure."

Noori refused to look at him. She didn't want to hear about the agenda. She was sick of his theoretical bullshit. He refused to factor in choice. It was an unknown and incomputable variable.

Before them was a pit of darkness. They stood on a five-foot ledge projecting out into it. Thirty feet across the pit was another ledge. Beyond it was what they sought: a doorway leading back out into the desert wastes of the planet. Noori could smell the dryness and feel the heat. They only had to reach that other ledge and a conveyance had been provided—a metal pole not much bigger than a flagpole connected the two ledges. It was just a matter of shimmying across.

"I can cross it in five minutes," she said.

"No, you can't do that. How can I make you see reason?" Slade asked her. It was all so rudimentary, so obvious to him. "The machine presents a pattern and we have been following it much like a drop of water follows a crack. We are being pulled in a prearranged direction towards the central attractor by making obvious, calculated choices."

"Enough, okay? Enough? We're not in a lecture hall or a theoretical physics lab." She kept shining her light below. Insane. It was as if the light was being turned back on itself. Physics were corrupted in this damn box. "We're in a survival situation here. We need to act accordingly."

"Which is what I'm trying to get you to see. Basic human survival instincts have already been factored into this. That's why we're being offered what we want the most—a way out. If you take that way, then you have no more free will than a river following a ravine channel to its attractor which is a lake."

"So what would you have me do?" she asked him, growing more angry all the time. "Stay here and starve? Die just to frustrate the machine?"

"Yes...no...maybe. If we deny the basal attractor, we become radical variables. The machine may accept that we are intelligent beings and not instinctive animals. This will upset the curve and nullify the equation. Hence, it will dispense with us. In other words, show us the door."

Noori breathed in and out slowly. "I'm crossing that pole, Slade. Accept it."

He leaned back against the wall. "Then you go to your death."

"Then I do."

It was pointless and he knew it. She would never listen to reason. If she couldn't see how ridiculously obvious and coincidental this all was, a simple way to freedom, then she was lost to reason. The box was a mousetrap and she was acting as mindless as a mouse. There was no hope for her.

She pulled herself out onto the pole. "When I reach the other side, you can come across," she told him.

"But you won't reach the other side."

"Shut up."

She shimmied about halfway across and then stopped. She gripped the pole tightly. "It moved," she said. "The pole moved."

Slade said nothing. He was tired of talking, tired of trying to impress common sense on someone inherently senseless. Her behavior had been predicted by the machine and factored into the equation. She could not escape her fate; it was preordained by nonlinear dynamics, only she was too much of a fool to see it.

"It's too late," he said. "I'm sorry."

The pole trembled, then it retracted and dropped. Noori fell screaming into the blackness beneath her. There was a splashing and her screams faded, echoing into nothingness. He didn't need to see what was down there to know she had fallen into a vat of some corrosive liquid, some unknown acid that had already rendered her to a skeleton.

The pole came back up, extended and connected the two ledges.

He stood there for some time. Finally, he said, "I won't use it. There's no point in going on with this."

The box seemed to agree. It opened another doorway and he stepped through.

He didn't know how much later it was that he found Pang, just as it was determined that he would find him. There was a reason for it. He knew that much.

"We have to be careful in all that we do," he told him. "We must consider our actions carefully."

Pang said, "The food was poisoned. I told him it would be. He wanted it and they gave it to him and he devoured it like a rat. He stuffed himself with it."

"And why not? Gluttony was in his nature and the machine understood that. He was easily predictable. A mousetrap for Mlyca. Rat baits for Rigler. A drowning pool acid bath for Noori. Each offered something they could not refuse. They did not think, they acted."

Slade had the feeling that it was lost on Pang, too. He had been reduced to an animal state of fear. His thinking processes were handicapped. He was no longer rational.

They followed a passage for some distance. Eventually, of course, it opened into a room. And that's where they found the doorway leading outside. It was much like the one leading in—a circular opening. Freedom was a matter of feet away.

"Do we chance it?" Pang asked.

"Of course not," Slade said. "It's bait."

"But it's right there." Pang had inched to within a foot of it. "I could dive right through it in a split second." He stared out into the desert world, licking his lips like a hungry man. "I would be quick."

"And dead."

"How do you know?"

"I don't. But evidence suggests escape will not be quite that simple."

At that moment, Slade knew, Pang was in a very dangerous place. His intellect recognized the foolishness of what he was contemplating, but his animal drive saw only freedom from the nightmare.

"Come away from there," Slade said. "Please, Pang. Don't be stupid."

And it looked like he was going to retreat, then bravado took hold of him and he dove through the opening. He made it roughly halfway through when a lightning-fast guillotine blade sheered through him, slicing him neatly in two. His upper half lived for a few moments, writhing in the sand like a dying worm. Then the doorway closed.

Slade turned away from the blood and carnage. "Show me another doorway," he said. "Show me the thing you want me to see."

A triangular door opened and he stepped through, deeper into the box. He was trying very hard not to be terrified, but it was no easy matter. He was the last one. The entire shuttle crew was dead. Maybe he had not been close with any of them—hell, he knew they found him irritating on a good day—but he really and truly had had their best interests in mind. He felt their loss and it pained him. For the usual reasons and for the fact that their deaths could have been avoided.

His intellect had kept him alive this long, but would it be enough? How long before he was reduced to a dumb animal? How long before he got desperate, too?

The passage led on and on. He became aware of how thirsty he was, how hungry and, more so, how exhausted both physically and mentally.

And it was about that time that he found a room. It was long and rectangular. There were bodies stuck to the walls, shriveled gray things, mummies with sprung jaws and clutching hands. It was the crew of New Horizon #2. They were all there, fixed to the walls.

"Flypaper," he said. "Of course."

One of them got stuck to the wall, then another and another. Others tried to help them, becoming likewise stuck, until the entire crew was trapped. The box flawlessly predicted human behavior— that they would keep trying to free each other until they were all in the same predicament.

There was a stray boot on the floor. He pressed it to the wall. Regardless of how hard he pulled, he could not break it free. His mind went back to a history class in college where they studied 20th century pop culture. There was a product they'd all found quite funny at the time. It was called the Roach Motel and the catchphrase was, *Roaches check in, but they don't check out.* A simple glue trap. And the box was basically the same thing.

"We aren't wanted in this part of the galaxy," Slade said out loud.

That's what the purpose of the box was: to keep the vermin down. The allegory was obvious. Save that there was a way out, if you were smart enough to find it.

"The equation is solved."

A doorway opened and he stepped out into the punishing heat of 18 Scorpii D. The box closed again. Humans weren't wanted out here. They were vermin to whoever or whatever left the box, infesting the galaxy planet by planet. But they would keep coming and they would keep dying. Slade knew it was the one constant in the equation.

"Somebody finally built a better mousetrap," he said as he walked towards the shuttle.

MIGRATION

L
ike anything bad, it had been brewing for awhile. But the first indication came that afternoon when they were out at the #6 substation shack and Isley was bitching about the heat.

"Gets much hotter, my dick's gonna melt," he told Holliman, scratching at the scraggly beard he wore that looked oddly like a nest of mating black worms on his chin. "It's gonna steam and melt right off."

Holliman was checking the pressure readout at the main coupler. "Well, won't be much of a puddle."

Isley ignored that, kept right on running down Zeta Cygni-5, saying how he could feel his nuts sizzling in his shorts like meatballs in a frying pan. How one of these days, those goddamn stuffed-shirt pricks from the Company were going to show up and he was going to drop his pants, let 'em get a good look at that burnt smoky link and the two charcoal briquettes which was all that was gonna be left of his manhood.

But, he had a point.

The heat on Cygni-5 was unbearable. Imagine a flat, burnt-yellow world of endless grasses that climbed up to your chest and sometimes right over your head and you had a good idea what the planet was like. It was hot and dry and monotonous. No hill, vale, or tree broke the repetitious landscape—in every direction, from horizon to burning horizon, just that motionless, burning sea of grasses. All of it washed down by the relentless heat which no breeze dared disturb.

It was called "the barrens" by those who called Cygni-5 home.

Isley stepped out of the shack and the sun hit him full and hard, sucking the moisture from his skin. It rode the misty, saffron-colored sky like a great blazing platter of hazy orange. Sweat ran down his face and immediately evaporated. With the scraggly beard and seamed face he looked like a prospector from old Earth.

"Man," he said. "I hate this goddamned place."

Holliman came out, slapped his bush hat on his head. It was khaki in color and, like everything worn on Cygni-5, banded with ancient sweat stains. "Guess we can head back to the compound."

But Isley wasn't paying attention. He had his head cocked to the side like a dog, listening intently. He held a finger to his lips when Holliman tried to speak. Then he shook his head. "Damnedest thing," he said. "Damnedest thing."

"What?"

He licked his flaking lips, swallowed hard. "I heard something...a sound...I'm not sure what."

Holliman's red-rimmed eyes scanned the grassy desert, seeing nothing but that infinite waste of yellow grasses, the ochre sky reaching down to touch it until they became one. Heat waves shimmered like the air from an oven. Nothing moved. Nothing stirred. Out there was a dead, arid world where the only sounds were the stalks of grass crisping and popping from time to time, but that was about it.

Holliman turned away, "I don't hear anything."

He refused to look or listen further, knowing that people had gone mad on Cygni-5, just staring out over that barren, scorched savanna. In those undulating waves of dry heat, you sometimes saw things and heard things that weren't there. Over the years, quite a few had lit out across the plains, swallowed by the grasses never to be seen again. Their bodies were still out there, hidden in that parched womb of sedge, bones bleached white by a sun that never set.

"Listen," Isley said and meant it.

Holliman did. He leaned up against the rover and the plastic shell was so hot he burned his hand. He snatched it away and heard, yes, heard a weird trilling sound that rose up to a whining like that of a locust and faded.

"What the fuck?"

Strange. There was no animal life on Cygni-5, at least not on the surface.

He opened the rover, dove into the air-conditioned cab, thumbed the radio. "Urmanski? You there? This is Holliman out at Six…are you there? Get your goddamn hand out of your shorts and answer."

"I'm here, I'm here," a tired, bored voice said from the speaker. "What's up your ass this time? Every time I sneak away to whack off over your wife's picture, you call me."

Holliman said, "Listen to me. You picking up anything weird out in the barrens?"

"No, not a thing. Why?" You could hear him punching his keypads back at the main compound. "No. Dead out there."

"No strange atmospheric shit?"

"Nope. I can give you the weather forecast, though. Tomorrow up to a hundred-twenty, dry as a spinster's twat. Next day, same. Next week, same. Next month—"

"All right, all right. We're hearing some sounds out here. Let us know if you pick up anything. We're making for Five."

Isley was still listening.

He heard it again, but farther away. He didn't know what it was, didn't know what it meant, but he did not like it. It made the flesh at the base of his spine crawl. Gave him a chill here on this blistering world where a cool day was ninety plus degrees.

Scared shitless, he climbed into the rover.

On Cygni-5 there were no roads as such.

Trails were cut through the grasses by huge automated mowers that worked daily to keep the network of passages open that led from the compound to the various substations. Currently, there were over two hundred miles of these shorn paths. But if mining operations increased, there would be more. The grasses looked dead, but they were very much alive, fed by underground water and nutrients, constantly growing.

When the rover arrived at the #5 shack, right away Isley knew something was wrong.

Gillis or Olger always came out to meet them. At the very least they heard from them on the radio. But today there was nothing. They couldn't even raise them.

"Maybe we should head back to the compound," he suggested.

The rover rolled to a stop next to the shack and they climbed out hesitantly, Holliman in the lead. The shack looked much like a long, aluminum Quonset hut. Inside was the machinery that pumped radioactive plasma from pockets deep within the planet's crust. The reason for human presence on that hot, empty world. If you were to have flown over the mining operation, you would have seen what looked like a wagon wheel: the sprawling, central compound and dozens of substations and storage tanks connected to it by innumerable arteries cut through the grasslands.

While Holliman went into the shack itself, Isley circled around outside. He checked the maintenance sheds, the footpaths, and saw nothing. Twice, he heard that weird, eerie sound out in the barrens. It rose up to a whirring drone, then died away just as quick. He couldn't seem to convince himself that it had no meaning. A sound like that...

He hurried back around to the front of the shed, popped the hatch and was expecting to feel the cool embrace of air conditioning...but what he got was a blast of hot, fetid air. Inside, everything was a mess. Cables were snapped, hoses ripped open. Pipes had burst. Electronic equipment had been shattered. It looked like some awesome, ravaging storm wind had blown through there, tearing and rending and smashing. Everywhere circuit boards and broken plastic and destroyed bits of equipment.

"What...the hell happened here?" he said, glass crunching underfoot.

Holliman just shook his head. He looked pale as cigar ash. "In there," he said.

Isley went through the archway into the crew's quarters, wished right away he hadn't.

Gillis was in there...or what he *thought* was Gillis. His body was bloated up like a barrel, his limbs swollen like sausages. He was nearly snapped in half, as if something incredibly strong had tried to make the back of his head touch the back of his ankles. He was bent in a lurid V, his eyes wide and staring, his mouth frozen open.

Isley, sucking in a sharp breath, kneeled down by him.

His flesh was the color of oatmeal, his glazed eyes full of blood as if every vessel and capillary had burst at the same time. The corners of his lips were ripped open right to his cheeks and his jaw appeared to be broken, as if he'd screamed so much it had snapped from internal pressure.

Isley left him. "What in Christ happened?"

Holliman just shook his head. "You find Olger?"

Isley said he hadn't.

Outside, they stood by the rover, both thinking, thinking.

And out in the barrens, a huge and manic buzzing shrilled like the lunatic drone of thousands if not millions of hornets. It cut through the stagnant air and then fell to a weird shrill whistling that echoed away into silence.

Isley was trembling. It felt like there was something stuck in his throat, something he just couldn't swallow.

"Listen," Holliman said. "Are you hearing that?"

It was a sort of secretive rustling, a stealthy motion plying through those dry stalks. A busy motion. Like there was something out there— maybe a lot of somethings—that were trying damned hard not to be heard. And the idea of that was worse than just about anything else. It filled Isley with a gnawing, dawning sense of horror that would not be ignored, would not be shut away by rationality.

"I think," Holliman said and his voice was just as dry as cinders in an ash bucket, "I think we better have a look…if it's Olger, well, he might need help."

Isley just stared at him, unblinking. "Do you really think that's a good idea?"

Holliman nodded, licking his lips. He was a big man and fear did not come easy to him. Yet, he felt it now; that much was obvious. "Stay here. If I don't come back right away…anything happens…you jump in the damn rover and get the fuck out. Understand?"

Isley tried to nod, but it seemed like everything in him had shut down. Something was telling him to breathe shallow, to stay still, to keep his heart rate low, and not draw attention to himself.

Like a rabbit in a field, he told himself. *That's me. Just waiting for the owl.*

Holliman stalked off. All he had for a weapon was a torque wrench from his tool belt. A pretty good weapon if you were going after a man, but if it was something else…

Isley watched him disappear around the side of the shack.

Through sheer force of will, he made himself move. He wanted to at least be able to see which way he went. He saw Holliman slip off into a footpath cut though the grass. He heard him walking, heard dry grasses crunching under his boots. Then the tall, yellow stalks enclosed him.

There was a short, high-pierced humming sound. Then a clicking noise.

Silence.

Five minutes went by, then ten.

The sun—61-Cygni to astronomers—blazed down hot as a torch. Out in the barrens, the grass crisped and popped. The silence was immense. Isley edged towards the path Holliman had vanished into. He pulled a cable cutter from his belt—it had a ten-inch, hooked blade. He began to smell an odd sweet odor. It reminded him of honey, but pungent, sickening.

"Holliman?" he called out. "Answer me, dammit!"

He heard a thrashing, stumbling sound and knew without a doubt that Holliman had gone off the path. Although the grasses looked dead and dry, they were very much alive. The dominant form of life on Cygni-5, the root systems below were very active. If you wandered off into the grass and didn't bust all the stalks in your path, then within fifteen or twenty minutes, they'd stand back up, erasing your trail.

If Holliman had gone out into the barrens…

Isley ran down the path. To either side, thick and bristling stems towered above his head. He saw a path broken through the yellow, dusty wall. *Dammit.* He moved into it, slowly, cautiously, calling out Holliman's name. Stalks brushed his face. All around him, there was a weird piping. He clutched the cable cutter tightly.

Holliman came plowing through the barrens like a man through a cornfield, fighting and clawing his way. He came right at Isley with a crazed, desperate look about him. Isley got out of the way, dashing back to the main path.

Holliman made it there himself, screaming now.

That noisome stench of sweetness was thick as taffy.

There were six or seven little forms clinging to him. Isley thought at first they were wasps or ants grown to obscene proportions. And that's what they looked like, except they were eight- to ten-inches in length. They had bright orange-red bodies and dun-brown, eyeless heads, their jointed legs and whipping antennae and forceps-like jaws were colored a brilliant, vibrant yellow.

Isley uttered a cry at the sight of them. He had an almost instinctive revulsion of them. As Holliman fell, he could see there were five or six others on his back, buzzing and clicking, hanging on by their spurred legs and immense jaws.

They had Holliman and as Isley watched, feeling utterly helpless, they began to bob their asses up and down, inserting fire-red stingers into him like seamstresses threading needles.

The effect was immediate.

Holliman went stiff as a board and then instantly began to writhe and convulse, legs going one way, arms another, and body yet another. A bloody froth vomited from his mouth and he jerked and twitched so violently, Isley could hear tissues tearing and bones dislocating. It all lasted about thirty seconds, until he was a broken, bleeding mess.

Isley, his head full of Holliman's death stink and that awful honeyed stench, began stumbling back as the insects abandoned the body. Something brushed against his shoe and he saw one of them poised at the tip of his boot, its antennae flexing.

Crying out, he stomped it under his boot.

It let out a maddening shrill cry. Isley tried to squash it, but it was too well armored. Like trying to squish a tick. He remembered the cable cutter and brought the blade down in a vicious arc, the blade entering between two thorax plates and impaling it. Its death cry was a wild, weird fluting, black bile dripping from the wound.

The others moved in.

Isley turned and ran as they buzzed and clicked behind him.

Still holding the dead bug skewered on his blade, he got in the rover and made for the compound, the squeaking, humming sounds of the insects echoing in his skull.

They tried to sedate him, of course, but he wouldn't hear of it.

There was no way he was going to be drugged and helpless now. Not after what he'd seen. He had to be awake, he had to be ready. And maybe the rest of them didn't understand that yet, but he did. Oh, Christ, yes, he did.

They were in the infirmary at the compound and Isley, after they'd calmed him sufficiently, had just finished his story. They probably wouldn't have believed it except that they were still unable to make contact with substation #6. That and the fact that he had brought the dead bug back with him.

Walker, one of the drillers, was pacing back and forth, looking decidedly unfeminine with her greasy coveralls and oil-smudged face. "So you left him out there?" she said, incredulously. "You left him out there with…with those *things?*"

"I didn't have much of a choice," Isley said. "You know, like when nature made you a woman and you couldn't grow that pecker you'd always wanted."

"Fuck you," Walker said, coming at him. "Goddamned stuck down here in this fucking oven and I gotta listen to your sexist bullshit. I'm sick of it—"

Gavlek stepped between them. "Settle down, Walker." And then to Isley. "I have to ask this—did they seem, well, intelligent?"

Isley told him he couldn't say. "I was too busy trying to get my ass out of there." His face was pinched and pale, his eyes drifting in a bloodshot soup. "You want, you could send Walker out with an I.Q. test, hand out some fucking pencils, see how they do."

Walker glared at him, simmering away like a goose in a pot. "Goddamn asshole."

Isley blew her a kiss. "You just want me."

"Want you? You're hung like a pipe cleaner, Isley. You couldn't make a field mouse come."

Isley managed a laugh, feeling some of the tension drain out of him. "See that, Skip? Goddamn women. They get pissed, right away they start making fun of your dick. But that's not sexist, no sir. But you or me? We say something about their saggy damn tits or how their hole's so big it flaps in the wind, right away we're sexist pigs."

"You are a sexist pig," Walker said. "If the sky is blue, you want me to call it green?"

"No, course not. Tell the truth, you damn cow."

Walker looked like she not only had one large, grade-A bug up her ass, but that it had just given birth and space was at a premium up there. "You fucking—"

"Take it easy, both of you," Gavlek snapped at them, sick of their constant bickering. He pulled on his neck like he did at moments of high stress. He shook his head. "This installation has been here... what? Eight, nine years now? And in all that time, all I've ever seen is grass. No bugs, no animals, nothing. Where the hell did these things come from?"

It was a good question. Cygni-5 had originally been surveyed twenty years before by a robotic probe. Five years after that, an exploratory team dropped down. They found nothing but grass, some simple forms of life below the surface where the water was—microorganisms, fungi, simple burrowing worms. Nothing else. They even tried to colonize the planet, giving up less than a year later when too many people kept getting lost in the barrens. Then the Company bought the planet to exploit the mineral wealth. It was a project that was just getting going. But one thing that had never been found on Cygni-5 were insects.

"I mean, have these things been here all along? Hiding? But if they're so damn ornery, why haven't they attacked before this?"

There were no answers to that one.

"All right," Gavlek said, running a hand through his thinning white hair. "I have to be wondering about these things, people. We make contact, there's a goddamn book I gotta fill out."

Two of the maintenance crew had shown up now, Jensen and Broeder. They didn't say a thing, they just listened.

Gavlek said, "Company's gonna be pissed. We're going to have to shut down. The Agency will have to send some eggheads out here, check this all out. You know how that goes, too."

Walker stood up. "That's fine and dandy, Skip. But you send word today, they're not going to be out here for six goddamn months and we all know it. If we've got some nasty bugs out there killing people...well, shit, we can't just sit around with our thumbs up our asses in the name of science. I'm from Arkansas, boys. We got ourselves bugs there, we step on 'em."

Isley brightened. "Exactly. Trust me, Skip, these mothers are mean."

Jensen and Broeder grunted in agreement.

"Way I see it," Walker said. "We gotta save ourselves. Fuck these bugs."

Gavlek thought it over, knowing full well he was hamstrung by regulations but also knowing the company was very clear on things like this—protect the project and its workers at all costs. In other words, science was great and little green men were wonderful, but if they got in the way of making money, spill all the green blood you had to.

Gavlek cleared his throat. "Okay. Anybody know where we can get a big can of bug spray dirt cheap?"

The Agency had one rule when it came to commercial projects on alien worlds: each colony had to have a biologist. And the biologist had to be paid by whatever firm was running said colony.

So the mining operation on Cygni-5 had one. His name was Stemick and he spent most of his days digging in the soil, taking cuttings from the barrens, playing in his little lab just off the supply bunker. He was the sort of guy nobody noticed.

But, today, he was a celebrity.

Everyone, except the crews monitoring machinery, were there, crowded around like vultures over tasty roadkill. Except this offering was anything but tasty. Stemick had the insect in a dissection tray, its thorax split open. It was a hideous little creature and gave off an awful sewer smell now that it was beginning to decay. It swam in a glutinous stew of black fluid.

"What we have here is an unknown arthropod," Stemick told them. "Unknown because it's never been documented—or seen, far as I know—an arthropod, because that term takes in just about any invertebrate with a segmented body, jointed legs—insect, arachnid, crustacean etc. This thing seems to be composed of all of these and has a few things of its own going."

He went on to explain how it possessed rudimentary circulatory and digestive systems and—judging by its stomach contents—ate mainly the roots of the abundant grasses. It also had, interestingly enough, a very complex nervous system. And there was a good possibility that it was intelligent to some degree. Its DNA was very similar to that of the other organisms on the planet and this would suggest it was native to Cygni-5.

"Some of you have joked that this creature looks like an over-sized ant or—what did you say, Walker?—a wingless wasp on steroids? That's good." Stemick tittered. "But, obviously, this is no ant or wasp as such. But there are similarities. These mandibles for example—" he forced the hooked appendages open "—are much like those of a tropical driver ant back on Earth. The jaws beneath are hinged and I believe they can be dislocated to hold enemies. It has no eyes. No evidence of nasal passages. But these antennae, they might be a generalized sensory organ. And these legs—" he pried them up from the black bile "—I've never seen an arrangement like this before."

The creature had what appeared to be four legs on each side, but there were in fact only two. Two thick limbs jutted from either side, but at the first joint they branched into two separate appendages.

"Preliminary analysis would suggest that this creature—we'll call it a Cygnan, since nothing else has showed up to claim that title— has something of a symbiotic relationship with the grasses. I might go so far as to say that our Cygnan here might be part of a social hive whose primary function is cultivation and pollination of the grasses. I've found pollen sacs on its legs and so I'd say that's not too far off the mark."

"How come we've never seen 'em before?" Walker said.

"Good question. They may be very good at concealing themselves. And if they spent their lives out in the savanna, we'd never see them anyway."

Gavlek nodded. "That's fine. But we've left them alone. Why are they attacking now?"

But Stemick had no answer for that. He told them he could only make a physical analysis, make extrapolations from what he'd discovered via anatomy, physiology, and biochemistry. Behavioral speculation would be premature and reckless.

"However, I can substantiate what Isley saw," he said. Using forceps, he took hold of the stinger which had now gone black. He held it up so they could all see it. "Holliman—and presumably the others—met their end via this little mechanism. It's hollow like the stinger of a yellow jacket. It's connected to a gland with an extremely potent neurotoxin. Once its injected into the human body, it would have the same effect as nerve gas."

That brought a heavy, measured silence to the room. It was bad enough that these things gave human beings the creeps, but to possess a weapon like that which could bring about such an appalling, agonizing death…that was just too much.

Stemick warned, "If anyone's thinking of fighting these things, think it over carefully. They are quite capable of defending themselves. If they're anything like other social insects we've encountered, they'll be ferocious fighters. Their individual lives are probably meaningless to them. Hive-mentality."

Again, that deadly silence.

It hung like that for maybe two, three minutes while Stemick began dropping tiny organs into preservation jars. Everyone watched, amazed at how the biologist could manage to touch the thing. He used plastic gloves…but still.

Then Urmanski came flying through the door. "Substations Seven and Twelve," he gasped. "They're under attack."

After Urmanski's announcement, the bio lab lost its appeal and the comm room was the place to be. The comm room was the nerve center. It was here that the artificial intelligence programs that ran everything were located. It was also here that contained the interfaces for the transmitters that could beam a message home.

Gavlek decided not to risk more lives by sending crews out to assist the beleaguered workers at #7 and #12. It wasn't a very popular decision. But he was in command and the rules of engagement with a hostile enemy force were quite explicit.

It had been several hours now since anyone had heard from either substation.

Gavlek had used codes only he possessed that locked down the compound so no one could get out short of blowing a hatch. There was one other work crew out, over at substation #3. But they were sitting tight. They had sealed themselves in and were following orders.

What was concerning everyone now were the odd series of sounds coming over the radio. Like distant chiming and high-pitched chirruping and pinging noises. Urmanski assured them that these were no natural emissions, no reflections or echoes. They were artificial and they were being directed at the compound from deep in the barrens, a dozen miles away.

Isley said, "If that's how they talk, they better speak up."

He didn't care for it. It was like something strange and disturbing you'd hear out in a black jungle in the dead of night. Shrill, insectile sounds. The noises beetles and spiders might make talking to one another.

Gavelek had been deep in thought for some time, just listening. "All right," he said, "let's give 'em the benefit of the doubt. You got a lock on where this noise is coming from?"

"Approximately," Urmanski said.

"Send those sounds back at 'em."

Stemick made a low groaning sound in his throat. "Not advisable. First off, we don't know what they're trying to communicate or if they're even communicating at all. We may incite an aggressive response. AI has a translator, doesn't it?"

"Sure. But it's not telling us shit about this business."

Stemick nodded. "What I'm saying is, the translator is programmed with thousands upon thousands of languages both actual, figurative, and symbolic, countless variations there of. Have it send, say, mathematical symbols at them in their own wavelength. Give that a try first. If they're intelligent, they'll understand we are, too."

"Yeah," Isley said. "Take it slow here. Don't be pissing 'em off."

Walker just sneered. "You want my opinion? We arm ourselves and we go find 'em. Kick in the door and introduce ourselves proper."

Stemick tittered. "You have a decidedly militaristic, belligerent turn of mind."

"Quit talking like that," Isley warned him. "You're turning her on."

"Go fuck yourself," she said.

67

Urmanski started broadcasting and almost immediately the sounds stopped coming. They waited fifteen, twenty, and, finally, thirty minutes for a response. The silence was heavy and tense. You could hear lungs sucking in air. Hearts pounding. Hair growing, cells dividing. The pitiless, unrelenting sun beat down on the roof of the compound, making the metal contract, rivets creak.

Then…more sounds, pinging and strident, drawn-out chittering noises, clickings and sharp ringing peals. The tone was definitely different this time around. Apparently they had gotten the message. If anything, they seemed to be aroused.

"Well, let's see how smart they are," Gavlek said. "Send this out on their wavelength. Have the translator run it through every language it knows and some it doesn't."

Urmanski's fingers played over the touchpad. "Okay, let her rip."

"Greetings, Cygnans. I am Gavlek. I come from the planet Earth in the system of Sol. We mean you no harm. Our intentions are peaceful. Please respond."

"Take us to your leader," Isley said.

Urmanski sent it out.

The sounds stopped.

Walker threw up her hands. "What the fuck's with you people? We're talking *bugs* here," she raged, feeling like the last person afloat in the gene pool. "Let's spray 'em, let's step on 'em. You don't negotiate with crickets for chrissake."

But no one was paying her any attention.

Isley was about to say something smart-assed, a comeback all set and ready to fly…but then a harsh, screeching static came over the wire. It was unpleasant, jangling, but not necessarily menacing. But everyone in the room felt it down into their bones—an awful, alien cacophony that sucked the blood from their faces and made their teeth grind together.

Then it ended.

Utter silence.

Stemick just sat there, nodding. "We can deduce that either they are intelligent or they're merely responding to the sounds you're sending. That noise…it really proves nothing."

But Walker wasn't so sure. "It proves they've got a transmitter, doesn't it? Can't you lock onto it, Urmanski?"

He just shook his head. "It's not coming from any one place, but from lots of places. I can't get an exact fix." He sighed. "I'm not even picking up any energy pulses out there. If they've got a transmitter, I have no idea how they're creating that signal, boosting it, or directing it."

Walker turned away. "Well, what fucking good are you?"

"Any thoughts, Stemick?" Gavlek asked.

He smiled thinly. "A few. We should look at the possibility of an organic technology."

All eyes were on him.

"By that, I mean a technology unlike anything we have. A wetware technology that doesn't require mechanical or electronic gadgetry. A *living* technology. I've seen it on other planets. Some of you probably have, too. Let me simplify that." He stood up, looked out the bank of windows at the burning plains beyond. "Some of you mentioned ants. Okay, let's go with that. On Earth, driver ants use a primitive form of this. They have no true nest. When the colony rests, the soldiers make bivouacs of themselves by interlocking their mandibles and leg spurs. They make living structures that protect and house the others. Their bodies are their tools, their houses, their everything. What I'm saying is the Cygnans might be like that. These transmissions we're getting might be originating from their bodies. A communal shortwave sent to us."

There was something sobering about that, something unnatural. Though it was anything but.

"Sure, fine," Gavlek said. "But are they really intelligent? Are they actually communicating or just sending out noise?"

"Good question. These sounds might be attempts to discover who and what we are or just their method of calling out to us in some base Cygnan language that any good bug would understand."

The static rose up again. It seemed to be not just a single noise, but hundreds if not thousands of them—high, low, sharp, dull, flat, piercing. A chaotic sound. But then the individual sounds rose up into a single, uniform, almost electronic buzzing that made everyone cover their ears.

"Turn if off!" Walker cried out. "Turn it off! It's...it's driving me crazy! I can't take that fucking noise—"

But then it stopped and her voice was loud and echoing. She looked at the others sheepishly, knowing she'd made a fool of herself. Or, thinking so at any rate. Truth was, they all felt it jangling in their heads, felt it rub their nerves raw, making them want to shut it out or crush it in any way possible.

"Interesting," Stemick noted, evidently intrigued by it all. "Like hundreds of voices calling out at the same time, a hundred minds that suddenly coalesced into a single shrieking thought. A hive brain composed of thousands, but in reality, a single brain. A single dominating, irresistible consciousness. Incredible."

Isley had found Stemick interesting before, but now he was just being a goddamn pain in the ass. Interesting? Incredible? Only an egghead would get a hard-on over something like this. Maybe it would have been a little different if he'd seen them all over Holliman, stabbing him with their stingers.

Urmanski pulled up multiple screens on the interface now, nervously fingering the touchpad. "Something's happening out there… Christ, Skip, they're on the move. I got a fix on 'em now." His face was tight, pressed white like a flower in a book. "The numbers…gotta be thousands of them…and they're coming this way."

Urmanski was right about one thing: they were on the move.

But he was wrong about the numbers. Not thousands, but *millions*. The entire Cygnan hive was on the move. A crawling, buzzing perpetual motion machine with millions of moving parts. It came out of the barrens, destroying and devouring everything, leaving destruction in its wake.

And the compound was directly in its path.

It was Gavlek's idea to stay and fight.

A lot of suggestions were bounced back and forth. One of them was to abandon the compound, get out of the Cygnan's way. But there was no guarantee of safety in that. Maybe they could avoid the main force, but what of the scouts? And who could say what the objective of the main force was? It might have pursued them wherever they went.

So, Gavlek decided they would stay.

On his order, the drills and pumps were shut down. The pipelines were closed off. All hatches were locked. Any holes in the compound structure were plugged. There was a fence around the compound, a solar collector shield that turned the rays of 61 Cygni into energy for operations. It wasn't intended as a defensive perimeter. But with a little ingenuity, it was turned into a barrier that surely even the massing Cygnans couldn't hope to penetrate. Gavlek had the maintenance crews run high voltage cables to it from the central fusion generator. There was enough juice in it now to fry gravel. The only breech in it was the drive coming in and this had been covered with metallic netting and likewise electrified.

If the Cygnans got through, they were going to be pretty crispy.

An hour later, everyone was waiting.

On the screens they could see the approach of the hive. The grasslands fell at their approach. The mowers couldn't have hoped to be this thorough. They cut a swath nearly four miles wide. According to Urmanski's scanners, the actual army was nearly five miles long.

"I think what we're seeing," Stemick said, "is a migration of the entire colony. I'm not convinced they mean us any true harm. We just happen to be in the way. Like driver ants on Earth, they're just on the move and anything in their path is going to be destroyed."

"Including us," Walker said.

But Gavlek did not accept that. "There's no way they can breach that fence. Just no way. It's sixteen feet high. Unless they're real good jumpers, they're toast. You didn't find any wings on that one, did you, Stemick?"

He shook his head. "But I believe it was a soldier. There's no telling about the others, the workers, drones, queens. Who can say?"

Isley had been in a few bad spots in his time, but never anything like this. Never anything that left him feeling so damn helpless, so damn frightened. Because he was scared shitless and he would have been the first to admit it. There was something instinctively abhorrent about great numbers of insects. It set the human mind on edge. Ant colonies. Hornet nests. Beehives. Swarms. Just seeing all those damn things congregating and wriggling, it set the skin to crawling. And it was much, much worse when the insects in question were nearly ten inches in length.

"Here they come," Urmanski said. "Less than three hundred yards from the fence and closing."

"I see em!" Walker said, face pressed to the window.

Isley joined her.

The barrens were collapsing. As if the Cygnans were armed with chainsaws, the great, tightly-packed fields of grass stalks were falling like tall timber. Then they were gone and the swarm pushed across the road at the fence. They showed no fear, no hesitation. The scouts moved directly before the colony, antennas waving and feeling and snapping like bullwhips.

"They can sense the energy in the barrier," Stemick said.

"Well, now we'll see how intelligent these bastards are," Isley said.

The scouts came at the fence with tight, economical jumping strides. The first dozen hit the fence and there was a popping sound as the electricity reduced them to burning cinders. But more followed. Waves of them attacking, soldiers and scouts throwing their bodies into the voltage as if they could overcome it by sheer numbers. Their blackened bodies clung to the fence like burning marshmallows. There was smoke and fire and arcing electricity. Those in the compound shielded their eyes from the blinding flashes.

The compound was equipped to do many things, but it was not made to filter odors. And right then, it was filled with an acrid, burning stink like seared meat and scorched hair. It filled the comm room in a nauseous, pervasive mist.

"Look at them bastards, will ya?" Isley cried out, fascinated as he was repelled by their numbers, their ferocity. "Christ, they're insane!"

And it seemed that way.

Thousands of buzzing and hopping bodies crowding for space at the fence. They hit it with everything they had, inundating it with sheer numbers, going right over the top of each other, crawling over burning corpses, attacking the mesh with their mandibles. A creeping, writhing, wriggling mass, more piling up all the time until you couldn't even see the fence any more. In fact, with all the fireworks and smoke, you couldn't see much of anything. But you could smell that hideous, incinerated stink and hear *them*. Oh, yes, you could hear them just fine. A droning, whistling, piping wall of deafening noise.

Those in the comm room were covering their ears at the din.

They could almost sense the anger, the rage, the torment of the Cygnans.

But they were not about to give up.

Isley thought: *They're not intelligent, they can't be goddamned intelligent. Intelligent creatures don't act like this, they don't attack in waves and die and keep dying.*

It reminded him, if anything, of wars he'd read about in history class. Human wars on old Earth. Human wave attacks. Bodies piling up so deep the second wave had to go over the top of the first and so forth.

Trembling, shaking, wanting to scream and maybe even needing to, he felt something cool and damp touch his fingers. It was Walker's hand. Their fingers found each other, joined together tightly. There was solace in holding hands. When the world—your world—was coming to an end, what else was there to do?

About that time, the lights started to flicker like all the bulbs were loose.

"Urmanski?" Gavlek said.

Urmanski looked like he wanted to cry. Maybe he was crying. "The generators, Skip…they're not made to put out this kind of juice. They're over-capacity now."

And everyone in the room knew what that meant: the fusion generators would shut themselves down, leaving the compound wide open.

Outside, in that flashing and arcing light show, the smoke cleared a bit and the fence was gone. It was covered in the burnt, sizzling bodies of the Cygnans. Thousands and thousands of them with more pouring over it every moment. It began to sag and then collapsed completely. The lights flickered again and died for real this time.

And the swarm poured into the compound.

The only lights inside the compound came from the sunlight streaming through windows and skylights of which there were many. With the generators down, it began to get warm in there. Without the air conditioning going and the air circulating, the sun heated the compound's metallic shell like a tin plate on hot asphalt. The atmosphere quickly got stuffy and thick.

At Walker's side, her hand hot and sweaty in his own, Isley watched the Cygnans flood forward, a twitching, chirring tidal wave of insect frenzy. So many. So goddamned many. It reminded him of maggots on a carcass, a busy canvas of worming, slinking, industrious motion punctuated by the monotonous, ceaseless droning wail of soldiers and workers and drones. He could feel the flesh at his groin creep, move in prickling waves up to his belly. His throat was as dry as salt. Trapped in that web of unspeakable horror, he had to remember to blink, to breathe.

The Cygnans assaulted the compound's main structure and everyone within drew tight into themselves. Had they been able to fold up and slide into a crack, they would have done so. Because the Cygnans were massing, by the thousands, the hundreds of thousands, engulfing the building like antibodies ingesting a disease germ. And the same thought was on everyone's mind: *How long? How long before they get in?*

"Christ," Walker said and Isley had never heard such a tone of quiet desperation in her voice before. "Dear Christ, I can't stand it!"

You could hear them on the metal walls and roof, their clawed feet like thousands of pencils tapping and tapping and tapping. It was a sound that went right through everyone in the dim, shadowy compound. That constant, hollow tapping.

It wasn't long before Cygnan bodies were pressed tightly against windows and skylights. They were pulsing and scraping and clawing and biting and stinging, trying desperately to breach the flesh of the intruder, to get at the soft internals that made it live, made it a danger. With blazing sunlight hitting them, their orange-red abdomens seemed to glow like sunsets—salmon, vermilion, scarlet, and coral. Like candlelight flickering through carnival glass, the Cygnan bodies appeared to be transparent, made of gelatin. Yes, beautiful almost, but so deadly and soon enough the light began to fade as skittering bodies heaped atop one another and a dire, twisting blackness fell over all and everyone.

Urmanski was whimpering pathetically.

You could hear others shouting in the corridors, crying out in desperation.

"You better do something, Skip," Isley told Gavlek. "You got fifty odd people trapped here and they're losing it."

And they were. And you couldn't blame them because you could hear all those mandibles and spurred limbs working and seeking, trying desperately to find a way in. Because they knew there was one just like they knew what was inside. The shell of the compound was humming, vibrating now with an awful, lunatic noise. It was like having your head thrust in a beehive. You could not escape the droning racket.

Gavlik's face was red and puffy, beaded with sweat. His lungs sucking stale, dry air. "What do you want me to do? What the hell do you want me to do?" he yammered, moving forward, then back, then in a drunken circle. "Can't you hear them? Can't you *feel* them? They want us! God, how they want us! In my head! *Ahhhh, God, they're in my mind, in my mind! I can feel them!*"

And Isley could, too. That central, relentless, irresistible hive intelligence worrying at the edges of his will, pulling, pushing, tearing, wanting in, trying to make him do things he did not want to do.

The walls were beginning to groan and creak now. Like an aluminum beer can in a crushing fist, they were beginning to give under the weight, under the force of those murmuring, creeping bodies.

Gavlik ran off and Isley smelled something foul and realized Urmanski had shit himself. He was insane now, pressed into some gibbering, frightened childhood corner from where he could never hope to escape.

But he was the lucky one.

Isley and Walker ran out into the corridor. Emergency lights had come on and bathed everything in a moonish, surreal glow. Crew members were attacking each other now. Hitting and being hit, stomping and being stomped. Some were trampled under the boots of marauding, screaming gangs that turned on one another after they worked a victim to his or her knees.

Isley was hit by a wall of bodies. He saw Walker go down. She tried to drag herself through a doorway, but hands yanked at her, boots kicked her senseless. Isley tried to make it to her and collapsed under a bevy of hammering fists. But as he went down, he knew, he knew, all right.

It was the Cygnans.

This wasn't simple mob mentality at work, something bred of horror and despair and madness. It was the insects, their minds channeled into a single, devastating thought: *kill, maim, kill.* They were pressing their primitive, barbaric will upon the minds of everyone. Working them into a fervor, taking them back to a darker, uncivilized time when the stocks had to be purged, cleansed.

Crawling on his hands and knees over the broken bodies and shattered faces of friends and co-workers, Isley caught sight of Stemick. He was using a cutting torch to melt the lock on the main door. In fact, he already had.

The lock hissed and fell away and the door blew open, a tide of Cygnans washing in, inundating him. And then they were everywhere, scuttling and wriggling and hunting. They were on the floor, on the walls, moving over the ceiling in a lethal progression. They fell on the crew members and gave each and all a taste of their venom.

Isley, shrieking madly himself now, saw a man with an even dozen Cygnans on him get stung repeatedly. He dropped and went into rabid convulsions. Blood and saliva flew from his mouth and his body snapped and flopped like it was being electrocuted. His head bashed violently against a concrete step until his skull came apart and a gray slop of brains splashed over his face. A woman came stumbling forward, countless Cygnans up underneath her coveralls, stinging the life from her. The insects dropped from the ceiling, vaulted through the air, fell over people en masse like tarps. The corridor was a thunderous wind tunnel of buzzing and trilling, thrashing bodies and airborne insects.

Isley caught sight of Gavlik.

He tried to run with a blanket of them on him. They began to sting and he threw himself violently against a steel bulkhead, shattering his jaw, his teeth spraying from his mouth like dice on a table. And then he was down, too, legs shuddering and arms slapping and body twisting. And it was like that for everyone.

Isley saw that the insects had abandoned one of the windows.

He broke through it with a hammer and dove out into the suffocating heat of Cgyni-5. The bodies of the attackers went to pulp beneath his weight. But he saw, *really* saw. There were so many insects that they were three, four feet deep on the ground. A living, chitinous carpet.

There was no escape.

But as he ran forward, screaming, trying to break his way through... the sea parted. Yes, the colony opened and let him through. Soldiers reared up on their hind legs, barbed mandibles clicking and snapping.

He could feel that communal mind in his now, like needles and knives ripping through his will, his sense of self. He could see nothing but Cygnans. The greatest army ever assembled. And he was caught within their numbers, seeing things no one ever had and no one ever would. It was a profuse, innumerable dominion, an infestation of creeping, crawling, droning, whirring insects. And then, as they continued to part, to press at him from behind and push him forward, he saw why.

There was a gigantic ball rolling in his direction.

A huge, rolling, peristaltic ball composed of workers, all hooked together via mandibles and claws and armored appendages. The ball rolled forward and then it stopped. The frenzy of interlocked workers began to melt away like snow on a roof and beneath, beneath—

Yes, the queen.

She was the size of a collie. A huge and bloated representation of her hive. Legless, her abdomen swollen with millions of eggs, she rubbed her mandibles together with an awful scraping, hissing sibilance. Unlike the others, she had eyes. Immense triangular orbs the color of green stained glass. They looked not only at Isley, but right into him and through him.

His mind was a puny, trembling thing under her gaze.

His brain exploded with white light, with thrumming waves of agony. His free will was stripped away like meat from bone and what it left behind was another empty vessel for her godless, black sentience. She filled Isley and destroyed every possible vestige of refusal, of free thought, of willpower, of defiance. These were unacceptable mutations purged by the hive. Obedience was the mantra of the colony and Isley was one with that now.

From somewhere, from a distant alien world of dementia, a voice was speaking. A buzzing voice like thousands of wasps attempting human speech: *"We are peaceable...we are one...you and yours built these structures in the ancestral migratory path...it could not be allowed...not during the festival the time of rebirth the time of life of filling and rending and seeding...now run off to a place that waits for you a secret and quiet place..."*

And Isley did.

For that was the world, *his* world: the grasses and those who tended them.

Something snapped in him with a wet, pulpy sound and then he was running through the colony and wanting only to see those grasses, those high yellow grasses. And then he did and burst through them as they slapped against his face and cut his hands and shredded his coveralls and he kept running until he fell from sheer exhaustion into that yellow, dry, hot world of coveting stalks. He buried his face in the crumbling soil. The stalks rustled now. They whispered and pushed in closely, holding him, keeping him. And the barrens, that infinite ocean of yellow alien corn husks, covered him and held him, erasing his path, shrouding him in a secret dark womb of madness.

DEAD PLANET

They were sprawled on the frozen crust of a lifeless world, staring at the remains of the *Polar Star*. It lay in the little rocky draw, sheared open amidships and crushed like a soup can. Shards of plastic, metal, and composites led away from it over the rise. If the aft compartment hadn't broken free when she slammed into the craggy bluffs, there would have been no survivors whatsoever. Not a soul to eulogize the passing of the merchant freighter.

"Where the hell are we?" Eckhaus said. "I think we should figure that out first. What do you say, kids?"

Yanami managed a dry laugh inside her helmet. "Sounds like somewhere to start."

Eckhaus nodded, his bulky envirosuit moving back and forth. The helmet lamp gave his broad face a yellow glow. He raised an eyebrow through his viewshield. "Okay. So where are we?"

"Damned if I know," Yanami said.

"You don't know? I thought you were a navigator? Isn't that what they pay you to do?"

"Yeah. Just like they pay you to mind the engines, Chief. But in case you didn't notice, I was in cold storage with you when we hit." She stepped away from him. Gravity was near-normal, at least according to what her suit told her. The sky was enveloped in a murky gray haze, so you couldn't even see the stars to get a position the old-fashioned way. "We could be just about anywhere."

"Jesus H. Christ. You hear that, Skipper? You hear that?"

Sellers was coming down the rise from the shattered remains of the *Polar Star*. "I hear, I hear," he said, calm as ever. "Bottom line is, people, that it doesn't really matter where we are. Company already knows we're down. The Agency will be sending a rescue ship, so there's no need to panic."

"Was I panicking?"

Yanami said, "Sounded like it to me. So much for those balls of yours. And after all the bragging you've done about them."

"You never mind my fellas, woman."

Yanami grunted. Inside her helmet, her face was olive-skinned, her eyes dark and exotic.

"Boy, could I go for a pizza," Eckhaus said.

"Why don't you?" Yanami said.

"What?"

"Go for a pizza. And don't hurry back."

Eckhaus laughed. "You want me and you know it."

They fell silent after that, staying close together. The e-suits would easily locate one another should they become separated, but they needed to be together. This was a desolate world, a cosmic graveyard. Black rock formations, hills, valleys, mountain ranges. Nothing more. The terrain was monotonous, repetitive. Patchy ochre illumination that was murky at best filtered down from above, casting dancing, lurching shadows whenever anyone moved. A heavy mist clung to the ground and the wind had a nasty habit of creating instantaneous dust storms.

Sellers found a jutting slab of stone, eased himself down on it.

Things like this were scary, of course, but there was no real need for panic of any sort.

The moment the ship plowed into this dead rock, it sent out distress signals on every imaginable wavelength. And if, for some crazy reason it didn't, the e-suits were sending out distress pulses every fifteen minutes. Their sister ship, *Polar Light,* was only three solar days behind them. The ships were uplinked continuously. When the *Polar Star* vanished off the scanners, her sister would go into immediate Code Red Sequence. Which meant that it would be screaming towards the *Polar Star's* last position. Already, no doubt, it was waking the crew.

No worries.

You could survive within the e-suit for two weeks and they'd be picked up long before that. It was only a matter of waiting. The e-suits were a real miracle of technology. They would keep you warm, feed you, protect you, dispose of your waste, keep you breathing, do just about anything. Once you climbed in, sensor receptors clipped to your skin and made an instantaneous analysis of your metabolism, your particular biorhythms. Everything from blood gases to brainwaves to heart rate. You needed a particular medication? No problem. The suit would manufacture it for you and dispense it as needed. Had a headache? An ache or pain? The suit would know it before you did, take appropriate action. You couldn't sleep? Couldn't stay awake? It could handle that, too. It knew when to warm you up, when to cool you down. The entire thing was controlled by a brainbox artificial intel package that in the old days might have been called a computer, but was as much like one of those archaic machines as a piece of broken glass was like the Hope Diamond.

"What do you got for me?" Sellers asked Yanami.

"Only the basics. We got ourselves a dense gas atmosphere, mostly hydrogen, helium, and ammonia. The ground fog is methane. Exterior temperature minus one-fifty. Not exactly a vacation spot."

Sellers looked around.

They were all thinking about the same thing, he knew. The twenty-odd colonists that had been berthed in the forward freezer chamber. All dead now. When the ship plowed into those spiky hills, the aft freezer chamber had broken free. Sellers, like the other two, had woken from two weeks in frozen hyperspace inside his e-suit. The freezing tubes automatically slid occupants into them at the first sign of trouble. Thank God for that.

"I'm gonna do me some exploring," Eckhaus announced, casting Yanami a rakish wink through his helmet visor. "Join me?"

"Gee, I'd like to. But I have a date."

"Don't go too far," Sellers said.

"Okay, Mom."

Sellers was the first at the crash sight. The first to see the forward compartment. All the tubes had been ruptured. Locked in the stasis of metabolic suspension, they were frosted up tight like strawberries in a freezer. When the tubes burst, their bodies shattered like fine crystal from the impact. And that's what it pretty much looked like when he reached that iron, mangled coffin—shards of broken glass everywhere.

Sitting there, he just couldn't get it out of his mind.

How the hell had it happened? How had the ship failed to see this goddamn planet? It just didn't seem possible.

"HEY!" Eckhaus called over the comm. "LOOK WHAT I FOUND!"

He was waiting for them when they finally arrived.

He was standing at the top of a blackened ridge, gesturing off into the distance at a group of crooked hills that jutted from the mist. Yanami and Sellers got up close to him, tried to see what he was seeing, then did.

"Damn," Yanami breathed. "Goddamn."

Sellers just stared.

Crowning the tops of the hills were the remains of what might have once been a city, but now were little more than cyclopean ruins. Carven towers, twisted spires, crumbling columns, rectangular buildings—all quarried from an odd gray-green stone.

"Wow," Yanami said in a husky voice. "A city…something…I don't know."

"Let's find out," Sellers said, glad for something constructive to do.

Eckhaus led the way down the slope. It was hard going, the hillside covered in a fine, black ash. At the bottom there was a plain of slippery, flat stones. They had all they could do not to be pitched on their asses in the bulky, day-glo orange e-suits. When you walked in the suit or turned or reached out to grasp an object, you really didn't do it at all, the suit did. Its receptors immediately knew what you were trying to do and did it for you, almost as if your nervous system was connected with the thing. After twenty minutes of cussing and sliding and inching, they stood at the threshold of the ruins. They towered above: ancient, omnipotent, and alien.

"Looks like they're about to fall on us," Eckhaus said.

And it did.

The monoliths and pyramidal slabs above seemed to be leaning in all directions at the same time. Forward, backward, to either side. A confused tumble of wild angles, an exercise in nightmare geometry. No human mind could've conceived of such structures; it made the brain ache just trying to study their lines, make sense of them—cones, discs, oblong spheres, arching columns.

"It's built to look like that," Yanami said. "Everything spills out at right angles from the base. Crazy. Almost looks like a growth of crystals, doesn't it?"

"High and hard," Eckhaus said. "Make you horny, Yanami?"

"Yeah, I'm wet," she said. "Why don't you slip out of that naughty suit and come over here?"

"Bitch."

Eckhaus led the way up there, through more of that sand or ash or whatever the hell it was. It took them another thirty minutes. The methane fog was growing heavier. Great swirling patches and clutching tendrils haunted the structure.

Yanami ran her glove along the stone. "Feel it," she said.

Eckhaus stroked her well-encased rump. "Oh yeah. Daddy likes."

She laughed. "Sexist asshole."

"You're much more sexist than me."

"The stone, I mean."

Sellers sighed. These two and their banter. They were both scared and he knew it, so they were laying it on thick to cover the fact.

Close up, the stone was not smooth as it had appeared, but pebbled, uneven, porous like quartz. The entire structure was convoluted, corrugated. No regularities whatsoever. Here it was jutting with irregular mounds, there it seemed to be formed of tapered cylinders layered over one another. Yes, up close, the entire thing was insane, like something a child had built out of odds and ends.

Sellers thought it looked like a colossal pile of bones.

Yanami took a black box off her belt. She pressed it to the material, stepped back. It clung like a tick, making a subtle whirring sound that the external microphones of the e-suits, of course, picked up. The object was a self-contained analyzing unit, or "magic box" as it was generally called. It could make detailed analyses of any object it came into contact with.

The whirring stopped. Yanami pulled it off. The results appeared on the inside of her visor.

"What's it say?" Sellers asked.

"Composition of material is unknown, but mineral in origin. Age is…oh shit…"

"What?"

"Captain, it says this stuff, these buildings, they were quarried at least fifty-thousand years ago."

Eckhaus whistled. "Goddamn. Might be something valuable inside."

"Yeah, like a personality. God knows you could use one."

"Oh, you're in such denial of my masculine charms," Eckhaus said. "Let's go inside."

"And how do you propose to *get* inside, oh wise one?"

And that was a good question. There didn't seem to be any doors, windows, openings of any sort. Yet, there had to be…didn't there? Black sand was pushed in banks up to the buildings, probably blown there by centuries upon centuries of wind. Chances were pretty good, Yanami pointed out, that they were only seeing part of the ruins, the rest were buried in the sand.

Undeterred, Eckhaus kept searching.

Yanami and Sellers followed behind, commenting to one another that Eckhaus was nothing if not amusing. He extended his middle finger and saluted them with it.

"Dust storm coming," Sellers said.

But they all knew that—their suits had told them.

High above, there were what looked like channels cut in the stone. But from their vantage point they might have been crazy, snaking ledges. About the time Sellers said they'd better find some shelter from the blow, Eckhaus found what he wanted.

There was an opening or part of one, anyway. A circular doorway, much of which was filled with sand. Eckhaus went down on his belly, crawled through and barely fit. His suit's exterior lights came on right away, cutting through the gloom. He was in a huge chamber of some sort.

"You okay in there?" Sellers asked.

"Yeah, c'mon in," he said. "Take a look."

They followed him inside. It was dark in there, murky, a cloistral haze hung in the air. The room was large, but empty. It seemed to serve no obvious purpose.

"It's like a fucking castle in here," Eckhaus noted.

And it was. Huge, empty, almost gothic with its lilting shadows and crawling network of passages twisting in every direction. Like the exterior, every square inch of surface was craggy and coarse, full of bumps and protrusions and knobby projections.

"Anthill," Sellers said under his breath.

He just stood there in the grainy darkness. Then: *"Jesus Christ!"* he suddenly cried, spinning around as fast as the suit would let him, his flesh literally crawling on his bones.

"What?" Eckhaus and Yanami said in unison.

Sellers was shivering and his suit immediately turned up the heat. "I don't know...I'm not sure. I thought..."

Yanami was a few feet away now. "Thought what?"

"Thought something brushed against me...something big."

There was really nothing to say to that. Eckhaus made a profane comment and Yanami said nothing. But her silence spoke volumes.

"Imagination," Sellers said, trying to reassure them and falling far short of the mark. "It's the dark...bothered me since I was a kid."

Eckhaus made a ghostly sound.

"Knock it off, dipshit," Yanami snapped.

It was an alien maze. The snaking passages not only wound off through the walls, but the floors and the ceiling, too. A labyrinth of utter blackness, cut only by the searching fingers of the suit lights.

"Be careful," Sellers said, inspecting a burrow in the floor, noticing with some unease that it continued long after his light failed. "You fall down one of those holes, who knows where you'll end up."

Eckhaus peered into the black mouth of a passage, disappeared into it.

"We shouldn't go too far," Sellers said, not knowing why. The suits, he knew, would map out their path and lead them safely back. And a rescue mission would pick them up immediately with thermal imaging on this frozen rock. Yet...he didn't want to go any further. The place was oppressive somehow, heavy and grim with the tenebrous atmosphere of a violated tomb.

And he was certain something had touched him.

"I've been thinking," Yanami said.

Eckhaus laughed. "Well, don't strain yourself."

"Piss off. The walls, the floors, the ceilings. Everything is bumpy, full of ridges and rises. When we build something, we build it smooth so we don't trip. But this place…it's like it's made so that whatever lived here would always have purchase, something to cling to or pull themselves along with."

"Yeah," Ekhaus said. "I'm starting to picture some real ugly bastards."

Yanami followed him into the tunnel. "Let's leave your family out of this."

"Long dead," Sellers said. "All long dead."

They followed winding, low corridors only to be led into more rooms. Some were covered in crabbed alien hieroglyphics, others just empty. Still others were crumbling to chalky dust. And everywhere, that haze and nameless darkness, pressing in from every direction. The farther they went, the more an odd, helpless feeling of anxiety grew. There was no explanation for it. It was just there—an almost palpable sensation.

Then they stumbled into the chamber.

It was immense. The vaulted ceiling was a good fifty feet above. Their lights couldn't seem to dispel the cloying blackness here, it was dusty and seeping. Like some mammoth cave, the chamber was honeycombed from floor to ceiling with elliptical cells. In each cell was a tangle of segmented spidery limbs wrapped around a central pear-shaped body that was heavy and armored. There was a cylindrical structure that might have been called a head. Its surface was covered with dozens of tiny, glaring orbs. In the center of these a slit, beyond which were something like serrated teeth. A face, maybe. But leering, hateful.

"They're dead," Sellers said, barely finding his voice.

Yanami stepped forward, placed her magic box against one of them. It whirred a moment. "Dead, all right. Petrified. Twenty-thousand years."

"What are they?" Eckhaus said, playing his lights over the cavities.

"Box says arthropods. Nice and general."

Sellers couldn't help notice that the creatures were not only residing in those cells, but connected to them. It was like they and this structure were only part of some huge biomechanical machine. *All these years*, he thought, *these mummies waiting and waiting in this mechanical crypt*. He examined one closer. It filled him with an instant atavistic dread, like a large spider or a scorpion, both of which it resembled. He'd come across plenty of alien life forms before…but these…they were loathsome, abominable.

"Don't you get it?" Yanami said. "We're in a gigantic alien mausoleum."

No more needed to be said on that.

"Let's get the fuck out of here," Sellers said. "All of us. We—"

Yanami screamed. A high, fierce, blood-maddened shriek.

"I saw it!" she screamed into their earpieces. "Something over there…*it moved!*"

She pointed to the mouth of another tunnel. There was nothing there, just stillness, oily darkness. Dust motes the size of snowflakes drifted in their light beams.

"You imagined it," Eckhaus said.

"Bullshit." But she would say no more on the subject. "Let's go."

Using her suit's guidance mechanism, she led them back the way they'd come.

She wasn't sure what she'd seen, just a blur of gangly motion. There couldn't possibly be anything alive in this frozen sepulcher…yet, there had been *something*. Though she wouldn't admit it to the others, this place filled her with a numb terror that she just couldn't put a finger on.

A hive of hideous, alien dead.

She wanted to break and run, to get away from it all. But she knew she had to keep her head. If you freaked-out, the suit would give you an injection of something to bring you down. And she didn't want that, not in this evil place.

They made it back to the original chamber. Outside, the dust storm was howling like a freight train. Visibility was zero. There was no way they could go back out in it.

"Let's just stay here," Sellers said, hating the idea. "Get some rest."

They laid together, the suits enveloping them in warm darkness, urging them gently to sleep. Despite themselves, Sellers and Yanami gave in, needing to shut it all down. They slept.

Eckhaus laid there wide awake, thinking, wondering.

And that's when he heard it: the music.

Low, piping, and melancholy. He could hear it clearly, but the others slept on. He asked the suit what it was. INSUFFICIENT DATA, it said. The general catchall for anything it didn't understand.

Eckhaus stood up, following the sound into the tunnels.

"Wake up," Sellers said, shaking Yanami roughly, dragging her from the depths of a nightmare into yet another, worse one. "Eckhaus is gone."

"Where is he?" she said.

"I don't know."

She asked the suit. "Where's crewman Eckhaus?"

UNKNOWN.

Unknown? Didn't make any sense. It should've been able to locate his suit.

"Let's find him," Sellers said, stalking off into the tunnels.

Silent, echoing, and very dead, the tunnels were a crazy lightshow of clawing, prancing shadows as their exterior lights cut a path in the claustrophobic darkness. Yanami overtook Sellers, who gladly let her take the lead. Though she was filled with a cold, crawling horror, she surged forward almost arrogantly. Needing to do this.

Finally, the burial chamber.

"If he's here," she said, "we'll find him."

There was no answer.

She turned, her lights bobbing and swaying.

Sellers was gone.

Frantically, she looked everywhere. Nothing but the creeping murk, the frozen alien dead, a grave silence.

"Where is crewman Sellers?"

UNKNOWN.

"WHERE THE FUCK IS CREWMAN SELLERS?"

UNKNOWN.

She went hot, went cold, shivered, sweated. The suit worked overtime to compensate, but there was no compensation for this. Inside her skull there was screaming white noise.

Steeling herself, she turned, carefully, thoroughly scanning every inch of the vault. If either of them were here, she'd find them. No way she could miss them.

This was how she found Eckhaus. He was standing against the cells, just waiting.

"Eckhaus?" she whispered.

No response.

She edged in closer, her breath coming in ragged gasps, her face wet with perspiration.

"Why doesn't Crewman Eckhaus answer?" she asked the suit.

UNKNOWN.

"UNKNOWN MY FUCKING ASS!" she screamed, her mind raging with awful imagery.

She approached the suit. The helmet view plate was a black mirror, her lights winking off it like suns. She reached out. Touched it. It fell over, collapsing, the helmet rolling away like a decapitated skull. It was empty. Eckhaus was not in the suit. There was nothing in there.

Well, of course not, a voice told her, *because—*

Eckhaus was nearby. He'd been taken apart like a puzzle, skinned, divided by saws, by knives, by an insane, predatory mind. He was very dead, his blood frozen to crystals, his limbs icicles.

Yanami stumbled backward. She would've fallen but the suit wouldn't allow it. Panic, terror, and mindless animal fear enveloped her. The suit would soon sedate her. She knew that. But she couldn't help screaming and screaming.

Particularly when the suit said: CREWMAN SELLERS IS BEHIND YOU.

And he was.

Or something was.

The suit was decompressed, yet something urged it forward. It moved all wrong, slack and dragging. Full where it should've been empty, empty where it should've been full. Yanami did fall now, crashing onto her back. Trapped in the coffin of her e-suit, she clawed and fought madly to be free.

And in her ears, music: mournful, shrill, eerie.

ERROR, the suit informed her. THIS IS NOT CREWMAN SELLERS. ERROR.

But she knew that as it dragged itself forward with a lurching, hopping motion. Closer, closer, reaching down for her as her mind went with a thundering wet snap.

That's when whatever was in the suit did the worst possible thing.

It removed the helmet and gave her a good look.

THE CITY
OF FROZEN
SHADOWS

The city was silent.

Blown by frigid winds, its streets and thoroughfares were barren as night came on. Trees were denuded and gnarled. No grass grew. No cats prowled. No night birds flew. Machinery was abandoned and houses were weathered gray, silent as bones. The stars looked down cold and pitiless and only ghosts walked its streets.

It was a graveyard.

Alone.

Charles Taylor was alone.

Alone in the dead urban moonscape. A pitted and gouged netherworld of shadowy buildings that were hulking, crumbling monoliths from a decayed and deceased civilization. Those that had built them were mummies now, drained of warmth and life and discarded like empty cans. All of them had been put to bed, tucked into sarcophagi and kissed by dust.

Taylor had red blood in his veins. He was alive and he was the last of the free men. Or at least this was what he told himself. It was easier that way.

The darkness was heavy and waiting, the wind cold. It was always cold. The world was wrapped in heavy cloud cover now. Light could penetrate it, but not heat. Nuclear winter. It had been this way for a year now since the Stygans came, since they had made Earth like their own world—frozen and stark.

He pressed himself into the shadows of the buildings, a 9mm automatic in his fist, a .38 in his coat pocket. He carried a knife, too. He was not afraid to use them. It had been quiet for days now and he did not like that. The hunters were out there somewhere. They looked like men and women and children, but they were not human. Mannequins animated by their alien puppet masters. Nothing more.

He thought: *The last one? Am I really the last one? The last breath of life in this sterile world?*

He looked up and down the streets. The city was effused with a surreal glow from the brooding, ancient moon above. He dashed from his hiding place and sought the shadows near a row of abandoned cars. He crept along them like a cat. In the distance he heard the peculiar sharp whirring of the alien war machines. They patrolled the streets and the fact that they still did said something. If he were the last man, why would the death machines keep up the vigil?

He licked his lips and his breath frosted into the night.

Sometimes he thought it was all a game with them. They had superior technology. No doubt they had methods of scanning, technologies probably light-years beyond infra-red. So why didn't they just pick up his heat signature and do away with him? He should have been easy to spot in the ice sculpture of the city.

He lit a cigarette, daring them to find him. His disobedience was a raw and hurting sore to them. Or, at least, he hoped so.

It was at times like this when the loneliness lay on him like concrete that he found himself thinking about Barbara. They were married two months when the shit rained down from the stars. And in love, oh God, how they'd been in—

Enough.

He couldn't think like that. Barbara was dead. She was part of the past.

Taylor grimaced with hate. The hatred cleared his head.

His face had long ago gone to leather from the bitter temperatures. His beard was thick and full. With the black watch cap pulled down over his ears, he looked like a burglar. But that was fine because he was one. It was how he made his living before they came and even now, crouched alongside a minivan, his pack was filled with cans of food he'd stolen.

Stolen?

No, it was hardly—

Quiet.

Yes, they were coming. A group of hunters. He sucked in a breath. His teeth wanted to chatter and his belly was filled with crawling things. He heard their footsteps. They did not speak. They marched with military efficiency, searching out stragglers. He saw them spill onto the avenue, five shapes cut from black cloth. Machines. Drones. They moved as one, remorseless, merciless, unrelenting.

They walked past the row of vehicles and stopped.

Taylor did not breath.

His heart did not beat.

His cells did not divide.

He went to stone and waited. Oh, God, he'd gotten so good at waiting, at silence. Only a marble bust was better at it. The hunters stood there, still as graveyard statues, all staring up the street. Then… they suddenly turned their heads in his direction, but all at the same time like they were hooked into a central brain. Which, they were. Dead, yes, they were all dead as such. Chips in their brains now. Their physiologies forever altered by alien biomedical technology.

Taylor knew he had to make a break for it.

He slowly backed into the oily pool of shadows cast by a Savings and Loan building. And they saw him right away. He knew by long experience that they did not hunt by sight or sound or even body heat, but by motion. And even the motion of lungs or the action of a heart muscle was enough. They could not pinpoint you, but they knew you were near.

One of them, a woman, spotted him.

Her eyes were huge and glistening red like pools of blood. No pupils, just black-red orbs swimming in unblinking sockets. She jabbed a finger at him and made a dry, hissing sound. The others began to hiss now, too. Like human insects, like locusts.

Taylor stood his ground, drawing them in like a fly into a web.

They fanned out, hissing like tea kettles, staring and pointing and hungry for the warmth that was in him. He let them get in closer. Their faces were pallid and etched by frost, painted yellow by the glacial moon. He kept the 9mm against his leg, made no threatening moves. They came on like marauding ants anxious to strip the carcass of an injured mouse.

Closer.

He smiled. "Not this time, assholes," he said under his breath.

When they were maybe ten feet away and he was certain he could not miss, he opened up. The automatic jerked in his gloved fist, gouts of flame spitting from the barrel. A man took two slugs that spun him around into another. A woman took hers in the belly. Her partner caught one in the chest, another in the throat. Taylor kept firing until they were all down and pissing that cold green sap they called blood.

They were all silent then, except one woman.

Half of her face hung from a grizzled thread of blasted flesh. Her lips pulled away from even, white teeth, eyes glowing with a malefic, cheated hatred. She began to hiss as gouts of green fluid spilled from her mouth. Her wounds steamed in the air.

Taylor shot her between the eyes.

The night grew heavy and black.

He wasn't worried about the hunters he'd drilled.

He'd greased them in a neighborhood far from his own. He'd only been there scavenging. Let them bring in their machines, let them level it. He was far away, laughing because maybe he was simply tired of crying. And killing them was the only true pleasure he had left. And this month, he'd clipped seventeen so far.

Fuck 'em.

He kept telling himself there had to be others. Brothers and sisters with warmth in their veins and fight in their hearts, comrades in the resistance. If he had survived, so had others.

His life was a tight, ceaseless circle of grim repetition.

Only through habit, through disciplined routine, had he survived this long. Nothing was left to chance. Impulse was unthinkable. All had to be plotted out—when to leave his hideout, when to gather food, when to sleep, when to eat, when to search for others.

Shortly after he'd gone into hiding, he'd raided a National Guard armory. He had handguns, grenades, automatic rifles, submachine guns, even perimeter mines. Things he'd used when he was a soldier years before. For a time, he'd booby-trapped old houses and buildings, leaving little surprises for the hunters. He only stopped when he thought he might accidentally kill living men or women.

He was sitting in the bombed-out ruin of a tenement. Waiting, smoking, watching the streets below through a missing section of wall. Watching the moon lord over the city. In the distance, he could hear the war machines. But not too often. Not like a few months ago.

Time to move.

He made sure his guns were loaded and ready, that his knife slid easily from its oiled sheath. *Check.* He stood up. There was a figure leaning up against a pile of rubble. Just sitting there, maybe trying to blend in.

A hunter?

He didn't think so, but he had to be sure. He slid his knife from its sheath. It was a K-bar. A fighting knife favored by the U.S. Marines once upon a time. It had a black, rubberized handle and a blue-steel blade, seven-inches long and sharp enough to slit a hair lengthwise.

He moved quickly and quietly like a cat.

The figure sat in a somewhat precarious position, back against the rubble, feet dangling into the night where the wall had once been. And nothing below but a three-story drop.

Taylor was careful.

He knew the Stygans liked to set out traps, baiting them with flesh and blood humans. More than once he'd been sucked into such a scenario. Once, they had used a child. Unthinkable, but it was how they were—cold, alien intellects that treated humans like insects to be used or crushed.

He came up on his quarry after he was certain there were no hunters hiding in the shadows. The figure was a man. He saw that much. He came up quick and put his knife against his throat. But he was too late—the guy was already dead. Maybe tonight, maybe last night, he'd slit his wrists.

"Why couldn't you have waited for me?" Taylor said to him. "One more night? A few hours? Would it have been that long?"

But he knew the lonely desperation of solitude, of being the sole survivor. He envied him. Envied his peace, his escape, his strength. He forced his hands away from the man's throat. The body tipped and fell into the night before he could stop it. It hit the walk below and shattered like glass.

And that, he knew, was more than mere cold. You didn't freeze-up like that from the wind. The Stygans had been at him. They had touched him. Whenever they touched someone, they went to ice, to crystal like they'd been dipped in liquid oxygen.

He remembered finding Barbara like that and how she'd broken apart as he touched her.

Taylor slumped over and wept.

The world was dead.

And death had come from the stars. But it hadn't come with flying saucers or comic book destruction, it had come quietly.

The old SETI network had picked up the first signal.

They called it a hyper-light transmission. It nearly overloaded their computers and took weeks to sort out the mathematical language. Finally, all the money spent searching the heavens for neighbors had paid off. The communication was from a planet called Styga. It was the seventh planet circling a star designated TXK221-B by the aliens, but known to Earth astronomers as Theta Eridani, a binary star, in the constellation of Eridanus, some 160 light-years from earth. They were uncertain as to our location. They wished to know more of our world and its people. They gave the SETI astronomers a precise bandwidth and were told they would amplify our signal in order to speed up the time lag which otherwise could have taken hundreds of years.

The astronomers transmitted the required info.

And the Stygans were never heard from again.

The astronomers promised it would take time, but years and years passed with no further contact. It was puzzling. Disturbing to some militarists who were against the SETI program from the beginning, considering it foolish to be broadcasting our position to anyone who might be listening. An invitation to invasion. And the idea was not simply paranoid, but backed by science. If evolution occurred on alien worlds the way it had on Earth, there could be great danger. For natural selection had generally channeled intellect to predators. Hunting and stalking required tactics, patterns, basic problem-solving—the progenitors of true intelligence.

Five years passed since the original Stygan communication.

It became the butt of jokes, the focus of both paranoia and conspiracy. Then an unthinkable chain of dire events began. A virus invaded Earth's computer systems and nearly overnight, anything with a memory chip in it shut down. Machinery would no longer function. The climate began to grow colder by the day. And lastly, an infectious plague swept the planet. Within a month, what remained of the human race (barely a third of what it had been six weeks before) we're swept into the Stone Age like hairballs into a dustbin. Civilization teetered, than collapsed entirely.

The Stygans arrived a year later in force.

The world was already beaten by then and this with no fancy light shows or Hollywood pyrotechnics. It was only a matter of rounding up the stragglers.

The predators, as it were, had arrived.

The hunters were on his trail.

Taylor was running and running, vaulting snowdrifts and skirting patches of black ice. The city reared up cold and dark and silent around him. He saw the subway entrance ahead opening for him like the maw of some primal beast. He slipped down there, waited on the steps with his heart thick in his throat. His lungs were full of fire. He had the 9mm out and he wished to God he'd brought a submachine gun with him.

He listened.

They were coming.

About twenty or thirty of them flowed into the icy streets, bleeding from the shadows. They carried no weapons; they didn't need to. They had formed up in ranks, marching in two single-file columns like automatons. The moonlight was reflected in the mirrored pools of their eyes.

Taylor went down the steps, urging his footfalls to be silent as drifting feathers. Down, down, down. He paused in the freezing darkness. It pooled around him black as tar. He had a flashlight with him, but he didn't dare turn it on. He stood on the platform and the darkness was a palpable thing, grainy, living, breathing. He moved quietly through it. He followed the tiled wall until he found the drop to the tracks. He hopped down there and stalked through the tunnel.

He guided himself using the wall, superstitious terror seizing him. He was alone in the dark…with whatever waited in it. But that was crazy, because there was nothing in the dark. Not anymore. Nothing haunted the dark but ghosts and memories and they were lonely, pale things. He kept pausing and listening, hearing nothing but his labored breathing, the blood rushing in his ears. Maybe, just maybe, he'd gotten lucky. Perhaps they hadn't followed him. He didn't use the subways much because they disturbed him…cave-like, claustrophobic, sunless, like being shut up in a closet or a coffin.

Sucking in a sharp, nervous breath, he dug out his Tekna flashlight and clicked it on. The brilliance of the beam was positively blinding. He saw the tracks winding off into the murk. A smoky haze hung in the air. Motes of dust danced in the beam like drifting moths. He saw a few skeletons heaped in the corner, a jawless skull farther up the track. Things like that had long since ceased to bother him.

Footsteps.

He clicked off the light, a pain ripping through his chest. He could hear their footfalls clearly now, echoing through the underworld. Yes, he'd fooled them for a bit, but now they knew where he'd gone. He heard their footsteps come down the stairs. Light, careful, patient. Then on the platform. He could hear them hissing and whispering. The tunnels caught the sound and amplified it.

He slipped away, boots placed softly, expertly. He moved on, keeping in contact with the stone wall. Sooner or later, he knew, he'd find what he was looking for.

Thud, thud, thud.

They were in the tunnels now, too.

Taylor started moving faster. They could sense motion and they could see in the darkness like hunting cats. He could hear them coming now, stealthily. Their hissings were echoing eerily through the passage. They filled his head with nightmare imagery—anemic faces and huge red eyes, killing fingers and cruel mouths. Close and closer.

He stopped dead.

Up ahead of him, another sound.

A slow, lumbering sound. A dragging noise moving in his direction. More of them? He heard it and then it was gone. His brain, inspired by too many Saturday afternoons of B-Movies, envisioned a giant spider living in the fathomless dark, the tunnels strewn with webs, festooned with dangling human remains.

But there was no time for imagination.

The hunters were very close now. If he squinted his eyes, he could nearly make out their shambling, shadowy forms.

He found a recess in the concrete wall and a door set into it.

He allowed himself to breathe.

A maintenance port.

The door came open, squeaking loudly. He slipped through it, shut it quickly behind him. There was a catch on the inside and he threw it. As he started up the ladder to the world above, he heard them at the door, fists hammering, nails scratching over rusting metal. The hissings and shrilling, and angry whispers. He only wished there was time to booby-trap the ladder.

He moved up it quickly.

It shook and groaned and he was certain it would pull from its cement housing, but it held. He saw light above, a street grating over his head. Shadows latticed his face. He peered through the slats and saw the city, the moon brooding above it full and lonesome. Below, they still worked at the door. They were nothing if not diligent. He swallowed a mouthful of raw fear and pushed at the grating. For a moment or two it wouldn't budge. He kept at it until the ice that welded it in place came free. It clattered onto the sidewalk and he lunged out, rolling through the snow.

Right away he heard the shrill sound of the war machines.

They were coming.

One of them prowled from the black mouth of an alley. It looked very much like an elliptical spheroid made of shiny blue-black metal that was crystalline like a diamond. A series of jointed mechanical legs, three on each side, supported it. The first time Taylor saw one he thought Earth had been invaded by giant spiders because that's what they resembled.

He crab-crawled into the shadows.

The war machine knew there was a human nearby, something alive. It moved in his direction, the tips of its legs ringing out with a subtle, hollow clanging as it approached.

Taylor, poised on the edge of a scream, ran into the confines of a crumbling building. A red light from the machine bathed the rubble, casting leering, dancing shadows in the night. He held his breath. Something suddenly growled in the blackness and ran over his legs and into the streets. A cat. A living cat. Taylor could scarcely believe it. He hadn't seen a cat—

It made it maybe halfway across the pavement when that crimson electric eye found it and a pulsing beam touched the cat. It froze up and teetered over, shattering. Taylor slipped through the wreckage and out of a cavernous hole in the wall. He was in an alley. He traveled down its length. It was L-shaped and veered off to the left. He darted down there and hid behind an overturned dumpster.

The alley suddenly lit up with an eerie, ethereal glow. It was ghostly and flickering. He waited. He had never seen anything like this before. What did it mean? His heart threatened to pound from his chest and cold sweat trickled down his spine. He heard that noise again: the one he'd heard in the subway tunnel. That heavy, cumbersome dragging sound. It was a dry, crackling noise like leaves crunching and static electricity arcing from blankets. It got closer and closer and louder. His skin was crawling and a tingling hole had opened up inside him.

Because he knew.

He suddenly knew.

He'd never seen a Stygan. He didn't think anyone ever had. No one that lived to tell the tale.

He peered from behind the dumpster to where the alley angled off. Against the frost-veined brick wall, that weird shimmering light played and pulsed and…a huge and gruesome shadow was thrown, swollen to nightmare proportions by the glow. Taylor saw a creeping, slithering mass of waving appendages and snaking limbs. Too much motion, too many things moving and coiling at the same time. He heard a strange, wet mewling sound.

He was cold and hot, his body thrumming with pure, animal terror. Because that dreadful and discordant mewling was the Stygan's voice.

Taylor screamed.

It was calling him by name.

An hour later, he was back in his hideout, his crib.

He dozed and woke alternately, covered in an icy sweat. He shivered with fever, his dreams dark and menacing. Finally, true sleep came and it locked him down. In his little basement apartment in the cellar of a ruined building, he slept amidst the trappings of survival and urban guerilla warfare. Tangled in black and forbidding shadow, a grim frost fell over him, wrapped him up tight and soundless like a winding sheet.

His eyes opened just before dawn.

He was not alone.

He knew that the moment consciousness flooded into his brain. He had been living by instinct, living like an animal for too long not to sense the invasion of his burrow. He came awake with the .357 Smith he kept under his pillow. He saw shadows upon shadows knotted and snarled together like jungle vines and creepers and leafage.

There was an escape route behind him. A passage that led into the sewers and to freedom.

THE CITY OF FROZEN SHADOWS

He saw a form in the darkness, heard it breathing. The eyes glistened. "You don't need the gun," it said. "Put it away."

He went white with fear: it was his wife's voice. *Barbara.* She had been dead these many months, frozen like an icicle and, like one, shattered. And now she was back, resurrected, it would seem, via Stygan technology.

He made a dash and clicked on the battery-powered light. Their kind didn't like the light. And true to form, she shrieked and hissed, covering her ashen face with long, pale fingers. She made a hissing sound and then seemed to control herself. "Please, Charles, turn off the light. Turn it off."

And he wanted to, it was blinding.

"You've come for me," he said. A statement. "They sent you."

Between the chill shafts of her fingers, her eyes were red neon bulbs. "It was time."

And he knew it was. She had not come alone—he could hear others outside, a ghastly knot of them trembling beyond the doorway. He thought he heard others creeping up his escape passage. They sounded like snakes gliding over stone. They had him. They were making it easy on him by letting Barbara—or the thing that wore her face—take him.

It was the most he could hope for.

He dropped the gun. So tired, so broken, so defeated. But the thought of those glacial fingers bleeding the warmth from him was unthinkable. He brought out his knife and, grinning, slashed his wrists open. But there was no blood, just thick, translucent green syrup. It hung from his gashed wrists like tree sap.

"Even me," he said, his world spinning into fragments. "Even me."

Barbara offered him a mannequin's smile. Nothing more.

The war was over. And had been for some time.

GHOST SHIP

I t drifted through dead space like a cadaver in a fathomless black sea.

A derelict, skeletal and forbidding.

Shaped oddly like twin submarines joined at the conning towers, its hull plating was blackened, superstructure pitted from meteor collision, aft thrusters sheared completely away as if by some tremendous impact.

On the bridge of the merchant vessel *Venera-12,* Boston, the first mate, studied her through the view screen, shaking his head. "Goddamn," he said. *"Goddamn!"*

And that pretty much said it all for those on the bridge. They sat in silence, wondering, waiting, staring at the derelict drifting an easy two hundred meters off the *Venera's* bow.

It wasn't five minutes before the old man showed up, chomping down on his pipe stem, his eyes set like concrete. "What do you got for me?" He stared out at the dead ship, not impressed.

"Derelict, Captain Wynn," Franz, the technical officer said.

"Yeah, I can see that, mister." He turned to Boston. "Got a number off her, Bosty?"

Boston nodded. "Late twenty-first century. Early freezer ship."

Wynn lifted his shaggy, unkempt eyebrows. "You don't say. Got a name?"

"Yes," Franz said, "she does."

Wynn turned to Franz at his console. "Are you going to tell me what that is?"

Franz looked from Boston to Wynn. "Yes, sir. I checked registry. Name of the ship is the *Croatoa.*"

Wynn's eyes widened. He pulled the pipe from his mouth. "You saying..."

"Yes, sir," Franz said almost proudly, seeing the look on his face. "The *Croatoa.* The one and only."

Jesus H. Christ, Wynn thought, *of all things.*

The *Croatoa* had left earth in 2087, one of the very first suspended animation ships. She carried a crew of twenty-seven. Her destination was the triple star system of Alpha A, Alpha B, and Proxima Centauri. Centauri A, long known to be much like Earth's sun, had always been a dream destination of astronomers. Round about 2081, the old SETI network picked up high frequency microwave pulses from an unidentified source. They were tracked to the fourth planet of the Alpha Centauri A system. First contact had finally been made. The *Croatoa* was the third such mission in as many years sent to investigate. Of course, some thirty years later, the first star drives were developed. Rescue ships sped out into the void and liberated the crews of the freezer ships.

Except one: the *Croatoa.*

"They never could find her," Franz said, though everyone knew the story quite well. "She stopped sending telemetry five years out. It was thought she rammed into an uncharted asteroid. Then in 2134, she was found. A warship named the *Lucia* encountered her fifteen light-years from where she could possibly have been."

The *Croatoa,* still functioning, was boarded, found to be empty. No sign of a crew. Escape pods were still in place. Everything was in order, except the crew was missing. The *Lucia* put a crew aboard and two solar days later, they, too, were missing after failing to report in after an interval of six hours. Another crew was put aboard.

"A few days later, same thing. They were just *gone.* After several days of fitful searching, his people ready to mutiny, the captain of the *Lucia* cut the derelict adrift." Franz paused, his voice having gone very dry. "And now, she's back again."

The silence was thick after that. No one spoke, no one moved.

There was a prevailing, breathing stillness that locked the bridge down hard like an insect in amber. The *Croatoa* was to space exploration what the *Mary Celeste* had been to Earth's maritime circles in the old days: a ghost ship, a hoodoo vessel. The subject of countless theories and speculation. The source of dozens of deep space horror stories. A modern myth cycle.

"Any life over there?" the old man asked. "Any systems still operational?"

"Life scanners show no organic activity. Nada. The freezer cells are functioning, but empty. The pile's still operating, believe it or not. She has gravity and lights, but no life support," Franz said.

Wynn stuck his pipe in his pocket. "Well, damn, if I'm not curious. You got a beam on her, Mister Franz?"

"Aye, sir."

Wynn smiled. "Well, reel the old girl in. We're boarding her ASAP."

Two hours later, Wynn followed a tungsten composite walk-wire from the *Venera-12* to the hulk of the *Croatoa*. Despite the superstitious fear the old ship inspired, the crew were falling over each other to join the boarding party. It was excitement, it was drama. After two years of tedious boredom hauling ore from the colonies, this was a big event. A real living mystery. The *Venera* was buzzing.

Wynn chose Franz, medical officer Alonzo, second mate Margulies, and an engineering tech name of Eagle, who was on her first voyage. They followed the wire down to a starboard escape hatch on the *Croatoa*. Eagle opened it with a burning bar and in they went.

They came in through the honeycombed maintenance tunnels where there was no gravity. They swam through grainy darkness until they reached the interior hatches. Once inside, it was a little better— the cabins were pressurized, artificial gravity still operating, emergency lights on in the corridors.

The sense of silence, of emptiness, was almost overwhelming. *Eerie* was the word for it. Like walking the shadowy byways of a ghost town. Memories seemed to linger in the air, suggestions of events long past.

Wynn felt it.

It got along the back of his neck, made his scalp crawl. He'd felt something like it only once before. Years back, he'd been selected to join a landing party on Beta Cygni-4. The colony there had been wiped out by a viral plague of unknown origin. It was horrible. Dead bodies everywhere, bloated up and covered with a blue fungus. Not a soul left. Empty homes and buildings, deserted streets. He could remember the almost claustrophobic sense of terror he'd experienced. He felt that now, fifteen years later.

But what was worse, more troubling, was the sense that this was all very familiar somehow. Déjà vu? Imagination? It was unsettling all the same.

The *Croatoa* was like a huge, drifting tomb, hushed and shadowy.

But nothing was out of place.

Supplies were untouched. Containers still sealed as they had been for the past eighty years. Personal belongings were still stowed in cabin nooks. Escape pods in hangars. The *Croatoa* wasn't a terribly large ship. Twenty minutes of searching and they didn't find a thing worth mentioning. Save a few items left by the *Lucia's* crew: flashlights, a few blasters, assorted technical equipment, now all hopelessly antiquated.

"Eagle?" Wynn said, his face slightly luminous from the helmet lamps. "You go up to engineering, see if you can get some more lights on."

"Yes, sir," she said.

Wynn stared at her face a moment or two longer than necessary. She was lovely, olive-skinned with huge almond eyes. Native American descent. Her beauty was only marred by a thin white scar along the bridge of her nose. And, somehow, that seemed to enhance it.

Wynn turned away. "Franz, go with her. See if you can do anything with the AI, find out anything. Marguiles, lend 'em a hand."

"Aye, sir."

Franz patted the plasticized container he had with him. The crew of the *Lucia* had tried in vain to tap into the *Croatoa's* brainbox, the artificial intelligence package that ran the ship, monitored all the systems, and kept things humming along. All they lacked was the proper technology. "This baby ought to do it," Franz said.

The transmitter in Wynn's helmet buzzed.

"You guys still alive down there?" Boston asked.

"Yeah, we're fine, Bosty."

"Anything?"

"Same as the *Lucia* found—nothing. We've been checking around, though. Looks like the freezer cells were opened manually. My guess is they rammed into something and the captain woke everyone up to see what it was. Just a guess."

"But where are they, Skipper?"

"I don't know. Maybe they sent out a distress signal—she's crippled without the thrusters—and maybe…maybe someone came to rescue them."

"Or some *thing*."

"I'll keep you posted."

"C'mon, Doc," Wynn said to Alonzo, "let's see what we can see."

Twenty minutes later, they had lights.

"That Eagle," Wynn said, "she's good."

"The best," Alonzo said.

Alonzo and he were standing outside the captain's quarters. The door, unlike the others, was locked down. Wynn desperately wanted to get in there. Somehow, it seemed important. He knew he could cut the hatch with his pulser, but he didn't want to damage it. When they towed this baby back to port at Ceti Station, there was going to be a major investigation. If Wynn or the others destroyed any evidence, there would be hell to pay.

He popped the access panel next to it, started fiddling with the components within. Jesus, there were actually wires and transistors. Wynn hadn't seen anything like that since he was a kid. "Where you going, Doc?" he said to Alonzo's retreating envirosuit.

"I'm gonna go down to sickbay, see what I can access there."

"Good idea."

Wynn kept working at the components with his tool kit, reconnecting, rerouting. It was work better suited to Eagle, he figured, but she had other things to do. So he kept at it.

Thirty minutes later, Franz buzzed him. "AI interfaced, Captain."

"Goddamn. Good going." Wynn was excited. "What do you got?"

"Ship's log."

"And?"

There was silence for a moment. "Some of it's damaged. I'll need the *Venera's* system for complete recovery, but I think I got the gist."

Wynn was about to snap at him to get on with it already when the hatch slid open. He wasn't sure what he'd done, but it had worked. "Franz? I'll be up in a few. Get together what you can."

He stepped into the captain's quarters, amazed momentarily how little the design of ships' cabins had changed in eighty years. But he supposed a bed was a bed and a desk was a desk and a—

There were two people in there.

At least, there were two Day-Glo orange envirosuits. One was lying on the bed, the other sitting at the commander's desk. Wynn, his throat dry, attempted suit-to-suit communication with them but got nothing. He told his suit to try all channels. Still nothing. He approached the suits. The helmet lamps were out, so he couldn't see inside them. He checked the power packs on each. Both long dead. There was dust covering everything, including the suits, years upon years of dust. So much of it, in fact, he had to brush it away like sand. Whoever was inside was dead. Had to be. The suit's internal atmospheres would have failed long ago.

But it bothered him. It all bothered him more than it should have because it was all wrong. How long ago had the *Croatoa* left earth? Eighty years. These suits were of recent vintage. They even had pulsers, modern side arms, standard-issue to both merchant and military vessels. Comm systems were modern, rebreathers were modern— *what the hell was going on here?*

Maybe, maybe, he thought, *these two were from the* Lucia.

But that didn't wash either. The *Lucia* had encountered the dead ship fifty years ago. They didn't have pulsers then either, just lasers and particle blasters. And they didn't have suits like these. They had e-suits, of course, but not like these.

Clicking on his palm light, Wynn inspected the helmet of the suit on the bed. Beyond the view plate, the face was horrible. Lips drawn away from teeth in a twisted grimace. The eyes were distorted, the irises filled with a mutiny of broken blood vessels. The lips were bluish, the face itself disfigured by a series of pinpoint hemorrhages. Wynn knew he was looking at a victim of oxygen starvation. Not an easy death.

Then he saw the white scar traced along the bridge of the nose.
Eagle has a scar like that.

Trembling now, he looked closer. He could see a braid in the helmet, that lustrous blue-black hair. Oh, Jesus Christ in Heaven, what the hell was going on here?

He went over to the suit at the desk. There was a blade in the gloved fist. The owner had been using it to scratch something in the table. Wynn moved the hands.

GET OUT WHILE YOU STILL CAN

Licking his sandpaper lips, he shined his light into the helmet. Something hitched in his chest, there was a distant echoing scream in his brain. He staggered towards the door, held onto the frame for support.

The body in the suit was his own.

Yes, yes, of course it is, his mind told him. *You've done all this before and it ends in this room.*

He accepted it. Revelation was much easier than he expected. A sense of calm fell over him. Now he understood the déjà vu earlier. He understood everything.

And then the lights went out.

"Captain? Where the hell have you been?" Franz said when Wynn finally joined them about twenty minutes later. "Why didn't you answer us?"

"Must be something wrong with my receiver," he said. His voice was feeble, barely even there.

They were in the engineering section. Eagle and Margulies were scrambling around in the darkness checking the panels with their exterior helmet lamps.

"What happened to the power?" Wynn asked.

"Something blew, sir," Eagle said. "This old junk...goddammit... it's not easy to work with."

Margulies said, "Junk is right. Those people must've been crazy to set out in a heap like this. Fucking death trap."

Wynn turned to Franz, saw the terror in his eyes. "Sir," he said, on a private waveband so the others wouldn't hear. "I can't get a hold of Alonzo. He's missing."

"We'll find him. Just relax. What did the log read?"

Franz sighed. "Five years out they rammed into something. Captain's freezer cell unthawed him first as it was programmed to. He checked it out before waking the others. They'd struck another ship. The *Croatoa* was badly damaged. He woke the others, told 'em that their ship was crippled. The alien craft that rammed them was still there…just drifting. The crew decided that maybe they could make use of it. So they boarded her.

"It was completely alien. Shaped like an elongated cylinder, it was just one huge hollow inside. All they found was a sphere. Apparently it had been suspended by a series of what they thought were light cables, but the impact with the *Croatoa* had damaged it. The sphere was empty. But it wasn't really empty…"

Wynn just stood there, shaking, remembering it now. "It followed them back to the ship."

"Exactly. It wiped out the entire crew in a matter of hours, an alien monstrosity, a predator. Captain," Franz said and came in closer now, "they thought that the creature wasn't merely travelling in that sphere, but *imprisoned* within it. They deduced it was of extradimensional origin. Like nothing they'd ever seen or anything we've ever seen. A real horror. Once loosed, it had an odd effect on everything—systems failed one after the other, instrumentation could not be relied on. Its physics were all wrong, it was distorting the material of this universe, corrupting matter, time…"

Yes, *time*. Wynn knew it did that. It fucked up everything it touched.

"Sir!" Eagle called. "I can't reach the *Venera!* I've tried on all channels."

Franz tried, so did Wynn and Margulies. Nothing. Lastly, Franz used his scanner.

"It's…*gone*." He tried different settings and, finally, in frustration, started shaking the black box madly. "It's not there. There's nothing within a thousand kilometers of the *Croatoa*. Even my uplinks with the ship…they're gone."

"Sir," Margulies said in weak voice. "Check your chronometer."

He did. It read that it was no longer today. In fact, it was three months ago.

"What the hell's going on here?" Eagle said, close to hysteria.

"All right, all right," Wynn said in the best soothing voice he could muster. "Franz, Margulies, you two make for the hatch. Maybe it's our instruments. Maybe it's this damn mausoleum. Go out there and physically check it out."

"What about you two?" Margulies said. "Shouldn't we stay together?"

"Negative. Eagle and I'll find the doc and rendezvous with you. Keep in voice contact. Keep your pulsers handy."

Madness closing fast now, they went their separate ways.

Eagle heard it first.

A dry, crackling sound like static electricity.

Then Wynn caught it, felt the hairs on the back of his neck stand up. He heard it get louder, shattering the stillness as it rose up to a thunderous snapping and popping. He could actually feel it *moving* through him, thrumming along his bones. It was as if, suddenly, without warning, a huge amount of energy had been released.

"What the hell is that?" Eagle asked him.

Wynn just stood there, staring at her face shield. "Franz! Margulies!" he called on the suit intercom. "What's going on? Do you—"

"I don't know, sir," Franz's voice came back and the crackling seemed even louder where he was, almost deafening. "I'm getting wild readings on my scanner...Jesus Christ, it's right off the scale! Margulies...it's...*GET AWAY FROM IT!*"

"What?" Wynn said. "What's going on?"

If Franz attempted to answer, Wynn never heard it. What he did hear was a shrill screeching and the sound of scuffling, cries, thuds. Then the hissing oscillations of pulsers being fired, of bulkheads being turned to scrap metal from the particle barrages they emitted.

When Eagle's voice came it was hollow: "Should we..."

"No. Not now. Not now."

At the end of the corridor, Franz came running. It was a stumbling jog at best in his envirosuit. He tripped, slammed into a bulkhead, righted himself, came on again, fell over completely and began crawling towards them.

He didn't respond to either Wynn or Eagle.

As he got closer, they could see his suit was damaged, external apparatus torn free. Eagle and Wynn went trotting to his aid in their cumbersome suits. When they were within a hundred feet of him, the shadowy corridor exploded with bluish, humming light. That crackling rose up again, louder than ever.

And they saw it.

The prisoner of the sphere.

It came on as an incandescent cloud of green-yellow mist sparking with tongues of blue. Contained within the cloud was a spiraling network of fleshy, snapping ropes, like hundreds and hundreds of knotted rags swirling and flaying in every conceivable direction, constantly in motion.

"Oh God," Eagle gasped.

Drawing his pulser, Wynn fired into it.

The beam struck it, was instantly absorbed and separated into a dozen harmless prismatic rays of light. The closer it got to the crawling figure of Franz, the more of it they could see. It was incredible in some nightmarish way. The rags seemed to swim out wildly from an ever-changing flux of gas and sparkling jelly held in stasis by that membranous cloud. The rags were like dark, coiling strands of snotty tissue one moment, and the next crumbling whips that flaked away into dust motes. It reinvented itself second by second with hallucinogenic speed and motion.

Eagle and Wynn kept firing at it with no effect.

They saw the insane, screaming face of Franz pressed up to his view shield and then he was drawn towards the thing, sucked into its noxious mass. Wynn saw a thousand rents open in his suit and then he disintegrated, anatomized into a blowing mist like a bag of blood in a wind tunnel.

Wynn pulled Eagle with him, towards the captain's quarters, where he knew they must go.

Behind them the thing kept coming, a tornado of flesh and gas. It left a destructive wind in its wake, a funnel of polluted air in which fragments and refuse of all kinds swirled and danced—papers, bits of iron, garbage, fragments of bone and flesh, pieces of itself.

Wynn pushed Eagle through the doorway of the captain's cabin and closed the hatch. The creature passed by outside, the metal door going luminous for a moment, and then it was gone. Wynn wondered for not the first time (and maybe the hundredth time for all he knew) if the thing was even remotely intelligent and not just some alien scavenger from the cellar of another dimension.

"What will we do?" Eagle asked him, sitting on the edge of the bed.

"We wait," he told her, sitting at the desk as he knew he must. "When it's quiet, we leave."

He checked his chronometer. It was two days ago now. The appearance of the creature distorted time and space. If it stayed gone… yes, maybe if it stayed gone, in two days' time they could rendezvous with the ship. But he knew he was kidding himself.

He took out a blade from his tool kit and scratched a message for himself, hoping this time he'd heed its dark import.

It drifted through dead space like a cadaver in a fathomless black sea.

A derelict, skeletal and forbidding…

THE KILLING JAR

he asteroid cored the *Polyphemus*, crippling her star drive, tearing her wide open amidships. The crew—what remained of it—stabilized life-support, but despite dogged effort, they were left with a very unpleasant state of affairs: the *Polyphemus* wouldn't be doing any star-hopping in the foreseeable future. In fact, she couldn't even make sub-light. The ship was adrift. They were stuck out in the great beyond, some fifteen parsecs from Earth and the Colonies.

If their distress call was picked up, great, if not, the *Polyphemus* would be drifting for millennia. There were only four left, Krist and Doc Mowfali, Chung and Dendro. The rest were corpses. The majority of them (those that hadn't been sucked out the jagged breach in the hull) had been gathered, in whole and in part, wrapped in sheets and placed in plastic, vacuum-sealed mortuary bags. It was the best that could be done under the circumstances.

Krist, the first officer, gathered the survivors together. "You know the situation," he said, his voice dire and very much lacking the optimism he'd once been known for. "We've sealed off the damaged sections of the ship which account for over two-thirds of the *Poly*. The drive is out, magnetic core is leaking plasma. Shit, even the auxiliaries are gutted."

"We are in a word, people," Chung put in, *"fucked."*

Krist shrugged. "That about sums it up. Even our escape pods were smashed. We got a distress call out and hopefully it'll be picked up and vectored. If not…"

"There's gotta be something we can do," Dendro said. The idea of dying out here was even harder on him than the others. He had a wife and two kids back in New Cleveland on Mars. "The *Poly* is a fucking star-clipper, First. She's supposed to have back-ups to her back-ups to the point of redundancy."

"And every goddamn one of them has been neutralized," Chung pointed out.

It went against the law of averages, but it had happened.

The *Polyphemus* had been en route to Magellan's World, the fourth planet of the Theta Centauri system. She was carrying forty colonists who were going to set up a permanent scientific survey base in the stagnant, steaming jungle hell of the southern hemisphere. And then they met the asteroid. Even the anti-collision/avoidance software hadn't picked it up. It had never even been mapped.

"Doc," Dendro said, looking to Mowfali, whom he considered the most rational person he knew, "tell me this isn't happening."

"Just take it easy," was all she could come up with.

But Dendro wasn't taking it easy. He looked ready to split his seams.

"If our distress was heard, a rescue ship can be here in six, seven weeks," Krist told them. "Problem is, we don't have six or seven weeks. The batteries will give us life support for two at the outside. We can gain another two in our e-suits. Either way, it's not enough. I say we do what we can, scavenge what we can for a few days. If we can't come up with anything better by then, we go into cryo and wait for rescue. The tubes'll keep us safe theoretically for several hundred years."

Dendro looked at them again like they were all crazy. "But my wife, my kids…Jesus H. Christ, I can't be frozen for twenty years or even thirty! C'mon, goddammit!"

"Just take it easy," Doc Mowfali told him, taking his hand in hers. "We're looking at a worse case scenario. Chances are, they'll come for us."

Dendro did not look convinced. He looked angry if anything, like he wanted to smash something. But there was no target, so he just went limp as the hope ran out of him. After that, he didn't say much. His family was his reason for living and if he didn't have that…

Krist wouldn't allow anyone to slack.

Things needed doing and they needed doing right now. Doc Mowfali was tasked with making sure the cryo systems were go if it came to that. There were only the emergency chambers left, the others had been destroyed in the impact. Krist made an extensive inventory of what they had that had not been sucked out into the void. Chung and Dendro went to see about the remote possibility of rigging solar batteries strong enough to charge the *Polyphemus*. It was a long shot, but it was worth a try. And if anyone could pull it off, Chung could.

Everyone settled in and got to work.

Krist was working on their food supply: how much they had and how long it might last them when the comm buzzed.

"Yeah?"

"First, you better get down here," Chung said. "We got incoming."

It was too soon. Nobody could have reached them this soon. "Tell me it's not another fucking asteroid."

"No. Nothing like that. It's a ship…and it's not one of ours."

Well, that was sheer understatement. What the scanners were tracking was coming in fast, 80% of light velocity. It had jumped out of nowhere, leaping out of hyperspace, and its trajectory was bringing it right at the *Polyphemus*. And the state she was in, there was no way in hell they were going to be able to maneuver out of its way.

"It's slowing," Chung said, having to work the controls manually because of the catastrophic damage. "Still coming at us. Collision in twelve minutes."

While Dendro and Doc Mowfali stood there wringing their hands and preparing for the worst, Krist tried to swallow down the dryness in his throat. "Give me those specs again."

Chung shook his head. "Unless this thing is malfunctioning, it's reading a roughly cylindrical mass of over sixteen klicks in length and five in circumference."

"Who builds a ship that goddamn big?" Dendro wanted to know.

When they'd first picked up its signature he'd been excited, almost gleeful, because he figured a deep-space freighter or a drone had picked up their distress call and was coming to rescue them. That had waned now. A ship that size...the implications were frightening.

"Still slowing and still coming at us," Chung said.

By the time it was less than a hundred kilometers away, it had slowed practically to a drift. The chances of a violent impact were negligible, but it was still bearing down on them.

"I've got magnification at max," Chung said. "Should be visible in a few seconds. Closer, closer...there it is."

It came out of the blackness of space, a massive dirty gray cylinder made of knobby overlapping plates with weird protrusions jutting out of it like tree stumps. Its fore end was like a huge black open mouth that gave it the look of a hungry monster. Whoever or *what*ever had designed it hadn't been much on aesthetics or style. It was a huge, ugly machine and that's about all that could be said about it. Other than the fact that it was perfectly alien and there was something unbearably disturbing about it. They could all feel it creeping inside them, but they didn't know how to put it into words.

"Why the hell doesn't it veer off?" Dendro asked. "It's got to know we're here. Why doesn't it try to avoid us?"

"Exactly what I was wondering," Mowfali said.

"Because it coming at us is no accident," Chung told them, wiping sweat from his brow. "I've been tracking it and it's made three course corrections to bring it right to us."

Even with magnification at normal, it filled the screen. It was coming for them and there was no doubt of it now. They were heading straight for its huge black maw.

"It's going to swallow us," Dendro said.

"Everybody in their e-suits!" Krist snapped. "Move! Move!"

They knew the drill. They were panicked, terrified really, but they were in their suits in a matter of minutes. The open maw of the alien ship filled the screen now. They were staring down its black throat. It was as if the stars had been turned off. The *Polyphemus* began to vibrate madly. There was a sound of metal fatigue as if they had been grabbed by a giant, squeezing fist. The ship shook itself like a wet dog and everyone was thrown to the deck plating. The auto gravity was canceled out momentarily and they began to float.

"It's got us in some kind of force beam," Chung said over the helmet channel. His voice was dry and rasping. "It's pulling us in…"

There was a great concussive noise like a sonic boom and then the gravity was back. They fell to the deck and pulled themselves to their feet.

"It's got us now," Dendro said. There was no hope left in his voice.

"What do we got out there?" Krist asked.

"We've got…" Chung said, working the scanners, "…normal gravity, a breathable atmosphere, median temperature of about fourteen Celsius." He looked at the others. "My guess is that we've been scanned and the ship has adjusted itself accordingly."

"The welcome mat is out," Mowfali said.

Inside his helmet, Dendro shook his head back and forth. "No…no way. I'm not going out there."

Krist sighed. "Son, what are you going to do? Hide in this broken hulk? Someone went to a lot of trouble to invite us aboard. If they'd wanted us dead, they could have crushed us with that beam. Let's go see what this is about."

Dendro didn't like it. He wanted to explain to them that the dread he felt inside had ramped up to something akin to pure terror now, but he knew it was hopeless. They wouldn't listen to him.

Krist opened the airlock and led them down the ramp into the gigantic alien craft.

They were in a huge bay or amphitheater of sorts. It was so big that their helmet lights and spots could not find its walls or ceiling. Krist had not given them the order to remove their pressure helmets yet and he wasn't about to. Not until he was sure.

Command and he had always been easy partners. It came natural to him to lead. But here, in this place, it weighed on him heavily because he knew that everything he did or failed to do might cost somebody their life.

Chung circled around them, shining his light in every direction. He had a scanner strapped to his left arm and he was taking readings.

"This room is about two city blocks in width, half that in length. Amazing." He kept scanning. "The ceiling is over sixty meters above us." He shook his head. "An area this large, yet they managed to pressurize it in seconds."

"Look," Mowfali said. "Down there."

They all saw it: a pale blue orb of light. It seemed to beckon to them.

"Let's go," Krist said. "But remember: as far as we're concerned, our hosts are friendly. Until they give us reason to doubt that, keep your pulsers on your belts. I want no shooting. Got it?"

They followed him towards the light. It was a long way away. When they reached it, it disappeared and an oval hatch opened. Before them was a long corridor with an arched ceiling. The first section of it was illuminated.

"Shall we?" Mowfali said.

There was really no going back and the wreck of the *Poly* was little enticement, so on they went. They walked silently. The floor, walls, and ceiling were made of the same shiny blue-black material that the scanner told them was a type of iridium-platinum composite alloy. It also told them it used a type of unknown plastic as a bonding element.

As they walked, the lights were turned off behind them. Section by section, the corridor was illuminated. They reached another hatch, but it did not open.

"Now what?" Dendro said.

The words had barely left his mouth when they discovered something disturbing: they could not move. Their boots were stuck to the floor and no amount of twisting or pulling could free them. Dendro began to swear, telling them he warned them about something like this. Then an aperture winked open above them and sprayed them with clouds of green gas. It only lasted for a couple seconds, but when it finished, they could move again.

Dendro brushed dry green flakes from his suit. "What the hell is this stuff?"

Mowfali noticed that it was evaporating quickly. "Decon," she said. "I think we've just been decontaminated."

"Makes sense," Krist said.

The hatch before them opened.

It was another corridor that spilled into another that angled off to the right, then terminated with yet another that climbed a low rise. It was a maze and the blue light led them deeper and deeper into it.

"This is insane," Dendro said. "We're so goddamned lost and turned around that we'll never find our way out."

"And if we could, where would we go?" Chung asked him.

"Back to the *Poly*. Even cryo is better than this."

"You need to stop getting yourself worked up," Mowfali told him. "If you keep it up, your suit is going to shoot a sedative into you. We don't need you dopy right now."

"She's got a point, son," Krist said.

The e-suits mothered their wearers. They heated you, cooled you, administered medicine if needed. If they thought you were in danger of an episode or a panic attack, they'd juice you with tranquilizers to mellow you out.

Dendro said nothing.

He could not verbalize the terror building in him.

They found themselves in an immense oval room with spouts jutting from the ceiling. What their purpose was, nobody could even guess. Chung tried scanning them, but the scanner had no idea what they were either. The entire ship seemed to be that way, Krist got to thinking, abstract, intangible. They were led deeper and deeper into it, but there seemed to be no rhyme or reason for any of it. They'd been in the ship well over an hour by that point and they were still no closer to understanding what the point of it all was.

We were sucked in here, he thought. *But it wasn't to make contact with whatever race built this. It has to be something else.*

Chung paced off the perimeter of the room, which was like being inside a giant egg. He scanned the walls, the floor, the ceiling. But there was nothing. There was no hatch to lead them out of there.

"I don't get it," he said. "Nothing makes sense. We were invited aboard so we could get lost?"

He'd barely finishing saying that when Dendro let out a fevered cry. "The door! The goddamned door isn't there!" He was standing at the point where it had been, but was no more. *"We're trapped in here! We're fucking well trapped!"*

Krist and Mowfali stood with him. There was no evidence there ever had been a door: the wall was perfectly smooth, not so much as a seam.

Chung made a quick scan. "I can't even pick up a passage on the other side."

Krist could feel the panic rising. As commander, he knew he had to do something, say something to calm them and bring them together, but damned if he knew what that might be.

Things began to happen.

It was Dendro that noticed it first. Out of one of the spouts overhead, a blue-green light began to flicker. "What the hell is that?" he said. Then a beam of light shone down on him. It was that same pale indigo and he was trapped in it. Agitated particles swam in the light like bubbles in champagne. He was trapped in it. They could see him trying to break free, but it was as if he was inside a glass jar. He was screaming, crying out for help, but there was no sound. The transmission from his helmet had been completely silenced.

When the others made to go to him, they were likewise encased in beams. It was all bad enough, but what happened to Chung was significantly worse. His beam began to fill with a black, oozing substance. It was like drops of India ink dispersing in water until his beam was so dark, they couldn't see him anymore.

They were all shouting, beating their fists against their prisons, but it was pointless. Krist kept slapping his hands against the beam capsule that held him and it was solid as if it was made of glass.

Then, just as quickly as it happened, the beams dissipated. They were all free save for Chung. When the blackness in his beam faded and the beam itself was turned off, he just stood there, arms extended as if he was still fighting to get free.

Mowfali was the first one to reach him.

"Careful," Krist told her, sensing something very wrong.

They all got in close to him. He still had not moved. His face behind the helmet bubble was hooked in a rictus of terror or agony and perhaps both. His eyes did not blink. Mowfali reached out to touch him, but at the last moment, she thought better of it. She prodded him with the slim barrel of a flashlight from her belt. He still did not move. She tapped it against his suit and it rang out as if he was made of granite.

"He's…he's frozen solid," she said.

And the idea of that had barely set in when he began to float. Nothing took hold of him or influenced him in any way (at least, that they could see). He became weightless and drifted up and up until he was near the ceiling, then a circular orifice opened and he was sucked through it. It slid closed without a sound.

The others stood there silently for a moment or two, then Dendro lost it. He seemed to spasm inside his suit and then he dashed himself at the walls, hitting them and bouncing off them. Rising again and again to do the same.

"LET US OUT OF HERE!" he wailed. "LET US THE FUCK OUT OF HERE! WE HAVEN'T DONE ANYTHING! YOU INVITED US! YOU YOU YOU—"

Then he went down in a heap as Mowfali went to him. He was like jelly as they hoisted him to his feet. Inside his helmet, his eyes were glazed and there was a disturbing grin on his face.

"He's been dosed," Mowfali said.

After a few moments, he could stand on his own. He was stoned on tranquilizers, unable to do much more than just stare blankly at them. But calm, very calm, and when he began to speak, oddly rational.

He giggled. "We're like white mice in a maze looking for cheese," he said. "We've been too busy to stop and think about what has happened and *why* it's happened."

"And you've got answers?" Krist said.

He uttered that silly laugh again. "It's obvious, isn't it? That was no asteroid that hit us. Did anyone see it? Of course not. Even the ship had no video of it. Don't you find that peculiar?"

"What was it then?"

He shrugged. "It was a projectile. A weapon. *They* used it like a slingshot to knock a bird out of the sky. They crippled the *Poly* with it, so we would be easier to collect."

Krist looked over at Mowfali, expecting her to flash him a look that said, *it's the medication, it'll pass,* but instead, she looked worried and gravely concerned.

"There's no way out of here," Dendro told them. "We're idiots if we really think we were sucked in here out of charity, because some fucking aliens were practicing half-ass humanitarianism. That they felt sorry for our plight and wanted to help us. *Sheeeit.*" He waved the idea away with his hand. "You know what's out there, you know what aliens are like. There's no goddamn alliance like in the stories. That's bullshit. They either hate us and want to kill us or they use us as cattle. They either have total contempt for us or they ignore us and wish we'd go away." He laughed again. "Do I have to site examples?"

He didn't; they were all fully aware of the horrors of alien races. The Vyrmid for example, were hostile and warlike. Wars had been fought against them. When they captured humans, they put them in death camps for medical experimentation. The Imperians were warlike, too, and they used captured humans as livestock. The Metalurians abducted humans (and any other races they could find) and put them in zoos. The Megra killed anyone or anything that was different from them. And the Etherians? Maybe they were not openly aggressive or unfriendly, but they liked to feed off human emotions and memories. There was no exchange of ideas or cultures. Humans were pets to them.

"We were brought here to be collected," Dendro finished by saying. "We'll never be seen again. When we got sucked in here, it was for a purpose. An ugly purpose."

Krist was gradually getting angry and mainly because everything he feared the worst was being said by Dendro.

"You need to stop with that, son. I'm not just asking you now, I'm ordering you."

Dendro just giggled again. He fell back against the wall and slid to the floor. After a time, he began to sob.

"Crazy talk," Krist said to Mowfali. "That's all it is. It's the drugs. Nothing he says makes any sense."

Inside her helmet, her smooth, dark face was pinched and pale. "Or maybe it makes all the sense in the world."

An hour later, they were released into another dark corridor. The same orb of blue light led them on. Hatches closed behind them—there was no possibility of retreat.

"Like toys being pulled along on a string," Dendro said.

If it wasn't for the helmet, Krist figured he might just slap him. He had never laid a hand on any member of his crew since he'd been in command, but that Dendro, goddammit, he would've made an exception for him. The wild, raving Dendro was better than the drugged up version. He was coming out of it slowly...*too* slowly...and sooner or later, he would lose it again. And be pumped full of tranks again. The cycle would endlessly repeat itself until—

Before them now, it wasn't a hatch that opened. The entire wall dispersed like smoke on the wind. There was an impenetrable blackness before them. Then lights came on from far overhead. Not the clear white light that they were used to, but again, that bluish illumination that revealed an immense chamber that Krist thought was easily as large as a football field back on Earth. It went on and on and on.

"Now we're getting to it," Dendro said.

Yes, certainly...but getting to *what* exactly?

Krist stepped in there with the others, but part of his mind refused to enter at all. It was still in denial. *What did you think this was going to be?* a voice asked in his head. It was more than a little hysterical sounding. *Did you think you would be greeted by benign bubble-headed, pointy-eared aliens and they would offer you a gesture of good faith and mutual respect like in some cheesy twenty-first century TV program? Did you think there would be glory and understanding? That you would be fawned over by your people for leading them into the light?* The alien ship seemed to laugh at his foolish naiveté and he could hear it echoing in his head.

He looked around with the others and what he saw made him want to cry. It sucked the wind out of his lungs and filled his brain with screeching noise.

"This is what it's about," Dendro said. "This and nothing more."

The room was filled with what seemed to be vinyl bags, row upon row of them that were suspended in midair by something they could not see. There had to be hundreds of them all lined up.

"Specimens," Mowfali said and there was a clear edge of anxiety to her voice.

Krist began to walk down a row of them with her. The bags looked like some sort of transparent plastic, but they were made of no plastic any of them had ever seen before. Each one was like a bag of liquid that held its form via its own surface tension. Mowfali prodded one with the barrel of her pulser and thick, torpid ripples ran through it like gelatin that had not completely set.

Inside each of them, floating in cloudy plasma, were specimens as she said—animals and plants in an amazing variety. Recognizable forms of animals like reptiles and mammals, insects and birds, and other things that were all these things and none of them, weird chimeras from all over the galaxy with too many eyes and limbs, fins and tentacles and appendages whose purpose were unknown and enigmatic. They saw alien creatures they recognized like Imperians and Sloth Worms, needle spiders and Trinary Quaalaks. Others that they had never seen before, weird spidery organisms and others that looked like blobs of fur or monstrous squid-like creatures covered in iridescent scales. Some were small as houseflies and others the size of whales.

"This ship must go from planet to planet collecting representative life-forms," Mowfali said. "It might be completely automated. A collector. A biological probe like nothing we can imagine."

Dendro was wandering freely from row to row, remarking on gigantic monstrosities to tiny insects to plants that seemed to be in the process of becoming animals.

"They've got everything! Everything! Anything that crawls or swims or flies! There's only one thing they're lacking—humans," he said. "Or *were* lacking but now they've got that, too. They've got four of them to add to this menagerie."

Krist, everything dried up in him now, wanted to tell him he was wrong but, of course, he wasn't wrong. They had been collected and it was only a matter of time before they went into the bags. Without really thinking about it, he had pulled the pulser from his belt and was ready to use it.

"What are you doing?" Mowfali asked him.

"I…I don't know," he admitted. "But I'll be damned if they're going to get any of us."

"They've already got Chung," Dendro said.

"Let's not be hasty," she said.

Dendro laughed. "She's right. First, don't be hasty. I mean, shit, why fight it? They've got our asses and it's only a matter of time before we're fucking bottled and labelled."

"Shut up," Krist old him.

He kept laughing like it was all the greatest joke he'd ever heard. "No, no, no! I'm not going to shut up! Why the fuck should I?" He raced off amongst the rows. "Hey, you bug-eyed fucking monsters! Here I am! Here I am! Come and take me! You hear me! *Come and fucking take me!*"

"Settle down," Mowfali called out to him.

But he wasn't about to. He ran around in circles, bumping into the bags and knocking them out of his way. And when that got him no response, he pulled his pulser and began firing it randomly, destroying bag after bag after bag.

"COME AND GET ME! COME AND FUCKING GET ME!" he challenged.

"Put that away! You're going to hurt someone!" Krist ordered, but there no was strength in his voice any longer. He felt weak and impotent against all this.

How far it would have gone was anyone's guess, but suddenly Dendro screamed as if he had been scalded. His cry echoed through the enormous confines of the chamber. He was far away from the others by then and they couldn't see him, lost as he was amongst the countless rows of specimen bags, but they could hear him just fine: *"Oh God...oh God! Krist! Doc! Help me! It's got me! It's fucking got me!"*

Krist and Mowfali raced down there as fast as they could and what they saw was not only insane but grotesque—something like a gigantic set of pincers had taken hold of Dendro. They came out of the ceiling above on a silver rod. They were not crushing him, but merely holding him up in the air like a curious bug worth studying.

"Don't move! Don't fight!" Mowfali said. "They might just be immobilizing you so you don't damage the specimens! Just try to relax and they might release you!"

Which Krist thought was some serious wishful thinking because Dendro had been collected by gigantic forceps and there was no getting around that. He aimed his pulser at the silver rod and fired, but it did nothing.

Or maybe it did.

Because Dendro was taken up and away, disappearing through an orifice in the ceiling much as Chung had been.

Two left now.

"There's no way out, is there?" Krist said.

"Not now."

"But they're might have been?"

"I don't know," Mowfali said. "Maybe. Maybe if Dendro hadn't caused trouble and..."

"And I didn't shoot?"

"Maybe."

He just grunted at that. She didn't seem to understand the gravity of the situation or maybe she had simply accepted it.

The lights were being turned off in the collection room, section by section until they were standing in the dark. It was all bad enough but this made it infinitely worse. The forceps could come for them at any time.

The blue light appeared in the distance.

It offered a way out...but to what?

They went after it because there was really nothing else they could do. They held hands because when everything else failed and the lights went off, it was the only thing left.

The light led them into the next chamber and it was equally as large as the last. And its purpose was even worse. But it had to end here sooner or later.

They were in a lab.

Maybe the scale was fantastic, but it was a lab all right. There were huge vessels of liquid that might have been made of liquid themselves. Tubes and hoses of the same material. Great round plastic trays like Petri dishes and clear rectangles that just might have conceivably been slides. There were bubbling vats and weird instruments hanging from the ceiling. But the most disturbing thing were the mirrored lenses high above.

"We're under a microscope," Krist said, pulling off his helmet and throwing it. "A goddamned microscope like fucking germs."

"We might not be anything more to them."

But he didn't hear a thing she said because he had gone to his knees, at first gibbering madly, then sobbing, and now laughing as Dendro had. Maybe he hadn't gotten the joke before, but he sure as hell got it now.

Krist steadily lost contact with reality.

He was a nuts-and-bolts kind of guy, a techie and an engineer by training. None of this made sense. It was a nightmare. It was a horror story. It was sheer unbridled lunacy. So, something in him pulled away from it. The idea of what the alien ship was and its purpose pulled the rug of sanity out from under him and he caved in. He thought about other deep space missions he'd been on. He thought of baseball games he'd played as a boy. He thought of the golden fields of wheat in Ohio where he'd been born and the horrendous dust storms on the red planet as a teenager. His suit provided him with food and water and would for several more days. After that—

But *after that* no longer existed for him.

Mowfali had wandered off, fascinated by what she was seeing. She had ceased to exist for him. He did some wandering himself and one of the first things he found was Chung. He had been sectioned into micron-thick wafers. It was like somebody had tried to slice him into a deck of playing cards. Each wafer—and there were literally thousands— was suspended along one of the walls as if they were drying.

Oh Christ, Krist thought. *Poor goddamned Chung. My right-hand man. The one guy I could trust and depend on. They froze you and sliced your ass like deli ham. Of all things.*

He found Dendro, too.

Poor stupid Dendro. Emotional, unstable, angry, happy, a stupid little puppy that had no business out amongst the stars.

He was fixed to a tray leaning up against the wall. He had been dissected like a frog. His internal organs had been removed and were pinned in relation to his body.

When Mowfali screamed, Krist went to her. Not at a hurried pace, mind you, but slowly and resolutely. What he saw made something twist up inside him but he really wasn't surprised by then.

"Help me," she said. *"Oh please help me..."*

But what could he do?

She was suspended about six feet off the floor. When Krist arrived, a long slim needle was jabbed into her belly and another into her throat. She stopped moving then. Things were sucked out of her or injected into her. Either way, she went limp and stared out at him with blank, unseeing eyes. The needles were removed and forceps took her away to be examined in more detail. Two plastic rectangular plates closed in on her and crushed her into a blob of jelly. Her bones were smashed, her insides mashed to sauce. She was smeared on another rectangular plate that was brought up to one of the mirrored lenses above for proper microscopic study.

"I'm alone," Krist heard his voice say and it sounded so much like that of the boy who used to play baseball that he began to cry. "I'm here all by myself and nobody cares. Nobody has ever cared. Maybe I've always been alone and I'm only realizing it now. Maybe I've been on this ship my whole life."

He couldn't move.

Like before, he was rooted to the floor. Colors began to swirl around his boots and a pink liquid bubble rose up slowly, encasing him. It felt very warm. Even through the suit he could feel its wonderful warmth.

Please don't let it hurt, he thought. *Please no pain.*

He didn't know if the ship heard him or could understand him or even cared. He was a specimen. That's all he was. A bug to be stuck on a pin. He had been born to die like this and become part of this terrible collection.

I will not scream
I'm scared to death.
But I will not scream.
I will die like a man.

But as those thoughts floated through his brain like gossamer, he knew that this was no way for a man to die. This was no way for a dog to die. No way for any of those things in the bags to die.

He sobbed and he couldn't help himself.

The bubble was up to his waist by then.

But please I'm an intelligent being.

But he knew with terrible certainty that to the master of this ship, he was not intelligent. He was an animal to be collected and studied. That's all.

"You didn't have to do this. Not to me. Not to Chung. Not to Dendro or Mowfali. We would have cooperated. We really would have."

But as the bubble engulfed him and he began to drown in the fluid which seeped into his suit now that his helmet was gone, he looked up one last time. He could see one of those gigantic mirrored lenses and the closer he got, the more its surface cleared, revealing a wiggly network of threads creeping around a massive bloodshot eyeball that looked down on him.

Then the fluid drained away.

He was numb, aware, but unable to move. He could feel nothing. Which was a good thing when the forceps lifted him into the air and a pin was driven through his chest and he was fixed to a foam board. Made ready. For the collection.

GRAVEYARD

Koreb.

The fourth planet in the Beta Andromedae system, a Class M Red Giant set in the Big Dipper. A star that stared out into the frozen blackness of space like a huge and angry eye the color of fresh blood. We fell into an eccentric, elliptical orbit around the planet, hung there like a fly in a spider's web, our perigee so damn low we nearly brushed the clouds on the first pass.

Within an hour, Brightenbach, the First Officer, called us up to the bridge and let us get a good, long look at that black and cryptic world spinning below us.

I said, "We're a freighter for chrissake, why the hell did we pull this? We're not military or expeditionary…we're merchants, we haul ore. This isn't our thing."

Brightenbach gave me his usual dour look. He was a round little man with a face just as red as Wisconsin cherries, the top of his balding head pink as a party balloon. He licked his lips. "There's a colony down there, Starling," he said to me, fixing me with his sharp blue eyes. "A colony with nearly two thousand people. Thing is, smart boy, nobody's heard from them in nearly two months—no subspace chatter, no telemetry, no cyberspace, not even a goddamn smoke signal."

I wasn't exactly moved. "Christ, First, we're not trained for this stuff."

"You're going down anyway, Starling. We're the nearest ship, so we get this. It would take five months for anybody else to get out this far."

Kurtz, running a hand through her spiky red locks, dropped me a wink. "C'mon, Starling. Where's your curiosity? Your sense of adventure?"

"I must have left it in my other pants."

Kurtz started laughing; she'd laugh at anything. Didn't matter what you said to her, she laughed. "That's what I love about you, Starling. Your yellow streak."

"Some people say it goes with my eyes."

Brightenbach sighed. "Trust me, Starling. I don't like putting people down there, but I don't have a choice. We already lost a drone. I need someone on the ground."

Penacek, the Third Officer, and Cuperly, one of the systems hacks, joined us now, staring down at Koreb below, not saying a damn thing. Penacek was pretty militaristic. His idea of civic action was a good carpet-bombing. Cuperly was quiet, real quiet.

Brightenbach looked us over, said, "You can take one of the shuttles down. Everything's already programmed in. You'll touch down just outside New Bayonne. You'll wear environmental suits just to be on the safe side. The power's out down there and the sun won't rise for another two weeks. Just look around. If you can't find anyone, just grab any records, any halo-spheres you can find. Track down the drone if you can. You'll be on the ground a couple hours, tops..."

He kept talking, but I wasn't listening. I was staring at Koreb down there, thinking and thinking. It was an ominous, lifeless world from what I could see, shrouded in heavy cloud cover like a mask it was waiting to remove at midnight. Thing was, midnight lasted for three weeks on Koreb on account of its lunatic orbit. The flesh at the base of my spine was literally crawling. The planet reminded me of some gigantic mausoleum, an alien spook house of creeping shapes and nightmare shadows. And we were going into it like a bunch of scared kids entering a deserted house in a dead forest.

"Any more questions?" Brightenbach said.

There weren't any.

"Just take your time," he said. "It's gonna be real dark down there..."

We broke through the lower atmosphere like a pebble dropped into a murky, stagnant pond and sank without a trace. Kurtz tried to lighten things up by insulting me, but she didn't get any laughs. Our humor had dried up like the spit in our mouths. We touched down on the landing pad at the perimeter of New Bayonne. The only lights were the ones from the shuttle. It was black as the inside of a body bag out there, the air full of wild, flying shapes like witches haunting the sky. Kurtz was quick to point out that what we were seeing were patches of mist.

But I had trouble believing that.

Penacek called the ship, told them we landed in one piece.

We pulled our helmets on over our strained, bloodless faces and Penacek broke the airlock and we stepped out into the forever night of Koreb. There was a good wind blowing and you could feel it hit you the moment you got out of the ship. It was a raging, frenzied dust storm out there, the air full of tiny fragments that peppered the outsides of our suits.

Kurtz had the scanner, being the only one proficient in its use. It looked like a black rectangle on her left forearm, its surface crowded with readouts and graphs. She had it set to continually scan for life-forms, give her constant info on atmospheric conditions. She walked in a semi-circle, her left arm held out. "There's nothing alive out there that I'm picking up," she said. "No feed from the drone. But this storm or whatever the hell it is…my signals could be bouncing right back at me. The city's directly ahead."

Through my ear mic, I heard Penacek say, "Something doesn't wash here, people. The brain-plex gave me a profile of Koreb before we came down. The air is clear here. Windy, sure, but it's not full of grit like this. If we tried to breathe this stuff it would be like, be like—"

"Sucking desert sand through a pipe," I finished for him.

"Right."

Cuperly was breathing hard; you could hear him. "Maybe…we should just get out of here."

Kurtz ignored him, said, "Yeah, something's wrong here. Scanner's telling me the air is breathable, but it's not telling me squat about all this dust or whatever it is."

Our helmet lights were full of it, motes of something flying and drifting all around us like snowflakes. Our bright orange suits were gray with the stuff. And the closer we got to the city, the thicker it became. Like wading through a vacuum bag filled with wind-driven cigarette ash. It wasn't only in the air, but layered on the ground, too.

The four of us plodded on through the darkness, staying in a tight formation. Four scared people in bright orange composite e-suits and those squarish helmets with the banks of lights running down either side. Suddenly, we could see the city rising up out of the murk, a huge and desolate graveyard beckoning to us. We saw nothing move out there, just a lot of prefab buildings and Quonset huts dipped in shadow, deserted and somehow deadly. A few narrow, winding streets. Just inside the city, we paused, speechless. In the glow of our interior helmet lights, you could see our faces—sallow and tight, eyes sunken into black hollows. We all knew something was terribly wrong, we just didn't know what.

There was a sudden crackling of static…loud, sharp, intrusive. I nearly fell out of my skin. But it was just Brightenbach up on the ship, checking in.

"Just wanted to remind you kids not to talk to strangers down there," he said.

A few of us uttered nervous laughter. The sort of laughter that's just this side of a scream. It was bad down there—bleak, haunted, and suffocating. It had all the atmosphere of a dank, wormy casket.

"You gotta love our First officer," I said. "He's some kind of funny guy."

"Yeah," Cuperly said. "Funny."

Penacek stooped down, picked up a glove full of that powdery material. "What is this crap, Kurtz? That box must have some idea."

She shrugged, though you couldn't really tell it in that bulky suit. "It's ash."

"I know it's ash," he snapped. "What *kind* of ash?"

But she didn't have any answers and on we went, staying close enough to touch one another. The city seemed like it was waiting for us. I know how crazy that sounds, but you could almost *feel* it. A waiting, endlessly patient sense of expectancy. Like it had secrets, surprises in store for us, and was holding its breath. Our helmet lights swept the buildings, creating ghastly panoramas of jumping shadows and casting distorted images of ourselves against the steel and stone facades. Motes of ash were caught in the beams like deep-sea silt. It was eerie and unreal. A ghost town 200 light-years from Earth.

"Where the hell is everybody?" Penacek said, tense. "I mean, Christ, show me some bodies here."

I understood what he meant: even a high body count would've been better than this. The ash was about six inches deep like a freshly-fallen snow. As we walked, we kicked up clouds of the stuff that twisted in the breeze. The grit in it crunched underfoot like dry autumn leaves. If you could imagine trudging through a crematorium ash pit, you get the idea. We were starting to see a lot of little heaps of ash that were gradually eroding in the wind. All that ash and no people. I think we were all starting to make some unpleasant connections by then.

Penacek stopped us. "Listen, I don't know about you guys, but I wanna wind this picnic up. Let's split into teams, work each side of the street, check the buildings. We'll get Brightenbach his precious spheres and then get the hell out. Fuck the drone. If we keep moving forward here, we'll find the administration building right at the end up there. Cuperly? You're with me. Kurtz? You go with Starling."

"How come I always get her?" I said.

We parted and moved up the walks on opposite sides of the road. Kurtz and I found a few locked doors, lots of ash, not a lot else. Finally, we found a place that appeared to be some kind of community center for the miners and researchers that called this cemetery home. Inside, we found a big cafeteria and some administration offices, a kitchen. There were announcements pasted to a pegboard. Everything looked perfectly normal. Except that it was dead and empty and dark. Too many heaps of ashes.

There were plates set out at tables, coats on hooks, a cigar butt in an ashtray. It reminded me of that derelict ship on old earth, the *Mary Celeste*. It was like that. As if the people had just walked out minutes before we'd arrived.

The piles of ash here were larger, mostly untouched. My throat was so dry you could've wiped up a spill with it. I was in one of the backrooms, gathering up some halo-spheres and hard copy when Kurtz screamed. I ran back out there, as best I could manage in my suit. I got out to the community room and she was standing there with her pulser out, ready to shoot down just about anything. Myself included. In her helmet light, her face looked to be the color of cheese.

"I saw something," she said, almost too calmly. "Up there…on the stairs."

I panned it with my lights. Just a set of steps leading to the upper story, a landing above. I saw nothing there, just that grainy darkness, a blizzard of drifting ash. I was expecting Penacek across the way to pipe in, wonder what the hell was going on. But he and Cuperly were out of range for helmet-to-helmet communication. They could only pick us up on the remote channel.

I took a deep, sucking breath. "Nothing there now. What was it?"

She studied my face, looking for some sign that I thought she was being a hysterical female. She found none. "Just…I don't know…I saw it out of the corner of my eye. Just a blur of motion, you know? I turned and I saw…I don't know…*something*. A vague, hunched-over shape." Her eyes were wide. She wiped a smear of ash from her viewplate. "You…you believe me, don't you, Starling?"

I told her I did.

Together, me in the lead, we went up the steps, our pulsers out. I think we both badly needed to hold hands, but there wasn't room. The stairwell was narrow. We went up step by step, wordlessly. Our lights were creating a ghoulish pantomime of slinking, crawling shadows. My breath was coming in short, sharp gasps and fear was rushing in my belly in thick, sickening waves.

We reached the top and entered a cramped corridor studded with doors. We stood there in the silence which was huge and menacing, listening to the beat of our hearts in our ears, the flow of blood. Nothing more. Just that immense, crushing dead absence of sound. But for all of that, our nerve endings were humming because we knew with dread, awful certainty that we were not alone. There was something here, something that exuded a phobic sense of…*occupancy*.

With a voice dry as cinders, Kurtz said, "You feel it, Starling?"

"Yes," I said. "I think so."

Have you ever been in a haunted house? Not a carnival attraction or a VR module, but the real thing? Every town or city has one, a place of vile deeds long since past, whether real or imagined. A shunned place tenanted by silence and dust and eldritch memory. I grew up in the Martian Colonies, New Baltimore to be exact. A mining town. There was an old refinery there that had been abandoned nearly a century before. And if you had the balls, the steel, you could go in there during the dead of night, walk those empty, desolate corridors. I did it once. Alone. I thought I saw a shape coming down a shaft at me and I screamed. And ran. I didn't stop running until I was home and safe. To this day, I'm certain there *really* was something there... something ancient and loathsome that had haunted Mars for centuries before we had even arrived.

At that moment, I was back in that bleak, isolated ruin.

We went through the rooms one by one. We found nothing of importance. On one of the beds we found a pile of ashes in the shape of a man. But it wasn't really surprising by that point. Both Kurtz and I knew what all those ashes were. If there was anything alive, we didn't find it.

Penacek opened a channel and Kurtz and I started.

"What's going on over there?" he asked. "Anything?"

Kurtz and I looked at each other, decided silently not to say anything.

"Not a damn thing," she said. "Starling keeps trying to back me into dark corners. I'm not sure what he's up to. How about you?"

There was a pause for a moment and it was pregnant with apprehension. "Well...I don't know...nothing I guess. Cuperly's freaking out over here, keeps hearing sounds, seeing ghosts."

Ghosts. It didn't surprise me. I swallowed down hard, thinking how welcome the clanking of chains or a disembodied voice would have been about then. Anything to break up that god-awful soundlessness. Even a ghostly figure walking through the wall carrying its head would have been welcome.

Cuperly said, "I'm not imagining anything, goddammit. I tell you we're not alone here, people. There's something out there. Something watching us from the darkness..."

I could feel gooseflesh at my spine, the back of my neck. Penacek was in command; we had to do what he said. If he said we had to search through this mortuary for spheres and what not, then we had to. Still, I was all for making for the shuttle and getting out.

Kurtz and I found a skywalk that connected the building to a mining office next door. We went over there and again, didn't find a damn thing. A lot of offices, a lab. Rock specimens. Dead interfaces. More heaped ashes. Like everything else. I was starting to wonder if maybe we were all letting our imaginations gallop away on us. Despite the horror that washed through me like a sterile, lifeless sea, I was beginning to think that very thing.

"Hey, Starling?" Kurtz said. "You ever did it in zero gravity? Man, now that's a trip. Bumping into walls and—"

I swung around suddenly, because this time *I* was the one seeing things. For just the briefest of instants—so quickly I had to wonder if I saw anything at all—there was a face at the window overlooking the deserted streets. A grotesque, inhuman face pressed up to the pane. I let out a cry, pulled my pulser and fired. A wink of cold blue light hit the window and melted it to blackened embers.

"What?" Kurtz demanded. *"What?"*

There was no air in my lungs. I couldn't seem to speak. I swallowed and swallowed again. "A face…something…I'm not sure. But it was there. I saw it."

"What in the hell's happening over there?" Penacek wanted to know.

Kurtz said, "Starling saw something. A shape. He's playing OK Corral over here."

"Take it easy for chrissake," Penacek warned me. "You're gonna kill someone."

Kurtz was checking her scanner. "I don't see any life out there. Bioscanners show zilch, no infrared signatures, no physiologic emissions. Nothing."

"Okay. I've had my fill," Penacek said. "We're scratching this. We need back-up here. We're not equipped for this. Everybody out into the street right goddamn now, we're making for the ship. Let's move, people."

We didn't waste any time. Together, Kurtz and I went out the door into that raging ash storm, staying so close our suits rubbed together. But that was a good thing. Company. Human company. I had never felt such a need for it before. We stood next to each other, waiting for the others. Our lights still burned bright, but there seemed to be shadows cavorting all around us. And the bad thing, the really bad thing, was that I didn't think we were creating them. Two, three, maybe four minutes we waited. An eternity when you're on a grim, vacant street with the wind throwing ash into your viewplate on some dire, alien netherworld.

"Where the hell are they?" Kurtz asked me and I could tell by her voice that she was distressed, frightened. Scared white, maybe.

"I don't know."

They were in a warehouse two buildings up the street. I knew that much. I tried to raise them on a remote channel and so did Kurtz, but we didn't get a thing. As far as communication went, they might have fallen into some black, rending void.

Kurtz said, "They're still in there. I'm picking up their life signs."

We made it over to the warehouse, having to plod through some deep piles of ash that came apart into a million buzzing fragments as we disturbed them. They swallowed us in clouds of debris like cyclones of spinning, angry wasps. Somehow, I lost momentary contact with Kurtz. Suddenly, she wasn't touching me. I spun around and was blasted in the viewplate with blinding grit. I started reaching out madly in all directions, crying out her name.

But she had only fallen and I helped her up. "Goddamn place," she said.

And maybe she would have said more, but right then our external mics picked up something that left us cold. First I thought it was the others, but no. That sound…we both heard it…an odd, light pattering sound. It reminded me of the sound of bare feet running on concrete. But tiny feet. Like those of children.

It was about then that Cuperly punched up a remote channel and started screaming. I had a feeling he had hit the channel scan by accident. For one second it was just me and Kurtz in that silent blackness and the next: "…help me, help me, help me…oh dear Christ, somebody help me…Kurtz! Starling! *They're everywhere, they're everywhere! Don't you see them…you must see them! Penacek! Oh Christ oh—*"

And it was cut off.

Kurtz and I drew our pulsers and made our way over there. We moved quickly. We were starting to get the hang of living and operating out of those damn suits, the trick of skating through the ash without going on our asses. Regardless, we made it up the walk and at first we didn't see a thing. The warehouse door was open. We saw nothing but darkness pooling in there, grainy and shifting. Then we heard sounds. Busy sounds. The motion of many things moving at once, whispering and creeping and rustling. There was a little alleyway that ran between the warehouse and as our lights hit it...something incredible, something shocking happened.

Kurtz said, "What the hell?"

It was like rolling over a rotting log and seeing thousands of ants scurrying and slinking. As our lights illuminated the scene, we saw, for a brief second, a quivering, industrious horde of...I don't know what, just a profusion of shapes and forms. They bled away with amazing speed right up the walls of the buildings. Light had the same effect on them as water poured into suds...dispersal. Complete dispersal. They moved off en masse and with such speed we never really got a look at what they were. About the time the shapes slipped away, we caught sight of Cuperly. He was being dragged off through a doorway. We saw his booted feet kicking as he was drawn into the darkness. It didn't look as if his helmet lights were operable.

Kurtz made to go after him, but I stopped her.

There were just too many of those *things*. Maybe you couldn't see them, but you could hear them—that buzzing, whistling noise they made like a swarm of locusts descending on a field. It made my skin crawl. It got inside your head, echoed around in there until you wanted to scream. And it seemed to come from everywhere: in front of you, behind, to the left, the right, overhead. Dear God.

I called the ship, requesting backup, but the channel was dead.

I led Kurtz around front or maybe she led me and we went through the entrance to the warehouse. We came into a sort of reception area full of desks and lots of ashes scattered everywhere. I could see the bootprints left by Penacek and Cuperly. Outside, we could hear that cacophony of motion again as the shapes returned. Kurtz made for a corridor and I was right behind her. I turned and looked and I saw...

I'm not sure what I saw exactly.

For one crazy second, I thought there was a toad standing in the doorway, frozen into inaction by my lights. It was like that. Hideous and bloated, a round-bodied thing with pebbly pale green flesh that was set off with pulsing blue vein tracery. It had long, broomstick-thin limbs that looked oddly atrophied, stubby legs, and an almost conical shaped head with three eyes just as yellow and bright as full moons. What I thought was long, flowing emerald-green hair was actually a mutiny of wormy fibers that squirmed and coiled. Sensory organs, maybe.

Then it was gone.

I think I screamed. I knew they were out there by that point… but to see one in the flesh as it were. Horrible. It inspired an atavistic fear in me, a primal loathing. Utter disgust like seeing some large, grotesquely-fattened spider stand up on two legs. Something inside told me to kill them, kill them all.

"It was one of them," I told Kurtz as she stood there looking at me.

She stepped away from the corridor, consulting her scanner. "It's not working…dead," she said. "Maybe the ash, maybe I bumped it… oh, Jesus Christ, Starling, what are we going to do?"

And maybe we could have thrown together some plan like getting out and getting out right goddamn now, but things were happening too fast. A figure came stumbling out of the corridor and by the size of it I knew instantly it was Penacek. He was a big guy. Problem was, you couldn't see much of him. Seven or eight of the things were hanging off him like ticks on a dog's belly, swollen up like beach balls. One of Penacek's helmet lights was out, the other was damaged and dimly glowing, casting weaving, bobbing shadows as he fought and writhed and slammed himself against the walls to get them off him.

Kurtz and I stood there stupidly, completely helpless, locked-down tight with some instinctual revulsion of the things. We had pulsers in our hands, but we didn't dare shoot for fear of hitting Penacek and we didn't march in and remove them because…because I don't think we could've touched those horrors.

Penacek's viewplate was fanned out with jagged cracks and you could hear him screaming and screaming as more of them leaped onto him. There was steam rolling off him in hissing plumes. It occurred to me then, that *they were burning through his suit.* He threw himself into the doorframe and two of them…*burst.* Like rotting, juicy grapes, they exploded with a rain of greenish fluid. Penacek was sprayed down with whatever flowed in them and pretty soon he was nothing but a smoking, sizzling mass as more of the creatures fell on him, leeching him with those appalling sucking mouths…dissolving him like meat in an acid bath.

The e-suits were real marvels of technology…self-sealing, radiation and chemical-resistant. Heat-proof. They even had a med nano system to repair anything from lacerations to broken bones. But against these creatures, the suits were useless.

I caught one distressing, last look at Penacek's contorted face pressed up to the viewplate, his mouth wide and screeching. I heard him let out a choking, insane wailing sound that went right through me: *"Oh Jesus oh Christ I can feel them I can feel them Starling kill me for the love of God kill me—"*

Kurtz and I opened up at the same time and by then Penacek, that poor bastard, was a cremated, flaking mass flopping on the ground, still alive, enveloped in those bloated little bodies. One of them turned and looked at us, its mouth wide and I saw it was roughly oval like the maw of a lamprey and studded with dozens and dozens of tiny, hooked teeth. Then the pulser emissions hit them, boiling them and Penacek into a twisted, blazing mass.

Kurtz and I made to go back out onto the streets.

No dice.

They were coming through the doorway, an army of obese, rubbery bodies, rolling and leaping and jumping like grasshoppers. They came through the windows. They slithered over the walls, the ceiling, the floors, all making that awful whistling sound. We ran back through the corridor, blasting five or six of them out of our path. We broke through a window and dropped into the alley. They were everywhere out there, the city a livid, seething carpet of them. The rooftops, doorways, alcoves, alleyways—yes, everywhere, nothing but hundreds, *thousands* of those luminous yellow eyes clustering and then scattering as our lights played over them. But what was worse, what really tore open my mind like a raw, hurting wound was that they were in the sky, too. Bounding and floating and drifting back down at us like dirigibles. They must've had some weird gas bladders in them that made them lighter than air.

And I knew, I knew finally—they had come from the sky.

For even then, more and more were descending like feathers on the breeze. The black sky was even blacker with their numbers, a verminous congregation spreading out like a flock of nightmarish birds.

What did we do?

We ran. We stumbled. We hung onto one another as the things parted like the Red Sea at our approach, their numbers tightening, but patient, so incredibly patient. They were above and behind and in front. Our lights showed us things we should never have seen in a sane world. Their numbers were swelling by the minute. They fell from the sky, bouncing on the ground and darting up into the air, jumping and vaulting and hovering like they were pumped full of helium. It was like being caught in a school of deep-sea jellyfish. As they rose they inflated themselves, as they fell, deflated. Like squids, was what I thought, and the air was their sea.

They started getting more daring, bumping into us, striking us from above, but not attacking. Not just yet. The world was a clamorous and resounding box of noise, echoing and whistling and shrilling. They seemed to be playing, if anything, darting about and toying with us like cats with mice.

We started shooting and shooting as they encircled us like a noose. We stepped on their bodies and they gushed that juice that ate away the soles of our boots. One of them hit me and dropped me on my ass and two of them vaulted at Kurtz and she cut them both in half. They exploded, washing her down with that gelatinous green filth. Her suit began to smoke and bubble, great rents opening in too many places. And then I lost sight of her as they fell onto me, blinding me by sheer numbers. I kept shooting and shooting and pretty soon, I'd cleared a path and I hoped, dear God, I *prayed* the batteries in my pulser would hold out because the shuttle couldn't be far now.

I charged through them, crying out Kurtz's name and then I heard her screaming and I caught sight of her. She was moving in a drunken, shambling circle, three or four of them hanging off her like leeches. Billowing plumes of smoke and steam wound her in a raging cloud. She tripped and fell and I saw that her suit was huge and puffy as if it was filled with hot gas. But, of course, it wasn't that—it was the things that had wormed into her suit, slithering and creeping in there with her, draining her dry as their acid-kisses burned her to ash. What was the worst possible thing was that her mic was open and I *heard* her suffering, those sucking sounds, that pathetic screeching as she begged me to kill her. *The feel of them,* she cried, *the horrible greasy feel of them…*

I wish I could say that I did, but it just wasn't possible. There were just too many hitting me from every direction and I was running and shooting and somehow staying on my feet as those acidic secretions of theirs turned my suit into a shredded, flapping rag.

And then I suddenly heard a beeping sound and I knew I was near the ship: it was the homing signal it had sent out for us. Ten or twelve of them clinging to me, I thumbed the button at my belt and the shuttle exploded with light—running lights, port lights, stern lights. The things made pained mewling sounds and scattered in every which direction… hopping away and floating right up into the sky.

I stumbled to the shuttle, bathed in that angelic light.

The airlock popped and then I was inside. I dropped into my seat and told the plex to take us up, up, back to the ship. The plasma jets fired and Koreb was filled with flames and light and up I went. I kept the exterior lights on and I could feel those fat, pulpy little things thumping and jarring as we blasted straight through congested storms of their bodies. They splattered against the view screen like water balloons full of Limeade and burned off as the shuttle exploded from that haunted world.

I saw the freighter and right away knew why I couldn't raise it on the radio, why I could never dock with it. My heart sank without a sound. The freighter floated there in a decaying orbit, completely dark, completely forbidding like some old world plague ship. Just looking at her, you knew she was dead. There was a great, mangled cavity in the side. I don't know if it was from a meteor hit or what, but I saw a stream of corpses drifting from that rent and knew the ship was lifeless, knew it was filled with those things. They rode the backs of the dead and clustered on the hull of the ship in a squirming, maggoty mass.

Apparently, they didn't require an atmosphere to ply their trade. Some free-living, self-contained hybrid migratory race of monsters.

I looked down at Koreb below. It was a great rotating tomb in the stark depths of space. I kept watching it, wondering what the hell I should do.

Then, as if on cue, a swarm of those things began lighting from the surface, swimming up through the clouds. They seemed to have no set destination, moved by the solar winds maybe, gravitational arcs. It was like watching thousands of flies abandon rotting meat. They drifted up at the shuttle like forgotten parade balloons, floating on some unseen, unknowable current…looking for another world to ravage.

I let the plex pick a trajectory and fired the rockets.

That was all three weeks ago now. I'm heading to the nearest colony which is about ten light-years out. The shuttle's survival package has food and water for six people for one month. Being alone, that means six months. Problem is, it'll take a year to make that colony at top speed. The ship is sending out distress calls every fifteen minutes on all wavelengths.

Maybe I'll be rescued.

Maybe not.

Thing is, the colony should have picked up my distress calls two weeks ago. I'm putting out a strong signal and I'm receiving just fine, yet all I'm reading is dead air. There could be lots of reasons for that, but I can only think of one. That's why I'm broadcasting this. You see, I'm hoping there are people out there to hear this.

But I'm beginning to doubt it.

NO LIFE ON MARS

hambers woke and he was alone.

The weight of the world was upon him like a dozen leaden suns. It crushed him, flattened him, pressed him into the folds of his bed. He wanted to move, but he could not. Or maybe, it was just that he saw no point in moving. Sometimes, it was better just to wait. Given time, the dream or nightmare would dissolve like a parting mist. And maybe, just maybe, reality would find its way home again.

He thought: *Just one more day. Just pull yourself together for one more day, because this might be the one. This just might be the one.*

He sat up. Outside, he could hear the frigid Martian winds blasting sand against the wall of his Quonset hut. And that was Mars—icy, rocky, a subzero desert of erosive sandstorms and memories and things long buried. One of the early explorers had said that Mars was a Pandora's box and that, given time, men would shake the lid free and regret what came out. Another said that if you looked for something long enough on Mars, you'd probably find it.

Chambers figured they were both right.

After he'd showered and forced some food into his belly, he suited up and went into town. He didn't need to; not anymore. He had everything he needed out at his place. The greenhouses supplied him with food. The solar batteries gave him all the power he needed. He had no reason to go into town.

But he found himself going, anyway.

The last man on Mars.

The town was empty like all the towns on Mars, but did not know it.

The AI programs still ran everything. Lights came on at dusk, went off at dawn. The automated street sweepers came and went. Water was synthesized and collected, pipes filled. The dome which held the town like a village sealed in a snow globe was still pressurized. The artificial atmosphere was not compromised. Sunlight was still gathered and amplified to heat the dome. Everything still operated with sparkling efficiency. But there was no one to notice.

No one except Chambers.

He was there now, his helmet hanging from the rebreather on his back. He walked up the main drag and thought how much it all looked like a city on Earth: the buildings stacked next to one another, the pre-fab structures sandwiched in between them. The Quonset huts and maintenance sheds sprinkled throughout. The little electric cars sitting at the curbs, waiting for occupants.

He looked for life and saw only black, empty windows staring back. They looked as he felt.

Sometimes, as he walked the streets, he found he could not bear to look at those buildings and homes for fear he would see someone looking back at him. It was impossible, of course, but it chilled him all the same. There was no one left…yet, the idea of someone suddenly reappearing after seven years of silence was disconcerting.

He walked and walked, visiting saloons and mining offices and hotels and restaurants. He sat in a booth at a barbecue joint. Back when Mars was bustling with pioneers and company men and colonists and government agents—all the people who'd wrestled cities and fortunes from the harsh red soil—this had been a place Chambers liked to go. It reminded him of being a boy back on Earth. Ribs sizzling on Uncle Frank's grill. The smell of the sauce and the hickory smoke.

He came here now because it was the place he had gone for so many years with his wife. With Sarah. Before the blackness had come and filled all the graveyards. It was one of the few places that he could go that gave him peace. Here, he could pretend and dream and imagine. He found that if he shut his brain down in just the proper way, suddenly the room would be filled with voices and laughter and forks scraping plates and that rich, heady aroma of the sauce smuggled from Earth via Kansas City (the recipe for which had never been revealed, now gone to dust with the brain that coveted it). In fact, Chambers sometimes found that if he squeezed his eyes tight and really let himself go, Sarah would be there across from him and he could hear her voice.

He whiled away hours dreaming like that.

It was a good thing.

And sometimes—

A phone ringing.

But Chambers knew it really wasn't ringing. Like everything else on that sterile world, the telecom systems still worked. You could call any one of a hundred cities that had sprung up across the globe and twice that many little villages and mining camps. You could call every number in the registry and all you would get was dead air. You would be calling graveyards and mortuaries and burial pits.

The phone was still ringing.

Chambers opened his eyes, his fingers trembling over the tangle of his salt and pepper beard. He was not dreaming now. He was wide awake. He saw the empty restaurant and its unoccupied booths and tables, stools lined up in neat rows like chess pieces before the bar. He saw the smoked glass of the windows looking out on deserted streets.

But the phone continued to ring.

His guts tangled in an electric knot, he rose and carefully, step by wary step, he approached the bar. The phone was back there near dusty pyramids of glasses and bottles of Earth-imported liquor. Filled with something he couldn't even begin to decipher, he ran back there and plucked the phone from its cradle. Terror, raw and thick, thrummed in his brain.

"H-hello?" he said and, God, was that sharp, airless trilling really his voice? He hadn't spoken in years. He cleared his throat, swallowed down what spit he could find. "Hello?"

There was no answer.

But he could hear something on the other end. The sound of wind blowing through desolate, dark, and hollow places. The voice of Mars and its empty quarters. But…something else. Yes. He could hear it now.

The sound of breathing.

"Hello?" he cried. "Hello? Hello? *Who is this?*"

As the phone fell from his hand he thought he heard a muted giggling.

Chambers remembered how they had all died.

He remembered how he had survived.

The plague was never actually named as far as he knew. It was called just that: the Plague. Once Mars was colonized and everyone started arriving and carving out towns, there was a matter of food. Water could be synthesized if the basal elements were available and they were. And there was always the frozen water beneath the permafrost. But food was the problem. The only answer was to grow it on Mars. Shipping enough to feed thousands was impractical and expensive. Martian soil was taken back to Earth, charged with organic compounds and seeded. Plants were genetically altered. And soon enough, gigantic greenhouses were in operation. The plague started as a simple blight. Despite every precaution, a simple Martian microbe was overlooked. In the presence of rich organics, it flourished and mutated. The plants were immune to it, but not human beings.

It spread like a pestilence.

Soon, the colonies were all sick and dying.

Ships from Earth arrived with cutting edge medical technology. But it was too late. The microbe—a virus—mutated hourly and was near impossible to eradicate; once a therapy was devised, it was useless. The virus had changed again into something else. The colonists left in droves. Those that made it to Earth were never allowed to enter the atmosphere. Later, any ship bound from Mars was destroyed well before it reached home. Martial law was declared. Mars was in isolation. No one could leave. No one could come. All interplanetary vehicles were crippled beyond repair.

In a matter of months, two-thirds of the population were dead.

But a cure had been found. It was expensive and complicated. A lottery was held. Chambers won it. He was given the cure. By the time he woke up from the exhausting and painful process (one that was never fully explained to him), Mars was dead.

After he left the hospital and its dead and dying, he found that Sarah had died nearly a month before. Eventually, within weeks he was alone. He jumped in a hovership and roamed the globe…but there was no one left, just empty cities and the huge, sprawling cemeteries that had sprung up on their outskirts. The streets were filled with the dead. The unburied were stacked in heaps like lumber.

He returned home, to the ghost town of New Providence.

He kept in contact with Earth for nearly a year until something happened. He never knew what. Maybe a meteorite had wiped out the communication satellite orbiting the planet. Regardless, he never heard from them again.

Chambers had been cured. He was immune.

But he was completely alone on an alien world.

He told himself that it had not happened.

When he left the barbecue joint, he assured himself that the phone had not rung. It was a hallucination. And he wanted to believe that, but something in him would not accept it. Then he remembered the noise on the other end—the wind, the breathing, and that muted, echoing laughter—and his flesh crawled.

He sat on the curb and tried to sort it out.

Was it possible someone, somewhere, had survived? He had never heard of a single case of natural immunity to the pathogen. And he was the only one who had undergone the cure.

He thought: *But say…say someone else did. Someone who has been alone these seven years like me. Maybe at first they searched for others, but then gave up. Retreating away into their shell. Going quietly mad.*

It was a scary thought: Alone on Mars with a maniac for company.

He knew he had handled the isolation well.

But he had always been a solitary man. If it hadn't been for Sarah, he would have had scarcely any social contact whatsoever. It was simply the way he was. He read and studied and worked and held out hope that a rescue mission would arrive. But would a very social person have survived? What would the solitude do to their mind? He could imagine the madness that would set in, the gnawing stark insanity, and the mental degeneration.

Dear Christ, could it be true?

Wandering around all this time and now, finally, they found someone. They found him. But their minds were too far gone to see him as companion or friend. An enemy? A victim? Yes. Another soul to torment, to press their anguish and horror upon.

Chambers sat there on the curb while lunacy whispered in his brain. He felt the city around him. For the first time in seven years, he *really* felt the city. He felt its bulk, its weight, its mass rising up around him. He felt its emptiness, its shadows, its dark lonely spaces, and the multitude of places that a madman could hide.

He found himself staring, watching.

His skin was shivering in waves, the hairs at the back of his neck charged with static electricity. He had been through too much to let his imagination deal the final blow. He would not allow it. He—

He jumped up, walking in crazy, confused circles. The sensation that he was being watched crawled over his flesh like ants. Eyes were on him. A single set of feral, probing eyes. A cold and malevolent intelligence was studying him, scrutinizing him.

He had to press his lips together like pages in a book so he would not scream.

It seemed there were shapes lurking in every doorway, every alley, every shaded window. Eyes watched him from rooftops. From cellars. From huts.

Charged with white, trembling fear, he donned his helmet and ran. He did not stop running until he was through the dome's airlock and out in the thin atmosphere of the Martian desert.

Even then, he ran.

Certain that someone or something was watching him from behind the rocks.

Twenty minutes later he was at his Quonset hut.

It and its interconnected outbuildings sat on a blasted table of flat rock in the shadow of great stone cliffs that made the wind howl and mourn and shriek. Sometimes, if you listened too hard, you could hear voices in that wind. But the air on Mars was thin and sound carried in a funny way. It was best not to listen to it.

This was his sanctuary, he knew. This was the place that was supposed to make him feel safe, protected. But it did not. As he stood before it and the Martian winds threw sand and pulverized rock at him, he was an empty jar filled to brimming with an insistent, inescapable terror.

He studied the shadows.

He studied the rocks.

He saw no one. Nothing.

He went around the side to the airlock and it was open.

The inner hatch was sealed shut which meant the atmosphere of his domicile had not bled into the Martian wastes. But the outer lock was open. He knew without a doubt he had not left it open. He was meticulous about such things. In seven years, he had never gotten sloppy or careless. He would not start now.

Which meant only one thing: He was no longer alone.

He checked his rooms. He checked the storage cellars. The greenhouses. The sheds. The workroom. Nothing, nothing, nothing. Nothing had been rifled through or stolen or dropped. All was as he had left it.

He stood there in the twisting silence, thinking, thinking.

No, there were no outward signs, but *someone* had been here. He knew that. A phantom had come and gone. When a man spent seven years alone in a place, he got to know the feel of it as if it was part of his own body. When it was invaded, he knew that, too. His rooms had most definitely been visited. The fabric of solitude had been woven expertly by him over the years. And now it had been shorn. There was an unpleasant, almost alien feel in the air. A sense of violation.

He dug in the old chest under his bed.

He found the gun right away. It was an old-fashioned .50 caliber automatic. It could punch holes through steel or tear a man nearly in half. He loaded it and strapped it on. He felt a bit better.

He wandered his rooms again, trying to put a name to that horrible sense of invasion he felt. But nothing had been touched. He remembered an old video he'd seen of some comedian from Earth, now long since dust. The comedian said he woke one morning to find all the objects in his room replaced with exact duplicates. Chambers had laughed. There was the rub: if they were *exact* duplicates, then how could he know?

But Chambers felt that now.

That subtle, yet overwhelming sense that something had been altered here. Library drives and VR spheres had been picked up, handled, and replaced in the exact same locations. Or nearly, perhaps. Just out of sync enough to be noticeable. Yes, someone had been here, had touched things, perhaps giggling and drooling with some sinister dementia all the while, mind sucked into some alien blackness like the yawning spaces between the stars themselves. Things had been touched. Drawers opened. Closets looted through.

Chambers pressed his face to the window bubble.

He could see Mars out there. Empty, lonely, forbidding. Winds sculpted it, brushed it, haunted it. Nothing but rocks and sand, hills and vales. Lifeless. Totally lifeless. Mars had been alive a million years before, but now it was dead. All that was left were microbes and tiny parasites frozen in the soil. The shadows were long and the hazy sky was feathered by elongated pink clouds.

He swallowed down hard.

He saw something he had hadn't noticed before. His interface screen. It was not blank, yet he had not sat before it in some time now. It was still uplinked with computers across the globe…but there was no one out there to contact.

On the screen, it said:

YOU ARE NOT ALONE
YOU ARE NOT ALONE
YOU ARE NOT ALONE
YOU ARE NOT ALONE

It went on and on like that. It could have been sent from another city, but Chambers knew it had been voice-typed here on the screen for him to find. He knew this just as he knew his heart was pounding in his chest and that there was a dizziness reeling in his brain.

He waited as night came on.

The Martian night was black and unforgiving.

It poured from all the dark and lonely places where nothing with life dared walk or breathe or exist. It seeped like the blackest oil from the desolate, shunned corners of the ancient planet.

And when you were alone, it was forever.

When you were the last man on Mars and someone or some*thing* was stalking you, it was infinity.

Chambers locked down his little complex well before true nightfall. There was no supper. No music. No books. No games. Terribly alone, he huddled on his cot in the darkness of his little bedroom, cowering like a mouse in a hole waiting and wondering when the cat might strike. He had his pistol in his hand and in his chest, his heart was encased in ice.

All that could be seen of the endless Martian plain was that illuminated by the dome lights of New Providence. Chambers could see it all through the little titanium-composite bubble that served as a window.

He sat there in the darkness, sipping from a flask of bourbon and wondering if maybe he had imagined it all. But the phone call? The messages on the screen? How could you imagine that?

No, huddled in clinging, damp sheets of paranoia, he waited.

He waited and listened to the voices of the wind.

Sometime near dawn as he dozed and the Martian night raged, the wind howling and spraying sand against the outer walls like an arctic blizzard, he woke up. There had been a dream in which he was stalked from one empty town to the next by a faceless, deranged enemy which never showed itself.

He woke with that awful, almost suffocating feeling of being watched.

He looked up at his window.

He saw a white and grinning face peering in at him. The eyes were black as burnt cork and the lips red as wine. He screamed and nearly put a bullet through the window.

Then the face was gone.

And he was alone and the night enclosed his little complex and scratched at the door to be let in.

In the city, a phone was ringing.

He heard it as he walked through the lifeless streets of New Providence. It was the very thing he dreaded to hear and, of course, he heard it right away.

He thought: *Please stop, please stop, please stop! I want to be alone again! I just want to be alone!*

But it did not stop.

He fell to the street on his knees and covered his ears and would not listen. In his mind, he kept seeing that hideous face looking in at him and all the implications of it. No human could exist in the thin atmosphere without protection. And if he had indeed seen it, then it wasn't human. But there were no true Martians, no intelligent race either existent or long-vanished. There were ruins on Mars, yes, abandoned stone cities and subterranean networks—but these were thought to be the works of a visiting extraterrestrial race. They left behind no physical remains. No indication as to who they had been. The most recent of the ruins were over 30,000 years old.

Ghosts?

There had been stories among the early colonists of things they'd seen. Forms stalking the shadows. Bent, hunched-over things seen lurking on ridges or slipping through the silent shadows of the ruins. But they left no tracks, no evidence of their passing. They were dismissed as the products of over-active imaginations brought about by the solitude of the new world.

Could he have seen a ghost?

A wandering, malicious spirit of the wastes that preyed upon the solitary, the frightened? A reflection of some early degenerate life form long since past?

Chambers opened his eyes.

And as he did so, he saw a form pass by a window directly across from him. He was scared, he was shocked, but he was also angry. He brought the pistol and fired two rounds through the window. It shattered instantly. He was on his feet then. He slipped through the doorway of the hotel and made for the stairs. He took them two at a time, the fear in him blossomed into a need for vengeance now. He searched the second floor, all those empty, dusty rooms. He found several skeletons, but no indication of anything alive. He found the bullet holes he'd punched in the walls. Nothing more.

"Where are you?" he whispered under his breath.

He heard it then: the sound of a door slamming down the corridor. Bathed in cool, stinking sweat he ran towards it. The door was ajar. He saw a shifting shadow cross the floor and then he threw the door open.

The room was empty.

He wanted to scream. He wanted to put the gun in his mouth. He wanted to sink into the sucking tar pit of himself and be lost forever.

The phone near the bed was ringing.

He reached out. Answered it.

"Hello?" he breathed.

He heard that noise again…like wind rushing, vague and distant. And something closer, a sullen ragged breathing like dusty lungs sucking in air.

"Who is this?" he asked. "Who the hell is this?"

A giggling. Shrill, eerie.

"Who the hell is this!" he shouted.

Silence.

Then, a voice, a cruel and mocking voice spoken through a mouthful of dead leaves: *"I think you know."*

He threw the phone and screamed with a high, mindless wailing. He ran out of there and into the streets again where he could feel the eyes, that malignant and lewd gaze, crawling over his skin.

That voice. He knew that voice.

It was his wife's voice. It was Sarah's voice.

And Sarah was dead.

〇

The graveyard.

It stood beyond the domes of New Providence in a little shadow-riven valley. The soil was stony, but loose. There were hundreds of simple stone markers and leaning crosses set out. Many had been weathered unreadable now by fierce Martian sandstorms.

But Chambers knew where his wife's grave was.

He found it, started chopping through the frozen soil, his hair streaked with white now. His red-rimmed eyes were fixed and staring, his face old beyond its years. A tic jumped in the corner of his lips.

Now and then he sensed motion around him, but did not dare look. His external speaker picked up crazy, lilting sounds. Just the wind, he knew, moaning through the rocks. But it sounded like voices.

He kept digging.

Two feet, three, four.

He had to dig because he knew that the voice on the phone and the face looking in on him had been Sarah's. An evil, depraved caricature of his wife. He could not explain it. And maybe he didn't want to.

The grave grew deeper and the pile of red Martian soil grew steeper. The squared-off hole was sucking the shadows from the world, gathering them, collecting them, pooling them here. They seemed to slither like living things.

Keep going, he told himself.

With a thud he struck the shell of her casket and it was like thunder booming across the land. A voice in his head asked him over and over again just what it was he thought he was doing, but he couldn't answer it. He just could not answer it. He broke the catches with the shovel and, the darkness hissing around him and crawling over him like snakes, he lifted the lid. His eyes were bulging from behind the dusty visor of his helmet.

His throat closed up.

Something scratched at the inside of his skull.

Sarah was there, all right. Just as they'd buried her. The dry, cold climate had shriveled her into a mummy, her skin brown and leathery, eyes sunken, lips withered from narrow teeth.

But the truly awful thing was that her mouth was grinning.

And her eyes were wide and staring.

Night.

It came and the winds began to talk and the shadows gathered in inky, lunatic silence. Chambers waited with the gun in his hand as darkness closed in around him. All he could see was Sarah's gruesome, mummified face, that terrible look in her eyes.

Mars was in her.

All the alien nightmares that dead world had spawned and dreamed of were embodied in that look. It was cold as the wind-swept plains and icy as the depths of blackest space.

Sarah.

Her gray, withered fingers breaking now from the icy crust of her grave—

Chambers was mumbling to himself.

Trying to remember prayers from childhood, he chewed his lower lip. His eyes were grisly holes gouged into his face. One pupil was dilated, the other a neat pinhole. His lips were pulled in a tight, gray line.

The air went electric and he knew it was about to happen.

Chills tingled up his spine.

He made a sharp, wet, moaning sound.

There was a knock at the door. Calmly, Chambers put the muzzle of the gun to his head and pulled the trigger.

It was all that was left for him.

They found him a week later.

Two men in pressure suits who had arrived from the mother ship. The plague had been beaten on Earth. The cure was a simple matter of an injection. So the ship came to search for survivors, knowing full well there would be none. They had not communicated with the colonies in nearly six years.

They found the cities still operating, at least, some of them.

And then they found Chambers.

"Is that the one?" the young lieutenant said. "The one they gave that cure to?"

The commander said, "Yes. That's Chambers, all right. I knew him well years back."

"All this time alone…it must have gotten to him finally. But he's at peace now, I guess. He's dead."

The commander squatted near the body. "He's been dead a long time," he said. "He put a bullet in the only part that was still really alive."

On the floor in a heap was Chambers. His brains were sprayed against the wall and out of his head hung wires and plastic mechanisms. An android. They had given him the only cure they could—a body resistant to all things, to all manners of infection and biological attack. But his brain had been his own, encased in that shell of steel and plastic and rubber. And it was this, the commander figured, that had abandoned him in the end.

The rescue team spent another day and night at New Providence.

And when they finally left, they were glad. Glad to leave that cadaver of a world behind to its shadows and graves and memories. At night, they heard things they did not like outside the ship. And it was enough.

But, sometimes, if you listened too hard, you could hear voices in the wind. But the air on Mars was thin and sound carried in a funny way. It was best not to listen to it.

Mars was a haunted planet.

CHARNEL WORLD

Xenos was a graveyard.

The second planet orbiting 61 Cygni, it was a charnel world.

A rotting green cemetery haunted by crawling tissues of mist. A poisonous primordial soup of rank growth and boiling putrescence whose soil was gray, moist, and noisome. Its nightmare geography was hilled by jutting rungs of stripped bone and monuments of black stone. And it was also the hunting grounds and slaughter yards of the most lethal predator evolution had yet spawned. A merciless thing neither flesh and blood nor ectoplasmic, but of a dire alien biology somewhere between.

Its killing fields were Xenos.

And Xenos was a graveyard.

The *Volarus*, then, was a knife.

A knife that came in low and gleaming, slashing open a single bleeding incision in the yellow, murky flesh of Xenos. It carved the wound wide, slicing deep into the seething, primal anatomy of the planet itself. On the viewscreen, there had been stars and black space and now there was just a pulsing skin of amber mist.

"I'm gonna go through this just one last time," Tate said to the others as he checked his weapons, his voice so sharp it could have slit a throat. "Three weeks ago, a passenger liner called the *Carus* sent out a distress call from this quadrant. Complete systems failure..."

But they all knew the story.

The *Carus* was a pleasure cruiser. Star-drive crippled, it fell into a decaying orbit around the nearest planet—Xenos. A world restricted by the Agency. Sometime later, losing life support, it ditched to the surface. There were twelve people on board. There had been no word since. Because Xenos was restricted, there would not be a rescue mission. Contact with the planet was strictly forbidden. But a man named Carlson who had a lot of money and whose daughter had been on board decided that wasn't good enough.

So he hired the only ones who'd dare break Agency by-laws: Mercenaries.

"We're gonna find those people, get the hell out," Tate finished by saying.

The others—Thorn and Sheckley, Dundee and Morneau—just nodded. They were checking equipment, steeling themselves for what waited below. They all wore black e-suits. But these were not the heavy enviro-suits worn by the freighter and expeditionary crews, but state-of-the-art fighting suits. Light, flexible, capable of instantaneously adjusting to any environment, they were sometimes called "mothers" because they doted over the wearer. If you were hungry, they fed you. Thirsty, they gave you water. They disposed of your waste, protected you from radiation, and doctored your wounds.

And as Sheckley pointed out, "If this sumbitch can give a good blow job, I ain't never taking it off."

Carefully then, the men checked over their suits, survival gear, and weapons. They were carrying pulser pistols and scatterguns, particle cannons and thermal grenades. Knives, machetes, throwing blades—they were loaded for bear. Or, in this case, something far worse.

"How long we got on the ground?" Sheckley asked, sucking on the unlit stub of a cigar.

"Twelve hours, no more, no less. We find those people or we find what's left of 'em."

"Aye, and if the Xenoid got 'em?" Dundee asked.

"We cross that bridge when we come to it," Tate told him.

"Xenoid?" Sheckley said, tobacco juice painting his lips brown. "I got that prick's number. We find it, fix it, and fuck it. That's what I say."

But the Xenoid was a great mystery.

Supposedly, it lived below on that hot, wet, yellow world. In that hellzone terrain of heavy fogs and miasmic gases, endless reed swamps and misty, bottomless bogs.

No one had ever actually seen one.

Not really.

At least, nobody who lived to tell the tale.

Forty years previous, a bio-survey ship called the *Pole Star* had touched down on Xenos to make a detailed assessment of its ecosystem. The crew of twenty was never heard from again. Two rescue missions were lost in the steaming jungles trying to find them.

Then by accident, ten years later, a Xenoid was brought back to one of the Rigel colonies. Within thirty-six hours, it had slaughtered every last colonist—some seventy people. The corpses were found eviscerated, half-devoured, heads taken for trophies. But the security cameras never recorded anything but a blur. The Xenoid was finally destroyed trying to slip through a force field and was burned up.

It was considered to be the deadliest predator in the galaxy, the most efficient killing machine nature had ever designed. It lived to hunt, to torment, to kill. It was so dangerous and so completely feared that Xenos was now a forbidden world.

So the mercenaries were going after the *Carus* and maybe, just maybe the Xenoid would let them do that.

The hatch finally slid closed, separating the mercenaries from the control room. The Ready light came on and helmets were slid over tense, sweaty faces. There was a rushing, hissing sound as the cabin was bled, its atmosphere hissing away. The e-suits responded to zero gravity, inflating chambers.

"Get into your harnesses," Tate told them through his helmet mic.

The men climbed into anti-grav harnesses which looked like old-fashioned diving belts with brass weights and control bars rising from them, a throttle for each hand to control ascent and descent.

The only one in the cabin besides the mercs was the crew chief. "Stand in the door!" he cried out.

The lights dimmed, went red, flooded everyone with thick, bloody illumination. The outer hatch slid open and a wind rushed through the cabin, creepers of dirty yellow fog. Though they could not physically smell Xenos through their helmets, their minds told them it stank of rancid swamp gas and mass graves.

Lined up before that rushing, cloudy netherworld, the mercs gripping their harness throttles looked like boys ready to ride their pedal bikes off into the great unknown.

"Get ready," Tate said.

The jump light went green.

"GO! GO! GO! GO!" the crew chief shouted.

And they went, falling into darkness.

They jumped at 40,000 feet, drifting down like fallen October leaves, punching five holes through the churning gases and vaporous mists of the forbidden planet. All they saw was liquid blackness. It wrapped them up in a moldering blanket and then they hit the ground—a sucking, gray mud that swallowed them up to their knees. They climbed out of their harnesses, pulling scatterguns and pulsers and immediately forming a defensive perimeter. No easy bit, stumbling around in that sluicing, bubbling muck.

Their helmet lights showed them Xenos—a rank, decaying jungle of heavy foliage dripping with a snotty dew. Shrubs and ferns. Flowering plants with black, steaming buds like bleeding eyes. Huge, limbless trees rose up into the miasmic fog, each raining down a profusion of knotted vines that coiled on the ground in carpets like tangled yarn. The gravity was near-normal, but the atmosphere was a deadly envelope of nitrogen. One breath would asphyxiate you and make nitrogen bubbles explode in your veins.

And though they could not smell the planet, they could hear it: an almost deafening, droning wall of insects.

Thorn was holding a metal box out before him, its surface covered in read-outs and graphics. "Something…" he began, moving the box from left to right, and back again.

"What?" Tate said.

"Got a fix, I think," Thorn said. "About five klicks, south-southwest. Yeah, whatever it is, it's artificial…auxiliary pile still operating. Must be the ship."

"You think so?" Sheckley said. "You mean it's not just a privy you've found…"

"Oh no," Dundee said. "You can trust Thorn, by Christ. Him and that box are tighter than bloody spoons in a drawer. Why, just last night I saw him making love of the finest sort to it."

Thorn chuckled. "Dundee? You ever heard the one about the limey with the pulser up his ass?"

"Oi! Heard it? Boyo, I lived it. Happened to me poor mother, God bless the old whore."

"Let's go," Tate said, not amused.

They fell into single-file behind Thorn. The mud sucked at them, pools of ooze splashing against their legs. Vines trailed over their helmets like snakes, leaving greasy trails on their viewplates. Everywhere, weeds and stalks and crawling patches of red-orange fungus. The mist was heavy and moist, roiling in thick gaseous blankets and billowing pockets. It actually had a physical presence, oppressive and weighty like moving through jelly.

Sheckley said, "Hey, Dundee, I wager you ten credits we run into that Xenoid…you up for it?"

"Aye, I cover that. And I'm bettin' you twenty more I bag that randy prick. I'll mount his lovely head next to me wife's. Hoo!"

Sheckley laughed. "Ha! Thirty says that ball-cruncher is mine."

"You two, always betting on everything," Morneau said.

"Oi! Did you hear that, Sheckley? That stream of piss spoke!"

"I heard it, all right. Twenty credits says the Xenoid kills Morneau first."

"Aye. Makes love to him first though, I'm thinking."

"Oh, it'll make love to all of us in its own way," Morneau said.

"Easy, easy with such talk, you're scaring Dundee," Sheckley laughed as he trudged along.

"Aye! And me the first week out of the seminary! Mary and Jesus and the bloody saints."

Sheckley was grinning with stained teeth. "Dammit, Morneau, look what you've done to the poor bastard!"

"Oi! I'll recover," Dundee said, making a show of breathing hard. "And Sheckley...if tonight, by chance, you were to feel something slimy crawling down the front of your pants, have no fear, for it's only Morneau's hand..."

"If you feel my hand, pretty boy, it won't be in your pants but at your throat. And they'll be a knife in it as I make a blood offering of you to the Xenoid."

The two of them went at it, falling into the slop, trying to fight free and falling again. Tate helped them up, keeping them separated. His viewplate was dripping with mud, his face angry. "Enough, goddammit!" he boiled. "Enough! We're here to do a job, we don't have the time for this nonsense!"

Thorn stood watching the evening's entertainment, amused to no end. When the barbs stopped flying and Tate stopped slapping helmets and shouting, Thorn said, "If you boys are done stroking each other, it might interest you to know we're no longer alone..."

Silence then.

Helmet mics picked up the sounds of water dripping, gases hissing, things cracking and popping and oozing in the flat-bladed jungle around them. Insects.

Morneau watched with the others.

Watched shadows surging and flowing, becoming solid then obscure dancing wraiths that slid off into the mists. Inside his suit, he was shaking. Ribbons of cold sweat ran down the back of his neck.

He had his scattergun up, was ready to anatomize anything that moved, breathed, or belched. He'd been in some ugly places, but nothing could touch Xenos. There was something...*pestilent* and malignant about this place. Maybe it was the mists and the jungle, the creeping gases and gurgling muck, the rotting trees and slimy vegetable matter...but maybe something else. Something that got down right inside him, made his balls go tight and the flesh at his belly prickle with waves of fear.

"Anything?" Tate said, raindrops running down his viewshield like tears.

Thorn shook his head. "This fog…it's giving me some wild readings. Biorhythms, organic pulses everywhere. I'm picking up lots of animal life…reptiles, mammals, insects, a few chimeras. But…"

"But what?"

Thorn licked his lips and sucked in a sharp breath. "Something… something big, something that makes no sense…it's there, then it's gone."

That landed hard. The five of them stood their ground, slowly sinking into the mud sea, but not daring to move. Not daring to do anything. Then—

Morneau cried out and opened up with his scattergun. He got off five or six random shots, knives of red flame blasting trees and scrub into glowing fragments that drifted earthward like tracers, sizzling in the damp undergrowth.

"What is it?" Dundee cried. "What in the Christ is it?"

Everyone had their guns up and everyone was firing questions at him, but Morneau could only shake his head slowly from side to side. His throat was filled with dust, molten iron in his guts. "I…I saw something," he managed.

"What?" Tate demanded.

"Aye, probably the fucking tooth fairy," Dundee said, but there was no humor in his voice.

"I…I don't know," Morneau told them, gasping now. "In those vines…something was watching us. Something with eyes. Bright, yellow eyes."

"Thorn?" Tate said.

But Thorn just shook his head.

"Let's go then," Tate said. "Take the point, Sheckley…"

On they went, cutting through heavy jungle and wading through sucking pools of mud. Nothing seemed solid on Xenos. Everything was soft and wet. Acid rain fell and globs of yellow sap dripped from trees. Huge insects the size of birds rose in swarms. Hairy arachnids with sawblade jaws dropped from limbs and skittered over the merc's suits.

"Fucking hellhole," Dundee said, brushing one from his view plate.

"Must remind you of your mother," Sheckley said, but it elicited no laughter.

"Quiet," Tate snapped at them. "No talking."

This was a dangerous operation and he wanted professionals, not little boys. An awful lot was riding on what they did or didn't do on Xenos. If they rescued the crew of the *Carus* or brought back their remains they would be rich. If the Agency caught them, they'd be spending the next ten years on a penal colony in some remote wasteland of the galaxy. He wanted to find the ship as fast as possible. The less time on the ground, the better.

He sent a signal to the *Volarus* to let them know they were still alive, that the mission profile was still intact.

A heavy sparkling yellow mist was seeping around them. It issued from the swampy ground in a shimmering, luminous cloud that swallowed them up to their waists. They could hear things moving in the jungle around them, some small and some quite large.

"Hold up," Sheckley's voice said in their helmets. "Something just ahead…I think…*shit!*"

They heard his scattergun erupt, pulsed charges tearing up the real estate. They charged forward until they were with him. Something was burning at the perimeter of the jungle with arcing blue flames.

"Xenoid," he gasped. "I pegged it! Do you hear me? *I pegged the sonofabitch!*"

Tate was unconvinced. He motioned the others to stay back while he checked it out. What he saw was a bony carapace hanging from a tree limb. It was burning.

"It's not a Xenoid," he said. "It's a Xenoid molt."

They all saw it now.

Just a shell. A huge armored exoskeleton that was nearly cracked in half. Like a crab or a spider, the Xenoid molted its shell from time to time, casting it off as a new one grew beneath. From what Tate knew from the findings of the *Pole Star*, it was speculated that it took many years to grow a new one. Even so, it was a horrible thing towering above them like some weird collection of jutting bones and spikes, interlocking plates and spoking shafts. Its skull was massive and double-lobed at the cranium, jutting out with a set of heavy tusks and smaller thorn-like projections, four empty black eye sockets staring out at them.

"It looks recent," he told them.

"Christ," Dundee said. "The size of it."

They were all thinking the same thing. The Xenoid must have stood eight-feet tall in life, gigantic and multi-limbed. A lethal monstrosity encased in an impenetrable shell of bone. Its arms had rows of barbs running down either side, all of them looking sharp enough to open a belly.

"Nice shooting, though," Tate said.

Morneau laughed nervously in his helmet. He prodded the carapace with his pulser. It swung back and forth like a skeleton in a haunted house. "The scattergun shot barely grazed it," he said. "We should have armor like this."

"It gives us a chance," Thorn said. "The creature that left it will not be so well protected. We should be able to kill it if it shows."

Morneau laughed again. "You're naïve, my friend. Our heads are practically hanging in its lair already."

Dundee stepped forward. "Maybe you should shut your cunting mouth," he said.

Sheckley ignored them. "Why was it left like this? Just hanging here?"

"Maybe it's what they do," Tate said.

"Scarecrow," Morneau told them. "It was left here like a scarecrow to frighten us. The Xenoid has been watching us since we got here."

Everyone looked around. No one disagreed with him because they could feel it out there circling them.

"Enough of that," Tate said. "Let's move."

As they plodded ever forward, ducking beneath clutching vines and avoiding massive luminous spider webs that were easily twenty-five feet across, Thorn said, "I wonder how many there are?"

"What's that love?" Dundee asked, kicking through a stand of black, glistening toadstools that exploded with lethal spores.

"How many Xenoids, I mean. We keep referring to the *Xenoid*, as if there's just one—but there must be a population of them. Thousands, maybe."

That stopped everyone. It was something they hadn't considered, at least openly. One was bad enough, but an army of them…it was inconceivable, terrifying.

"They're solitary hunters, territorial," Tate said. "I rather doubt we'll see more than one."

"Rank speculation," Morneau said.

Dundee swore. "Somebody shut him up."

Sheckley grunted.

"It's all we have. Now move out," Tate ordered.

The ship.

They found it twenty minutes later.

It had come down hard, gouging a ragged hole in the slimy foliage and coming to rest in a bog of steaming, oily water. There was a great gaping rent amidships, the port thruster pod sheared away. Its shiny silver skin was blistered and burned black.

Tate and Sheckley went in while the others stood guard.

The atmosphere was gone on the *Carus*, but the pile was still operating. Sheckley got some lights going, but they were dim, creating shadows and wild, leaping shapes.

Tate kept his pulser in hand.

Thorn had already told them via the magic box that there was nothing living in the ship. But Sheckley wasn't so sure. He kept sensing movement around them, phantasmal forms slipping into dark pools whenever he sought them out.

His face was bloodless, his eyes wide and unblinking.

He didn't like what he was feeling. He didn't like being scared shitless.

They checked the ship cabin by cabin, found bloodstains, some soiled dressings, but not so much as a scrap of flesh. The interfaces were burned-out, so they couldn't access the ship's log.

"They must've…left," Tate said, his voice hollow.

"Where to, chief?" Sheckley wanted to know. "Where to? Out there? Out in that pissing, rotten soup?"

But Tate would not look at him. "You got a better theory?"

Sheckley did. "Way I'm figuring it, something knocked at the door…and then they opened it…"

Outside, they watched the *Carus* sink.

Tate and Sheckley barely got out the starboard hatch before the cruiser gave out a terrible groan of metal fatigue and rolled over on her side like a sick dog. Mud and black, jellied water pulled her down, pouring in through her wounds and open hatches. Five minutes later, the nose went under with a foaming hiss.

End of story.

Tate knew what they all wanted to hear, but he wasn't giving that order. They were not pulling out. Not until he had a few bloated bodies to take home for Carlson. He owed the man that much, after all the money he'd spent throwing this little party together.

"All right," he said, "let's start a grid search, let's…"

But nobody was moving.

They were watching Thorn. He was the team's scout and he had an uncanny knack for sensing and locating the enemy, with or without his high-tech toys. And right then, they knew he had found something. He was frozen in a crouch about fifteen feet from the others, peering through a mutiny of wet, blue-green ferns hopping with tiny red beetles. He just waited there, like a hound that had located a fox.

"What is it?" Tate asked him. He did not move; he waited with the others, feeling something building in the air. Something savage and terrible.

They could hear Thorn breathing over the mic. Short, sharp breaths like knife blades. "I don't know…but *something's* out there… something's watching us…"

"The box?" Dundee whispered.

"It says there's nothing…but there's *something* off in the trees. I can feel it there, staring down at us." His respiration was getting faster now, his voice dry as cinders. *"Oh yes, I know you're up there…I know, I know.* I think…I think it has been following us since we touched down, shadowing us. Whatever it is…it's real good, real quiet."

Tate looked over into that green, blossoming wall of leafage. Water glistened from vines and tendrils, shoots dangled in the air. Clots of that snotty slime dropped into the mud below. *Plop, plop, plop.* His helmet lights picked out hulking shapes that melted away like wax just as quickly.

Thorn was giggling low beneath his breath. It was a pained, demented sound. *"Oh…Jesus…I can feel it…feel it hating us, God how it hates us—"*

"Stop it," Sheckley said. "That's enough! Dear Christ, that's enough."

Tate felt it at least as much as the others.

The blood had drained from him now, his skin was white and blotchy, his face corded with muscle and tendon like a man on the verge of a coronary. Sweat dripped from the tip of his nose and moths were being birthed in his stomach, fluttering up into his chest.

"Cover me," Thorn said.

He moved forward, slipping through the muck almost too easily. He barely made a sound. He moved up and over a deadfall of fungus-covered trees that looked like a seething pile of bones. The vines came down, coiled around him like mating serpents and then he pressed himself into their fetid, undulating depths.

There was nothing but silence after that.

A silence broken only by falling tree limbs, dripping water, and the constant bubbling organic stew that brewed around them. A flock of scythe-shaped insects rose from a bed of barbed shoots, disappearing into the fog with a low whirring sound.

Then Thorn's voice came over the com, panicked. "Right ahead…*I can see it.* I think I'm seeing it. It's green and yellow and blue…it keeps changing shape. I can see through it one minute, the next it's—"

Then they heard him screaming.

But it didn't last long.

They all started shooting this time.

They vaulted forward, blasting the foliage to incandescent fragments that exploded and rained all around them like flares. But it wasn't enough, by God, it wasn't enough. Tate was screaming for them to cease fire, cease fire, but they charged through the muck, splashing through algae-scummed mires and sinkholes, shooting and shooting. When it was over, they were encrusted in mud like shit-worms, swearing and panting, staring at the huge chasm they'd blasted through the sweating greenery.

"You stupid sons of bitches!" Tate railed. "If Thorn was still alive, you just burned him down!"

Dundee chuckled sickly. *"Alive?* You heard that scream by Christ... anything screams like that is being torn apart like a paper dolly."

"He's right," Sheckley chimed in, cigar butt still wedged in his teeth.

Morneau just stood there, shocked and terrified.

Tate resisted the impulse to knock heads...or helmets together. "All right, all right, goddammit, I've had enough of this shit. Let's go bag that cocksucker..."

So off they went.

Off into that crawling, slimy green hell. Beyond the hole they'd incinerated, the jungle was thick and suffocating, a dripping, hopping, tangled maze of shoots and stalks, vines thicker than a man's arm and flooded undergrowth they had to chop their way through. Weird insects buzzed and trilled around them, creeping over their suits and nipping at their face shields. They saw things like twenty-foot worms the color of fresh blood twisting in the trees, two-headed rodents, and armored spidery/crab things that spun funnel webs from their own feathery flesh.

Tate had them perform an ever-widening grid search, the four of them stealthily moving deeper into the weed-choked lowlands and swampy cuts that were thick with shivering tarps of mist. There were thickets of thorny bushes that did their best to slit open the suits and stands of trembling knife-grass just as sharp as razors. They found hideous clusters of morbid, spongy mushrooms the size of footballs that pulsed like they were breathing and mewled like kittens if they were prodded.

"We should call the ship," Morneau whispered, "get us out of here..."

But nobody paid any attention.

Dundee was just ahead on point, dappled with tentacles of ground fog and splotches of viscous, clammy mud. He was moving through a gelatinous pond of slushy water, making his way around green, rotted tree trunks and mats of sparkling pink moss that hung all around him like garlands.

Then he stopped, lifted his left hand up, signaling them to halt.

He was investigating something. Finally, he said, "Have a look at this, why don't you."

They sloshed forward, helmet lights spoking shafts of illumination in every which direction. The fog caught it, threw it back at them. What Dundee had found was Thorn's magic box. It was neatly strung from a forked tree branch…still dripping with the man's blood.

"Now ain't that fucking convenient?" Sheckley said. "Left here all high and dry so we can follow Thorn's blood trail? Our host wants this game to keep rolling, me thinks."

"Then let's not disappoint him," Tate said. He took the box and interfaced with it, getting it to sniff out human blood. Which it did quite easily; nothing on Xenos being based on the carbon atom. "Let's go."

He pointed the way and Dundee led them forward, crouching low under overhanging branches and fans of slippery vines. Morneau kept complaining and Sheckley kept calling out for Morneau's mother, but told him that, alas, the Xenoid was off buggering her in the trees.

Dundee pushed through a forest of stalks like purple-blue bamboo and just as he got through, they heard him say: "Well, would you lookee here…"

And Tate suddenly felt a black, crawling anxiety in his belly, but it was too late. There was a sound of exploding mud and plants followed by something like a meat cleaver shearing through a pumpkin.

They all slopped forward through that sea of phlegmy oatmeal.

What they saw floating in the mud made Morneau moan and Tate suck in a sharp lungful of air. Sheckley moved before anyone else. There was something like a ten-foot black blade jutting from the silt. It was curved like a scimitar and sharp enough to cut through steel. Dundee had been split in half, crotch to helmet, neatly slit lengthwise like a giant pair of scissors had sheared him in two.

"Booby-trap," Sheckley said, biting straight through the butt of his cigar. His face behind the shield was glistening with sweat, arteries jumping at his temples. "Fucking mantrap. Dundee...he must've tripped a wire, something."

Mantrap. Sure, it rolled through all their minds. Dundee went to pick something up, breached that tripwire and was sheared in half by the blade. It was not made of metal, but of cellulose. The flat spike from some horrible plant. And this, more than anything up to that point, really hit home. It meant the Xenoid was intelligent. Not just some mindless killing machine, but one driven by a sadistic, thinking brain.

"Why not?" Sheckley said. "A good hunter always uses traps..."

They pretty much had to put a gun on Morneau to get him to move after that.

But it was in all of them, too. A terrible, gnawing fear that crushed them with its immensity. It slithered in through their suits, filled their bellies with ice crystals and shrapnel, made their flesh literally crawl in serpentine waves.

But it was worse for Morneau.

He was nearly mad by that point. He was chattering his teeth and mumbling and talking to Dundee and Thorn and his father who'd been in the grave no less than ten years.

So when he saw it, saw the Xenoid clinging to a tree trunk twenty-feet up like a tree frog, he did not say a word. He just watched it. It was much larger than a man, looked to have four arms covered in protrusions like gleaming hooks. It had two spidery legs and seemed to be composed of curling, slithering vines.

But he saw its eyes.

Yellow, bright, obscene.

He saw it for only a moment, than it became something like indigo looping snakes that slid up into the trees and were gone.

He thought only one thing: *Chameleon.*

The reed swamp.

It was where the blood trail led them.

A fetid, simmering morass of segmented reed stalks that grew in a clotted profusion like sugarcane. They climbed high over the head of the mercs, swaying and bobbing with some unseen wind. They were so congested, you had to physically push yourself through. Ten feet later, the stalks pressed back together, erasing your trail. They pulled you in, locked you tight like iron bars, coveted and held you, wanting only to press your carcass into the bubbling, simmering mud where your remains would feed them.

Tate led the way and Morneau stumbled along blindly at the rear, his helmet light playing off those tall, narrow stalks that brushed against him, snagged his equipment, seemed to whisper with a high, profane sibilance.

Fifteen minutes into that sodden nursery, Tate died.

It happened very quickly.

He stepped into a small clearing of stagnant, leafy water. There were twelve poles cut from tree limbs jutting from that rippling sewage and on each, a speared human head. The passengers of the *Carus*. Their faces were blue and green and spattered with blood that looked oddly brown. Scarecrow heads…stuffing and straw poking out everywhere, confetti dangling from throats. Long, greasy worms were sliding up nostrils and investigating eye sockets.

Tate found them, stumbled forward…and something rocketed up from below: a living bear trap with huge, serrated jaws. It grabbed him, swallowing him up to the waist, nearly biting him in half before it pulled him back down into the muck. A few ripples. A floating helmet. That was about it.

Sheckley started laughing. "You see that, you silly little fuck?" he said to Morneau through his mic. "You see that? Armored fish or mud-crawler…shit in a box, that bastard was quick."

Morneau was beyond laughter or tears by that point. His face was chipped from white ice and somebody had stuck on a couple black shoe buttons for eyes as a gag. Those buttons shined, they reflected, but they didn't really see. "It was made of steel," he said numbly. "Some sort of metal…"

"Bullshit. It had eyes. I saw it."

Morneau accepted the idea of a living booby trap. In some dark corner of his flyblown mind, he found it almost amusing.

They didn't say much after that.

But Sheckley had come up with this idea, see, and Morneau was a big part of it. It was gonna be good, real good.

At gunpoint, Sheckley marched Morneau through the reed swamp, the barrel of his scattergun on him the whole while. He made him march a good twenty feet in front of him, but no more because that steaming, billowing yellow mist would have tucked him away somewhere secret. So Morneau, divorced of his weapons, stumbled blindly forward, not knowing, not caring, his brain gone to sauce and his mind fractured to the point where he felt like he was on some special, mystical level with Xenos. He could feel it inside him and outside him. The reeds were his brothers and anytime he wanted, they'd accept him. Make him a nice little cozy spot to rest.

Sheckley, cursing under his breath, his eyes bloodshot and set hard, pushed Morneau through slopping, foul water that came up to their waists, through the forest of reeds, and into a tight, black thicket of knotted plants that looked like rose stems but were well over six-feet tall. They were fibrous, bleeding a bright purple sap, set with thorns three-inches long. By the time the two of them fought their way through, their e-suits were riddled with gouges and ruts, their viewplates latticed with scratches.

They found a clearing of short marsh grass.

"Walk out there," Sheckley said, panting and gasping, "that beast is hungry…let's give it something juicy."

So Morneau, knowing he was bait but not really caring, walked out into that turgid pool of black slime, little islands of marsh grass undulating in his wake. He stood there, his back to Sheckley and waited.

Thank God he wasn't alone.

Thorn was there, telling him jokes but leaving out the punch lines as usual. Tate was telling him he had better straighten up. And Dundee was laughing in that annoying brogue, reminding him that if his mother had kept her legs crossed, it would've saved the galaxy from a scratch of shit like him. Yes, yes, yes, yes. They all were talking at the same time, why didn't they ever shut up?

Then there was a splashing sound like a crocodile rocketing from a swamp...and silence.

Morneau turned around and Sheckley was gone.

Morneau began to scream.

Sometime later, running and running.

Morneau was covered in silt and mud and weeds. He kept shambling forward, falling and sinking and rising up again. He thrashed through the reeds, hearing the others calling out to him, beckoning for him to join them in dark, stygian pockets of jungle.

That's how he found the city.

The reeds unzipped and there it was, a sunken city. A cyclopean series of ruins—leaning standing stones, rectangular uprights, columns and arches, squat low buildings sprouting with reeds and shoots and tangled vines. The entire place was flooded, crumbling and falling into itself, pitted with worm-holes and cracks. Like a city made of blocks a child had tired of and kicked asunder. It reminded Morneau of a cemetery. Vaults and headstones, mausoleums and sepulchers all covered in slime and fungus and oozing shrouds of moss.

He moved through the ruins, avoiding the murky hollows where things called him by name. He came to a wide central plaza that was lifted above the mire, constructed of huge diamond-shaped slabs of black stone. Overhead, a vaulted roof was made of a crisscrossed ironwork that was knitted with ropes of green growth.

This was the Xenoid's place.

A butcher shop, a trophy room.

The passengers from the *Carus* were here, as well as the other mercenaries. Their heads were missing, some tanned and mounted on stone pillars. Their bodies had been dressed out, skinned and cured. Joints of human meat dangled on vines from the iron rafters overhead. A belt of hands and a girdle of feet had been meticulously threaded together. Limbs were stacked like firewood. There were weapons leaning against a wall...black, razored things made of the same stuff that had slit Dundee in two.

A hunter's forest retreat.

But what really caught Morneau's attention were the bones. They were stacked in intricate piles, interwoven in sculptures of jutting femur, tibia, and scapula. Ribcages and spiraled vertebrae and gleaming slats. Some bones were human, but most were alien. Some tiny, some immense. These sculptures were topped by skulls that might have belonged to rodents and saurians and saber-toothed hunting cats. An ossuary. The collection of a deranged, perverted brain.

And that's when he found Sheckley.

He was hanging upside down, his suit and helmet still in place…or most of it, on account he had been severed at the hips. A weird, webby netting of shimmering pink material had grown into his waist and up into the rafters where it held him, swaying gently from side to side. A gossamer series of tendrils and filaments that looked very much like a neural network. When Morneau touched the material…little arcs of blue flame ran through the fibers.

He was still alive.

Inside his helmet, his eyes were open and staring with a vibrant lunacy, his mouth trying to form words. His mind was long gone, but the sparkling network kept him alive.

Morneau stumbled away, went down on his knees, his brain filled with a warm, wet madness. He could hear it dripping and slopping in his skull.

Then, prostrate in this slaughterhouse, a huge and black amorphous shadow fell over him.

He knew what it was, of course.

Just as he knew he didn't dare look a god in the face.

But slowly, very slowly, he turned his head upwards, looked through his view shield…and saw.

Yes, the Xenoid.

A serrated, razor-edged sculpture of bone and armor.

What a marvel of evil engineering it indeed was.

A blasphemy of perfection. Over eight feet tall, it was sinewy and plated like an insect, green and blue with a brilliant orange thorax, then morphing instantly to a dun yellow. Solid one moment, then the next, nearly transparent like a breath of ectoplasm. It had four rawboned arms that were set with rending spikes and jagged thorns, colossal four-fingered hands ending in talons like sickles. Its head was huge with arching shelves of bone, the cranium double-lobed like a human brain. It looked like a living alien skull, huge upward curving tusks projecting forward. Between them, there was a gaping black mouth set in a vertical chasm.

Morneau screamed, sobbed, then cackled madly.

The Xenoid looked down at him with yellow, luminous eyes upturned in narrow sockets.

Glutinous steamers of crimson drool dropped in clots from its mouth, oozing down Morneau's face shield in runny glops.

But its eyes, those yellow malefic eyes found him, held him, showed him what was in the mind of a Xenoid. It gave him a tour of that black, charnel wasteland of cold alien depravity. There was nothing remotely human in its thinking; it saw all lifeforms as things to be conquered, to be stalked, hunted, and brought down. Things to toy with and torment.

Morneau lost what was left of his mind then.

Felt it run from his skull in a cool and easy flow. "My Lord, I offer thee my flesh and blood," he said.

Grinning madly, the Xenoid's nitrogen breath on him like toxic waste, he awaited sacred benediction.

He did not wait long.

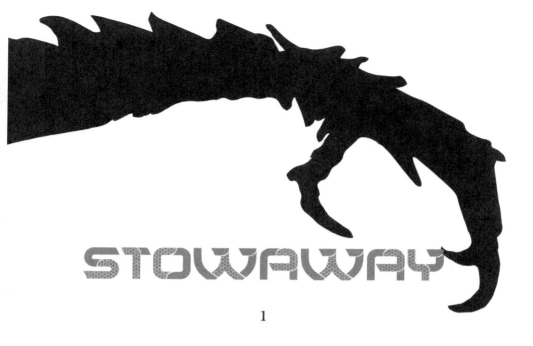

STOWAWAY

1

I t wasn't until after the survey team came back in from that blasted chunk of frozen rock known as BX-66 that the extraordinary happened. And the thing was, nobody seemed to notice. The crew went about their jobs entering the vital data into the interfaces concerning asteroid BX-66, because that was what was expected of them. They were some 419 light-years from home and to a man (and woman) they kept busy, knowing they would not see the green hills of Earth for at least five years and possibly six. And when you had that kind of time staring you dead in the face like bleak eternity itself, you did everything you could to keep from thinking about husbands and wives, children and parents. Last thing you wanted to be doing was remembering the caress of a lover, the smell of fresh-cut grass, or how it made you feel deep inside when you saw your daughter picking daisies in a spring meadow.

Boredom and memory were enemies aboard the *Taurus*.

And the crew fought them at every turn.

So the techies were squirreled away in Geolab testing rock samples and putting the drones in storage. The maintenance boys were checking systems. The flight crew was making preparations for lift-off, the AI neuro-plex already plotting a path through the asteroid belt.

And in his cabin, Captain Egan was playing with toothpicks.

He always played with toothpicks. Some had their cybergames

or holograms, VR diaries or interactive fuck-books (a great time passer known as "digital masturbation" to the crew), but Egan had his toothpicks. He was studying the monitor, the craggy, black landscape of BX-66 before him, thinking how every goddamn one of these asteroids looked exactly the same.

And, yes, thinking about patience, too.

How the toothpicks taught you patience and you didn't belong in the service if you didn't have some…patience, that was.

He was a short, round man whose skin was uniformly pink and polished. There was a perfectly-squared King Tut beard at his chin and his eyes were gray and watery like roe in a spawn bucket…and just about that animated.

Right then, he was putting together a scale model of the Tower of London and had already used over fifteen-thousand toothpicks and figured it would take five or six times that many to finish the project. Last voyage he'd slapped together the Leaning Tower of Pisa and the voyage before that? Buckingham Palace and the Colonnades of Mars. But his favorite was—

The door buzzed.

"Come in," he said.

It was Dahl, the systems tech. Dahl with his nervous twitches, scraggly black beard that looked oddly like something a spider had spun.

"Sir," he said, seeming unable to catch his breath, "something weird has happened…"

"Really?" Egan did not look up from his toothpicks. He was filing a collection of them to be used on the castellated walls. It was exacting work, not to be taken lightly.

"Yeah…I was checking over some of the external video feeds—"

"I have my own video feed here as you may have noticed," Egan said, dismissing whatever it was Dahl was going to say next. "The Tower of London. What do you know of it, mister?"

"Sir, I—"

"Come now, son, the White Tower? Traitor's Gate? Bloody Tower? Surely these names mean something to you? Did you know, Dahl, that they executed Sir Thomas More and Ann Boleyn there?"

"No, sir, I guess I wasn't aware."

Egan set his files aside. "Now, if there's nothing more, you can see how busy I am…"

"Yes, sir."

Dahl left in something of a hurry.

2

Kregan said, "Silicate rock composition…trace amounts of magnesium, cobalt, titanium, platinum, and iron. Extractable pockets of methane and hydrogen in crust. Iridium negligible." He looked up from his scope, sighed. "I'd classify her C-type, carbon rich."

"Log her so," Orhane, the first officer, told him.

He had heard it so many times by that point it meant absolutely nothing to him. They'd mapped out sixty-six asteroids now in the belt of thousands situated between the planets Omicron Ceti-4 and -5. Omicron Ceti, sometimes known as 68 Ceti or Mira A, was a Type-M red giant star of the M6 spectral type with a Type B companion star, a blue Dwarf known as Mira B with a 500-year orbit. But to the crew, even the hard-bitten scientific sorts like Kregan, it was just a big, ugly ball of red shit that would burn your eyes out of your head if you stared at it. Beyond that, it served to remind them all how damn far they were from home.

Dahl came through the hatch of Geolab. He looked around at everyone, swallowing continually, his Adam's apple bobbing up and down like a bird at a feeder.

"Chief," he said to Orhane, "I need to have a word with you."

"Sure," the tall, bearded man said, "gimme a minute here."

Pach, the biologist, a tall and striking redhead with upturned Nordic crystal blue eyes just shook her head. "Dahl, what do you want here? Go keep that neuro-plex chugging, why don't you? I'm in the mood for some porn tonight. You know how I like my porn."

You could almost feel the testosterone spiking in the room. Pach had been teasing every man on the ship for sixteen months now and there was no end in sight.

"Course, boys, I like to watch my porn *alone.*"

Weise laughed. "You're such a bitch, Pach."

"Don't I know it and don't I love it." Pach studied the screen. "Nope, this rock is just as dead as Dahl's dick."

"Fuck you," Dahl said.

"No thanks, honey. I made a promise to myself years ago that I would only mate within my species."

Weise broke up over that one.

Dahl was shaking, scratching angrily at his beard, entertaining fantasies of what he'd do to Pach if he ever got the chance. Bitch wouldn't walk straight for a week. "Dammit, Chief, this is important…"

Orhane was looking at him now. "Yeah? Go ahead."

But Dahl was not going ahead. He looked around and saw that all eyes were on him, staring, wondering. There were no secrets on the *Taurus*—other than whether or not Pach really masturbated to porn or it was just a gag—and everyone's supposedly private thoughts had pretty much been dragged from one end of the ship to the other, been used as rugs and rags, material for jokes.

Dahl just said quietly, "Alone."

"Oooo," Pach said, "do I sense the budding flower of young love?"

"Shut the hell up," Orhane told her, leading Dahl out of Geolab.

In their wake, before the hatch slid shut, there was a great deal of whispering and speculating. If Dahl had something to say, something he couldn't say in front of everyone, it had to be good. Better than your average social disease.

"What is it?" Orhane asked him, dead serious now.

But Dahl insisted they go into the First Officer's Cabin. When they got there and the door was shut behind them, Dahl keyed up Orhane's monitor.

"I've piped the feed in here," he said, as an image of BX-66 came up on the screen. "You've got to see this."

And maybe, Dahl hoped, when he saw it, when he looked at it dead-on, then maybe his skin would be crawling, too.

"What am I supposed to be seeing?" Orhane wanted to know.

But Dahl wouldn't say. "If I told you, you'd think I was nuts. Just watch."

Orhane sat down.

It was a video playback of the survey party out on the surface of the asteroid. It had been taken some three hours before from a port camera. The team in their heavy orange e-suits marching single file back to the ship, a whirlwind of murky dust whipping around them, obscuring them. Sometimes they were visible in the hull boarding lights, other times swallowed by the blowing debris. The party made it to the boarding ramp and started up.

Orhane just shook his head. "I'm not seeing it, sorry."

"You're not looking, Chief." Dahl backed up the feed. The survey party was at the boarding ramp again, starting up. "Now, watch, and while you watch, remember this: There were five people in that party."

"Yeah, but…"

Orhane got it now.

It hit him hard like a fist to the jaw. He licked his lips, backed up the feed, watched it again. Watched it three more times, in fact. His skin had an unhealthy grayish tinge to it now, his eyes huge and wet.

"Jesus Christ," he said. "Five people went out—"

"Yeah, but *six* came back in."

3

Orhane didn't say anything after that, not for a minute or two. He was running the import of those words through the methodical, precise reels of his brain. And it was a good brain. On a ship where insults had taken the place of greetings and the sexual preferences of everyone's mothers were open for debate, that was saying something.

He watched the feed yet again, staring intently at it. He sighed, arched an eyebrow. "All right, let's think this over."

"Shouldn't we…I mean, shouldn't we sound the general alarm or something?" Dahl said, chewing on his lower lip. "Declare martial law or…Jesus Christ, Chief, I'm *freaking* out here."

Orhane made him sit down and take a few breaths. "Take it easy, just take it easy."

But it was not as simple as that. Unless the equipment was totally screwed up, unless there was a serious glitch in some program, they had more than a ghost in the machine—they had one walking among them.

"Now, is it possible this could be a technical problem? A reflection? A patched of charged mist? Anything like that?"

But Dahl just shook his head. "I checked everything. Twice. Shit, three times. I ran every test I could think of and some I couldn't.

Look at it, Chief…does that look like a reflection or a patch of gas? It looks like a sixth crew member coming right in like he or she or *it* belongs here."

And, yes, that's what it looked like, all right.

When slowed down frame by frame, the sixth figure looked oddly filmy, insubstantial…as if it was composed of some weird, ethereal material and the light was not just reflecting off it, but passing *through* it in places. It was hard to be certain, of course, for all that blowing dust and grit completely obscured the survey party from time to time.

"I suppose we should tell the Captain—"

"Tried it, Chief. That fucking whacko is playing with his toothpicks. He won't listen."

Egan was crazy and they all knew it. He stayed in his cabin twenty-four-seven and in the past sixteen months, even Orhane himself had only seen him a dozen times. Orhane ran the *Taurus* and everyone knew it.

"He's your commanding officer, mister. Show him some respect."

But Dahl just laughed. "Oh for fuck's sake, Chief. Egan's nuttier than a peanut butter factory. We both know it. You're in charge, we all know that, too. That…*man* isn't fit for duty."

But Orhane would not belittle him.

He was very professional. He was not inflexible, but he did things by the book and followed a rigid set of personal ethics. Officer and a gentleman. Unlike the majority of the crew who were civilians, Orhane was regular service. A lifer. Besides, he was up for his own command and the service didn't look kindly on junior officers who had no respect for authority.

And, hell, given the state of surveillance technology, you honestly never knew who was listening. They had gadgets the size of your thumbnail that could see right through six-inches of tempered steel. And sometimes that fly that landed on your arm was just a fly, but other times…well, you just had to be careful. The service had strict policies concerning privacy. All their ships were set with anti-bugging equipment, but who could say? Pach, for instance, was certain that Dahl watched her in the shower with a micro camera, so everyday she made a big deal of soaping her breasts and sliding a phallic-shaped sponge between the cheeks of her ass. She hoped it made him squirm.

"Yes, well, I'll oversee this one," Orhane said diplomatically, clearing his throat. Then he turned back to the feed. "Can you blow this up, Dahl? I mean *big?* I want to see that last form up close and personal."

"No prob...which frames you want?"

While Dahl ran the frames, Orhane showed him the ones he wanted.

"Particularly that one," he said, jabbing a finger at the screen. "See that...right there?"

Dahl did, all right, and it gave him the creeps. It looked, well, it looked like that last *form,* as Orhane called it, had turned its helmet in the direction of the camera as if it knew it was being watched. Turned and stared momentarily. But it was probably just a coincidence.

Dahl fingered the touch screen, making images on the monitor jump and explode. Then he had it. Swallowing, he ran the feed frame by frame again, but this time the survey party's helmets filled the screen. You could see the lights reflecting off their suits.

"Oh, Jesus Christ," Dahl said, suddenly going white and board-stiff. He began to breathe very hard like he was hyperventilating. His hands shook and the blood ran from his face. "Did you see it? Did you—"

"I saw it, all right," Orhane said, his concrete-solid demeanor beginning to crumble around the edges. "Dear Christ, what is this about?"

The monitor was frozen on the frame where the form had turned its helmet in the direction of the port security camera. You could see the black plastic face shield and behind it...two glowing red orbs like luminous eyes staring at the camera with malefic hatred.

4

Orhane's plan wasn't much, but it was something.

Both he and Dahl were armed now, both carrying pulser weapons which were about the size of playing card decks. Small or not, they could burn a man to ashes with a flick of a thumb. Over the loudspeaker, Orhane told the survey party to report to the conference room and said it very calmly, casually. While he did that, Dahl got behind his terminal and began a bioscan of the ship...if there was somebody or something that didn't belong, the scan would pinpoint them.

And it began.

5

"What the hell is this about?" Pach wanted to know.

"It's a simple debriefing," Orhane told her, waiting for the others.

"Since when? We've never done that before."

"We are this time."

When they had all assembled—Weise, Pach, Kregan, Huckstep, and Tsumada—Orhane played them the video on the big screen. They all watched it two, three times, firing questions at him and then Huckstep, the engineer, saw it.

And when he saw it, they all did.

Pach said, "Incredible, incredible."

Weise did not say a thing.

Kregan just narrowed his eyes.

Tsumada said, "What the fuck gives here?"

And that pretty much summed it up.

"Seems we picked up a rider out there," Kregan said.

"That rock was dead," Pach insisted. "There was nothing alive there, no indication that anything ever had been."

"Well something was," Tsumada said, "you must've missed it."

But Orhane did not think she had missed anything. It was not like her. He had a couple ideas, not very scientific, but they explained a few things. He figured that this thing—whatever it was—had played dead so that Pach's scanners had not picked it up. It seemed far-fetched, but Orhane had been in the service some fifteen years and he'd seen some very insane, impossible things amongst the stars. Besides, if this thing could imitate a crew member in an e-suit, it was obviously very adaptable. Was it really so ridiculous to assume there could be a life-form that could evade instrumentation?

Orhane told them what he thought.

"That's crazy," Huckstep said.

Pach shrugged. "Maybe not. There are lots of creatures that mimic others for their own protection. A defensive adaptation, nothing more.

There's a giant mud worm on Draconis-3 that can shift itself into an armored, three-headed serpent. It's perfectly harmless, but it'll scare the pants right off you. And on Beta Hydri-7, there's a sentient fungus that mimics anything it thinks is threatening it. I've seen it. It's spooky. It became *me*. I was standing there, staring at myself, a living breathing duplicate. But again," she pointed out, "completely harmless."

"Granted," Kregan said. "But I was out there, we encountered nothing, threatened nothing."

"How can you be so sure?" Pach asked him. "Our presence might have been a threat."

But Tsumada just shook his head. "Bullshit," he said. "If something's afraid, it might mimic to scare a predator off…but do you know of anything that *joins* up with the predators to save itself? Shit, I'm just a navigator. I'll admit that. I went out on the survey because I was goddamn bored. But if you ask me, this thing was trying to be us so it could get *amongst* us."

"That's paranoid thinking," Pach said. "Just because we encounter a new Unknown Lifeform, it doesn't mean said ULF is a predator."

"Galaxy's full of fucking predators," Tsumada put in.

Kregen nodded coolly. "Surely. If there is one universal constant back on Earth, the Colonies, and out in the most far-flung worlds, it's that life exists by feeding off other life."

Orhane listened, absorbing it all. They all made interesting points and gave him more angles to consider. With all the talk of predators, it made him think of a few of his own. There was a supposedly dead, frozen world called Karnek orbiting Alpha Arietes. A world of perpetual dark and cold. It was home to an invisible creature, a predatory flux of radioactive plasma. It fed off the energy fields of other life-forms. And that in itself sounded quite antiseptic and bloodless until you discovered *how* it lured its prey. It could replicate human voices perfectly and would call out to you in the voice of a friend or crewmember, drawing you in and assimilating your atomic field.

Was that the sort of thing they were dealing with here? He had a feeling in the pit of his belly that whatever this was, it was certainly not a good thing. He agreed with Tsumada: it had mimicked a crewmember to get amongst them. And there was only one reason it would do that.

"I don't know about the rest of you," Huckstep piped up, "but I say we arm ourselves and hunt this sumbitch down."

Before anyone could disagree with that, Orhane told them, at that very moment, Dahl was making a security sweep of the ship. "If it's here, the scan will find it."

"If it's *alive*," Tsumada said. "Looks kinda like a ghost to me."

"It's not a ghost," Pach said.

But Kregen and the others were not as willing to dismiss that. Not just yet. Orhane had them tell him about the survey, if anything unusual had happened.

"Not a thing," Pach said. "We didn't even find a stray fossil."

"There was that blip on your scope," Weise reminded her. "Remember? In that cave…"

Pach remembered, relating it to Orhane. Just a momentary blip and then it was gone. The portable bioscope was an impressive piece of engineering. It could detect things as minute as a bacterium in the soil. It scanned not only for life processes—respiration, circulation, electrical fields associated with living things—but for organic molecules, mere biophysical reactions. It could even detect inert fossilized organic matter. But it wasn't perfect, she pointed out. Sometimes it would blip, finding certain organic chemicals in close proximity, but then mere seconds later, correct itself with a second scan, realizing it was in error and that the components were inorganic, unorganized. Atmospheric conditions, environmental factors, residual radiations could confuse it…at least for a moment or two.

Orhane let out a deep breath. "Well, this time I don't think it was confused."

Weise told him that the cave was a low natural tunnel and it was there the bioscope had blipped, thinking it had picked up something.

"Yeah," Tsumada said. "It was too tight in there…we couldn't go very far."

Orhane looked at all of them. Gone were the usual insults and wisecracks. They were a very somber group, very far from home. Whatever happened or didn't happen, it would be up to them. It would take six months for help to arrive and everyone knew it.

"Now, granted," Orhane said, "I'm not a scientist. But is this feasible? There was a lifeform in there. It saw you people coming, waited, then you scanned it and it immediately cloaked itself so you wouldn't know it was there?"

"That's a little fantastic," Pach said.

"Maybe. But is it possible?"

"Why not?" Kregen said.

And on that note, all hell broke loose.

6

The corridors were echoing now with the whine of the alarm siren, its red hazard lights flashing. Huckstep raced off to his engines, certain that someone or something had gotten at his antimatter pods. Everyone else came running out of the conference room and met Dahl running up with a pulser in hand.

"Jesus Christ," he said. "It's Zerecki...she's dead."

They followed him up the companionway to a garbage disposal chute. Zerecki, a maintenance tech, was hanging out of the chute, upside down. She was white as plaster, oddly shrunken and compressed looking.

Pach checked her over. Her flesh was like ice.

"Well?" Orhane said.

She swallowed. "I'm guessing...but I think the blood's been drained out of her."

And she was right. Zerecki had been bled white.

7

But the action didn't end there.

Things were just heating up.

They had just gotten Zerecki bagged up when Huckstep came on the intercom, telling everyone to get up to the infirmary. Weise was in there and she was out of her mind. If they didn't show in the next thirty seconds or so, he said he was going to burn the bitch down.

But Weise was standing there with the rest of them.

"I'm...I'm right here for chrissake," she stammered, a heavy apprehension behind her words. *What the hell is this?*

193

And Huckstep's voice came back, strained, "Then it must be your evil twin, Weise."

The group went down past the crew's quarters to the infirmary. The alarms were still ringing and none of it had served to rouse Captain Egan. His toothpicks absorbed all his time. That and degenerative mental illness. He seemed to be symbolic of what was happening aboard the *Taurus* now.

Huckstep was waiting for them with a pulser in his hand just outside the door. His face was sweaty, his eyes fixed and filled with terror. "In there," he managed. "In there…"

Orhane went in first, with Pach and Weise at his heels. Pach didn't want trouble, but she was incurably nosy. And Weise? She wanted to see what sort of freak her "evil twin" was. Something in her needed this.

What Orhane saw made something in him suck in tight, suck in and knot up. His heart was rattling like a garbage can lid. Blood was sprayed over the walls, the floor, loops and whorls of it spattered over medical equipment, diagnostic units, drug cabinets. Its stink in the air was raw and nauseating.

But Weise's twin was worse.

Her back to them, she slowly turned with an almost mechanical stiffness.

"Sonofabitch," Orhane said under his voice.

She was completely naked, her skin impossibly white and shiny like oiled rubber. It stood out in stark contrast to the blood smeared over her breasts, dripping from her chin in ribbons. It looked positively black next to her flesh. She had gotten into the blood cabinet, had managed to rip open no less than a dozen bags of hema-synth and right at that moment, she held one to her lips, sucking it dry with a revolting leeching sound like a child slurping the last drops of juice through a straw. She saw her visitors and walked slowly towards them, stepping on a vacuum-sealed bag of plasma that burst and splashed over the floor.

Orhane found that there was a pulser in his hand.

He did not honestly remember putting it there. He brought it up, let his thumb hover over the firing button. He tried to speak, but his voice felt thick in his throat like he was trying to speak through a clot of grease. "You…whatever you are, just stay there, just stay back…"

The Weise-thing paused, cocked its head like a puppy. But the effect was neither cute nor innocent. Strands of dark hair hung over her clown-white face in coils and corkscrews like mating snakes. And her eyes…black, depthless nebula flecked with silver. There were no pupils, just that shiny blackness. She/it made an angry hissing sound, stopped, then began to laugh with a hollow cackling that made goosebumps rise on the crew.

"Burn her," Huckstep said, his blood hot, a villager lusting for the death of the witch. For at that particular moment, he was not thinking right. Things like compassion and mercy had become abstract and indecipherable. He saw only the witch and in her, limitless sin and corruption.

"No, let's take her," Orhane said.

They began to circle around her, the stench of blood making more than one want to vomit. Orhane advanced slowly on her, Huckstep and Tsumada circled around behind her. Pach and Kregen came from either side. Weise stayed by the door, unable to move, and Dahl was in shock.

The Weise-thing cocked her head again, seemed almost amused. She grinned and a gray worm of a tongue flecked over her teeth. There was a necklace of blood at her throat, streamers hanging from her lips.

"Now," Orhane said.

They came at her and she was no longer amused by them. Her face pinched into a tight mask, lips pulled from teeth in a snarl. There was hatred in that face, but not human hatred. That was impotent next to this. This hate was ancient and alien, the sort of hatred born in bleak cosmos and blown in noxious rivers down black intergalactic gutters.

Orhane was on her first.

She seemed to draw him in, pretending she didn't notice his violation of her space, then she came at him with an amazing speed. Her fingers became hooks and her nails became razors. Before he could get a good hold on her, those fingers opened his face in a dozen, bleeding wounds. With a cry, he let go of her shoulder, covering his face. He slipped in the blood and went on his ass with a short scream. But it was hard to say if this was out of pain or surprise or just because of the *feel* of her. Because her flesh did not feel like flesh, but like a plastic membrane beneath which cords and bunched cables were writhing and snapping. It was feverish and hot, repulsive.

Pach and Kregen charged in, took hold of her and Tsumada did the same. She hissed and made slithering sounds, undulating like a worm in their grip, seeming positively boneless. Ropes of blood vomited from her mouth and Huckstep jumped in, cracking her over the head with a tension wrench from his tool belt. She folded up at their feet, swaying back and forth on her knees like a cobra in a charmer's basket.

Tsumada said simply, "Fuck this," and punted her head with his size twelve.

She fell face first into the gore and blood bags. She did not move.

Everyone just stood around her, panting and shaking.

8

Though the *Taurus* was designed primarily as a deep-space merchant freighter and a fast one at that, it was lightly armed and had two confinement cells. These could be used for quarantine or for violent offenders and in the case of the Weise-thing, both.

She had been in the cell for six hours now.

Six long hours.

She had woken after the third and sat up on the edge of the cot that was bolted to the wall. She had been sitting like that ever since— staring, still, silent.

Orhane and Pach decided to pay her a visit.

They both carried pulsers. When the security shield went down, they both stepped in there, but very carefully, keeping their distance and a clear field of fire.

"Move one inch, bitch," Pach promised her, "and we'll fry you."

The Weise-thing just stared at them with black, fathomless eyes. Her mouth was twisted into a crooked grin that was malevolent, totally evil.

"Who are you?" Orhane asked. "Better yet, *what* are you?"

She kept grinning, her diabolic face punched through with black, soulless eyes.

Pach was running a scan on her with the bioscope and coming up with nothing. As far as the scope was concerned, the only living things in that cell were herself and Orhane. The Weise-thing did not register on any setting. A nonentity. An enigma. It was the same thing Dahl had run up against when he scanned the entire *Taurus,* stem to stern. Only human life and all accounted for, but nothing else. Pach ran a few more scans, but it was hopeless. The scope told her that, *yes,* there was something sitting on the cot, but it was inert, inorganic.

Maybe Tsumada was right, maybe what they had here was a ghost, a shadow, a shade. Something that did not really exist at all. Just a wraith that drank blood. Pach thought these things, started thinking about viruses. Some of them were not necessarily organic in nature, only acting alive when they came in contact with living material. Maybe this thing was like that, an entity that could *react,* but not act.

"What do you want with us?" Orhane tried again. "Blood? Is that it? Do you need blood? We can get it for you…if that's what you need to survive. You don't have to kill for it. If you're intelligent, we can reach some sort of agreement."

He felt like he was wasting his time, but it was strictly SOP. Rules stated that every effort had to be made to communicate with a "highly-evolved, extraterrestrial intelligence." Even if it was a killer. And this thing was all that. An autopsy-scan had been performed on Zerecki and Pach's deduction was correct: she had been drained of blood. Her carotid artery had been opened by means unknown and her blood emptied. And quickly, according to the med-analyzer.

"Scope says she's not a living thing," Pach announced.

And that made the Weise-thing turn its gaze on her. Pach flinched at the ominous, glaring hatred she saw in those eyes. Was it even intelligent? She couldn't be sure. Its eyes were like those of a spider—predatory, flat, insectile, but completely lacking in anything associated with a higher order.

"Tell us why you are here, what you want," Orhane tried again.

The Weise-thing licked her lips, looked upon him like he was something to be eaten and began to laugh again. The sound of it went right up his spine. A mockery of laughter, but with no warmth or even sarcasm behind it. A machine would laugh like that.

Then the laughter stopped and the grin widened. And in a low, ragged voice, the Weise-thing said, *"I was hungry."*

And then she leaped.

She made it maybe a foot off the cot before Pach's pulser hummed, letting out a blue pulse of light that slammed into the creature and knocked it to the floor in a smoking mess.

"So much for that," Pach said, trying to be funny and failing miserably.

Orhane found his lungs, put some air into them. "Thanks," he said.

9

Huckstep rarely called it a day without one last pass through the Engine Control Room. Although the neuro-plex ran everything, he still liked to monitor its operations. It soothed his worrisome soul.

Tonight, though, he needed to get to his cabin.

In the back of his mind, it was a necessity. He couldn't put a finger on why exactly, but it had never seemed so important. He wasn't especially tired. More wired than anything with all that had been going on. He told himself he just needed a safe, quiet place where he could be alone for a bit and think things through.

It made perfect sense to him.

On deck #2, he cut down the corridor to his cabin and right away he began to feel funny inside. Physically, he was sort of light-headed and sluggish. *Rest,* he thought. *Boy, do I need some rest.* Psychologically, he felt done in. His mind was filled with memories of Earth and a subtle, deep-buried terror that he would never see it again.

Clump-clump-clump, went his boots down the corridor.

Strange, but the sound of them seemed very loud, echoing all around him and, more particularly, inside his head with a morphic, hypnotic sort of rhythm. As disturbed as he was by it, he was also comforted. It reminded him in some absurd way of his mother's heartbeat. *Clump-clump-clump.* Now why would he think something like that? And as he thought that, he remembered a beagle puppy he'd had as a kid. They used to put a clock next to the dog at night because it mimicked the heartbeat of its mother, comforting the animal.

Now wasn't that just a crazy thing to be thinking about?

At the end of the corridor, his head filled with fuzz and cobwebs, he just stood there, trying to make sense of things. Reality felt unreal, dreamlike. He began thinking of Weise. Not the monstrous creature that had imitated her, but the real Weise. Sometimes, he thought about her. He had a thing for her, though he would never have admitted it. Pach was beautiful and most of the men lusted after her, even though she made it abundantly clear that she had no interest in them. But women like that that bordered on perfection were cool and distant like faraway stars. They were untouchable. But Weise…she was the girl next door sort of pretty. Approachable. Like someone you had a crush on in the 10th grade that lingered there in your mind, a warm ember that would never completely go out.

She had dark hair and simmering dark eyes.

He'd always had a thing for women like that.

Standing before his cabin, his head whirling, a thought came to him that she was in his cabin, waiting for him. The idea made his heart skip in his chest and a cold terror rise from his belly. He had a mad, childlike urge to run away as fast as he could.

Then it was gone.

Weise, he thought. *In my room. Alone. Waiting for me.*

He pressed his hand to the identity pad and the door swished open. Almost mechanically, he stepped inside, feeling light and happy in his heart. Like a kid that had stepped into a fairy tale. A nightlight burned, but nothing else.

Weise waited there for him.

Her first name was Carolyn, he knew, but his tongue was numb and he couldn't seem to form the word. She was naked, her long legs splayed out, her small, perky breasts wanting to be touched.

She reached out a hand and he took it. Such a soft, lovely hand. Ice-cold, but wonderful in his own.

"Do you want to?" she asked him, her voice uncharacteristically husky. "I need you to make me feel unafraid."

His hands roamed her smooth flesh just as they had in his fantasies so many times. Her skin was so soft. He could feel the beat of her heart beneath his fingertips, the play of muscles. He could feel himself growing hard, wanting to be inside her, to feel her lips on his own. As he touched her breasts, exploring them, it suddenly occurred to him that her flesh was not smooth at all but sort of pebbly and that there were tube-like growths projecting from her body, dozens and dozens of them that suckered at his fingers like small, hungry mouths.

"Do you like me?" she said.

The tubes dripped a warm, oily slime that burned his fingers as she pressed herself closer, attaching herself to him. Somewhere during the process, he began to scream. But only for a moment as a scaly appendage sealed his lips shut. As the world went dark, he went limp in her arms as her many mouths sucked the blood from him.

10

The next morning, Orhane stood outside the morgue.

"Morgue" might have been a lofty title to describe a high-ceilinged stainless steel room with zero gravity and no life support, but that's what it was called. Most voyages, it was empty. But on this particular trip, it was starting to fill up. The bodies were stored in plastic shrouds that were wired to the ceiling. Zerecki was in there, revolving slowly in zero gravity. The remains of the Weise-thing were next to her. And this morning, Huckstep and Kregen had joined their ranks…both drained of blood.

And there lie the problem.

If the Weise-thing had not done it—and that seemed likely given the blast she had taken—then who or *what* had?

All Orhane knew for sure was that it was trouble.

Big trouble.

Paranoia was setting in and everyone was keeping a close eye on everyone else, wondering who was human and who was not. But a discreet bioscan of the occupants of the *Taurus* showed all to be perfectly normal, no deviations.

Then what had gotten to Hucktep and Kregen?

Orhane, saddled with just too much now, decided it was time to rouse Captain Egan from his slumber.

And in the morgue, the blackened corpse of the Weise-thing opened its remaining good eye.

11

Captain Egan listened to what his first officer had to say, but found very little of it to be of interest. An alien life-form was among them? Really? Where was his proof of such? A ghostly image on video was hardly concrete evidence in his way of thinking. And the Weise-thing? Interesting, he thought. Quite interesting. And the postmortem had shown what? Ah, that the body was filled with a black, glistening jelly. Again, interesting. But the neuro-plex insisted the jelly was not organic in nature? It was composed of no toxic substances, had normal radiation saturation levels? Why, it sounded quite harmless.

"Captain," Orhane said, trying to control a sudden urge to scatter his commanding officer's toothpicks to the four winds. To trash that silly collection of towers he was intently gluing together. "Captain. We've got three dead. They were drained of blood—"

"Vampire?" Egan seemed interested now. "Did you know, mister, that in seventeenth-century Europe there was a plague of vampirism? That village after village had countless residents simply 'pine-away', as they called it? Pale and sluggish, anemic even, they would die in their sleep. But once certain graves were opened—opened to reveal uncorrupt cadavers with staring eyes, mind you—and the traditional methods employed, these pestilential plagues vanished? Did you know that? And did you know that when stakes were pounded into these uncorrupted bodies, that they sprang to life inside their coffins, screaming and gushing with blood? Yes, they were swollen-up with blood, mister, *human* blood. Blood purloined by night when they left their graves…"

"Sir, that's superstition."

"Is it?" Egan chuckled. "How quickly we dispense with the testimony of learned men throughout history when it conflicts with our own tenuous world view. And though the majority of these vampiric victims were certainly peasants, those investigating these matters were surely not. Surgeons. Military officers. Clergymen. I wonder, I just wonder."

"Sir," Orhane tried again, "we need to concentrate on reality and not medieval folktales."

Egan grunted. "Do we? Do we indeed, mister? And who is to say that our medieval vampires were not extraterrestrial in origin to begin with?"

Orhane just stood there, feeling like the blood had been sucked out of him, too. Here he was on a starship under assault by an invidious alien entity and it was commanded by a lunatic.

"Sir, listen to me. I've given order to scrap the survey. I've had a course laid into the nearest sizeable colony."

"Yes, yes, a wise choice." Egan was methodically sharpening toothpicks now with a stencil knife. "And may I suggest, mister, the application of certain traditional methods?"

He offered Orhane a sharpened toothpick.

It was hopeless.

If he decides to take charge again, Orhane thought, *I'll have to relieve him of command. I'll have no choice. Because if he's in charge we'll be pounding stakes into corpses and hanging fucking garlic and wild roses from the bulkheads.*

Egan sharpened a few more toothpicks, then went back to working on his moat. "Was there anything else, mister?"

But Orhane just shook his head.

And kept shaking it as he waltzed out the door and into the comparative sanity of the ship.

12

The conference room again.

All hands but Captain Egan.

The tension was so thick in the air it was a palpable thing. The survivors—Pach, Weise, Tsumada, and Dahl—were listening to what First Officer Orhane had to say. Taking it in and down, one swallow at a time, and it was obvious from their faces that they didn't much care for the flavor of the day.

Dahl's fingers were trembling on the tabletop. "Oh, this is just beautiful. We've got something sucking people's blood and now Egan has finally wigged out all the way."

"Take it easy," Tsumada said in an almost fatherly tone.

"Yeah," Pach put in, "now would be a good time to act like a man, Dahl. Time to pull your mouth off mommy's tit."

"Quit running your mouth," Tsumada told her.

Weise listened to the exchange, but said nothing. There were brown half-moons under each eye, her corneas shot through with red. She kept licking her lips like she couldn't moisten them.

"As we speak," Orhane began, "we're pulling out of this asteroid belt. By this time tomorrow, we'll be out of this system and we can all bid 68 Ceti a fond farewell. Now, I don't know how this will affect what's been happening on board. Obviously, we have a hostile parasitic life-form—"

"Shit, you think so?" Dahl said, tittering nervously.

"—*and* how this entity will react to us leaving BX-66 is anyone's guess. Pach, Weise, and I have discussed this in some depth. The bottom line is, we don't know jack about this sucker…if you'll excuse that one. It's like nothing we've ever seen before. Alive, yes, but perhaps not in our sense of the word. It seems to be biological, physical in nature, but, again, of the sort that defies our science. But that does not mean there is anything supernatural here. It feeds on blood, so obviously it needs something in the blood, something to energize it, allow it to metabolize. So it must be alive, just not alive as we understand life."

Pach took the floor then. She told them of the post that was run on the Weise-thing, that black jelly the body was filled with. "The AI neuro-plex has in its memory, the molecular, biochemical, and physiological breakdowns of thousands and thousands of alien life-forms. This does not even come close to any of them. In fact, the plex is certain the jelly is not alive. Yet, *yet,* it did give us something, something that hints of life as we know it—cellular structure. The jelly inside the Weise-mimic's body was not multi-cellular, but held in stasis with a single membrane of unknown protein which hints at it being a single-celled organism. By our standards, primitive. Yet, obviously…functional."

"Can't be too primitive," Dahl said, "it's knocking the shit out of us. A blood-sucking amoeba."

Nobody paid much attention to that, so Pach went on.

She had a theory. Unproven, yes, based more on guesswork than any scientific method. But it seemed to work. "I think this creature is so utterly alien in design and intent, that its basal processes can even fool bioscans. Maybe that's its strength. Ultimate survivability. It may not even be from this galaxy. Imagine, just for a moment, a creature that can exist on an asteroid in zero gravity, zero atmosphere, withstand tremendous cold and pressure and lack of both. Then imagine a creature with these attributes that can alter its physical form at will, moving from the organic to inorganic as easily as you or I pass through a door." She let that lie for a moment, her blue eyes shining like icebergs. "When we were in that cave, all we saw were rocks. No jelly, no organic substance of any sort. But what if this creature *was* there, but we didn't see it and our instrumentation only detected it for a moment before it shifted shape."

Tsumada just sighed. "I'm not getting you."

"Okay, okay," she said. "What I'm hinting at here is a creature that encompasses, in its natural rhythms, the four states of matter—solid, liquid, gas, and plasma. It can shift between them as it sees fit. It can become organic or inorganic at will. The ultimate survivor."

Dahl's hands were really shaking now. "Yeah, but is it intelligent?"

Pach shrugged. "Maybe, maybe not. We often spend too much time classifying organisms by their intelligence. This may be a creature that has a tremendous potential for intelligence, but has no practical use for it. No use for technology, no use for organized systems of knowledge. Its entire universe would be itself. It could mimic intelligence just as it mimicked Weise's, but given its primitive structure it may very well be no smarter than a virus. For essentially, it's very much like one: The bridge between the living and non-living.

"Now, with all that in mind, it may be very highly evolved for its kind or have no use of natural selection whatsoever. Now, when it mimicked Weise, it appeared to be almost, well, *evil*. Unscientific, surely. But we all felt it. It got inside of us and we did not like it. But I don't believe for a second that it *is* evil. Just as our definitions of life don't apply here, nor do our cultural mores. It may know what scares us and uses it to its best advantage, but realistically, it's no more diabolical than a house spider. Just following its natural proclivities."

"Okay, since you already confused the shit out of me and scared me with this booger," Tsumada said, "where do you suppose the prick comes from?"

But Pach had no idea. "Its origins could be anywhere. It could be as old as this star system or come from another star completely, another galaxy even. Possibly Andromeda. Maybe that's why it does not conform to biology as we know it. I can't see time mattering to something of its kind. A million years could be a day to it. Who knows? Now, this asteroid belt we're in is the result of a disintegrated planet that broke up roughly eighty-million years ago. This thing could have been a native of the planet, the last of its kind."

"Or maybe it was *put* here," Dahl suggested. "Imprisoned here who knows how many centuries or millennia ago. Put here where it couldn't cause trouble."

"Then we came along," Weise said, smiling, finding humor in that.

Orhane sighed. "All this speculation is fine…but the bottom line is that we have a dead one in the morgue and obviously a living one on the prowl. Kregen and Huckstep didn't drain their own blood off."

Pach said, "We're probably dealing with only one. At least, right now. Just a guess, but it feels right. Just because we killed the Weise-shell, doesn't mean we killed *it*. It may be still around, wanting us to think it's dead, but very much alive in one form or another."

But what form was that? A drifting gas? A solid like the Weise-thing? A liquid pooling in the darkness? A jellied plasma? There seemed to be no good answers. But Pach suggested that it could be an energy field of some sort, the most advanced life form imaginable. If that was the case, leaving the asteroid belt might free them of it. It could no more pursue them than an electron could leave the charged orbit of its atom.

"Or it could be right here with us now," she finished by saying.

"What do you mean?" Dahl demanded.

"I guess…well, we should accept the possibility that one of us here may not be who or what they seem to be."

That hit like a bomb.

Everyone was looking at everyone else then, the paranoia seeping in their eyes like poison. Gradually, everyone seemed to inch away from who they were seated by.

Orhane had been waiting for something like that. "Settle down," he said. "That kind of thinking is dangerous."

"He's right," Pach said.

"Enough talking. Let's find that prick, burn it, dump what's left in a jar and let Pach and Weise sort it out," Tsumada suggested.

"And if we can't find it?" Weise asked.

He shrugged. "If it's alive, we can track it. And if it's alive, it'll show itself sooner or later, am I right?" He shrugged again. "If not, we put the ship into hyperspace, jump into the freezing tubes, and shut all life support down. That ought to kill it."

"Fuck that," Dahl said. "If you think I'm sleeping away frozen up like a steak while this bug-eyed monster roams the ship, defrosting us one at a time when it gets hungry, you got another thing coming. I mean, shit, if it can survive on that asteroid, it can survive hyperspace."

Orhane agreed. "Exactly. We're not about to jump into the tubes and hope this entity dies out in zero gravity and zero atmosphere. What we have here is an undocumented life-form, possibly intelligent and certainly dangerous. We have to find it and destroy it. We have no other choice, way I see it. We can't be bringing something like that back to an outpost. I think you all know what the penalty is for bringing in an undocumented organism of predatory or pathogenic nature to a populated area."

They all did. After the horrors of monstrosities ranging from alien plagues to flesh-eating insects, the courts became very specific about these things: life on a prison colony without parole, no exceptions.

"So, we better kill it before it kills us," Tsumada said, liking the idea.

Orhane and the others agreed. But he was bothered by Weise's state of mind. Though never terribly outgoing or bubbly, seeming very often like an appendage of Pach, she was obviously withdrawn.

"Weise," he said, "what's your opinion on this?"

She had been studying the tabletop, pale arms wrapped around herself. Now she looked up and began to giggle. Then she opened her mouth and that glistening black jelly began to pour out.

13

What happened next, happened fast.

People fell out of chairs, trying to find their feet and bring pulsers to bear, screaming and shouting. And Weise just sat there, the stuff pouring out of her like somebody had pulled a cork. It pulsed and sluiced and oozed, black jelly that glistened like wet steel. It came out of her mouth and nostrils, her ears and ass. It came in rivers and oceans, slithering ribbons, ropes, and tentacles. The jelly was very much alive, organized, and aware of its purpose. It immediately sought the chairs where the others had been. It flooded over the table and serpentine coils of it sought those who tried to escape.

And then Orhane opened up on it.

Pach and Tsumada did the same.

They hit it with spears of blue light that melted Weise and her slimy, seeking appendages into a bubbling, smoking flood of fire. But that was hardly enough. The pulsers hummed again and before they were done, the air was thick with a twisting, greasy smoke and there was nothing left of Weise and her inhabitant but flaking ashes. Even the chairs and table had been burned right down. The titanium-composite deck was pitted with holes.

Orhane in the lead, they stumbled out into the corridor.

"Where's Dahl?" he said.

"Ran off," Tsumada said, blowing air through his nostrils, trying to get the stink out of his head. "Saw him…saw him crawl out the doorway like his ass was on fire."

"Was he armed?"

"I think so."

They leaned up against the bulkhead, pulsers in hand. Each hoping the other was human.

Pach said, "Weise…she slept in my cabin last night. She seemed fine. She…seemed just fine."

"Maybe she was…*then*," Orhane said.

Tsumada seemed to recover first. He stood up. "We better find Dahl. In his state of mind, who knows what he'll do?"

14

Like it or not, they split up.

They had to.

There was no other way to canvas the *Taurus*. Five decks. Countless empty compartments. Storage bins. Maintenance shafts. While Tsumada and Orhane fanned out, Pach went up to the neuro-plex sphere to begin a comprehensive bioscan of the entire ship. It was the quickest way to find Dahl. She was also hoping, that if the entity was still aboard, that she might find *it*, too.

But Orhane found him first.

He was in the auxiliary control booth. The entire ship could be run from there and particularly if you had Dahl's knowledge of the ship's cybernetic brain and nerve pathways.

"Keep away from that door, Orhane," he said. "It's electrified. I don't want to kill you, but I will if I have to."

"C'mon, Dahl," Orhane said, weary beyond words. It had all been too much. The last thing he needed was this puerile nonsense. Way he saw it, there were only a few of them left now. And those few had to do the job, like it or not. "Dahl, listen to me, will you? I don't honestly have the time for this shit. Come on out of there, I won't bite you."

"So you say." He was silent for a few moments. "I just need some time, that's all. Then...yeah, sure, I'll open the door. But not until."

"C'mon, Dahl, you can trust me."

"Can I? I'm not sure I can trust anyone. How do I know who you really are?"

There was no way Orhane could argue with such logic; it was flawless, really, in its closed system of paranoia. He could beat his head against the wall, insist that he was the first officer, but what proof was there? What could he offer to break down Dahl's delusions? It was like arguing the existence of God, any god: pointless.

After about five minutes, Dahl said, "I know you're out there, Orhane. You're just hoping I'll open the door so you can infect me. Well, guess again." He was giggling now. "Oh, no. No, no, no, I know your game. I know what you're up to out there. You and those other creatures."

"We killed them, Dahl."

"Maybe. But to be certain, Chief, I'm going to be shutting off life support..."

15

Tsumada stood before the morgue door, pulser in hand.

The passage was shadowy, oddly dim. Almost as if there was something wrong with the air itself. Like some unknown gas that refused the penetration of light. He reached his hand out, thought for a moment he could feel it moving around his fingers, pebbly, grainy, as if it were filled with dust—

Thud.

He licked his lips. That sound...it had come from inside the morgue. Impossible. No atmosphere in there. Sound could not carry in a vacuum. But he kept hearing it, echoing through the corridors of his brain. And something told him that if he was two decks up, he would still hear it.

What're you gonna do about it?

There was the question. The whole damn ship was a morgue now and they were imprisoned in it. Like being trapped in a haunted house drifting through space.

He stood before the door, pressing his hand against the metal hatch. Cold, very cold. But was that just his imagination or something more? He peered through the glass port into the airlock, expecting to see the dead in there, reaching towards him.

But he saw only the empty airlock.

Sometimes your mind played tricks on you, he knew. Ask anybody who had been in the service as long as he had. Twenty years come next winter. That was a long time. A damn long time. Too many years spent on freighters, tankers, and deep-space rigs. Lonely outposts, desolate stations a thousand suns from good, green Earth. While other people fell in love, and had children, and built lives, he had been out in the great beyond, alone in the company of strangers, looking for something he could never find. Within and without him, some gargantuan emptiness that could not be filled, could not be—

Jesus Christ, what was that all about?

Like a dream, that's what. Tsumada was standing with his hands and face pressed up against the morgue door. He had shoved his pulser in his pocket and had no memory of doing so. He listened, waiting for more sounds. They were either gone or he'd been hearing them for so long now, his brain had shut them out. Like the sound of his own breathing. He did not hear it; but it was always there, always present.

Yes, yes, he was hearing sounds.

Something in the morgue was making noise.

Could not be, but was.

Thud, thud.

He went down the corridor, not really thinking any longer, just reacting. He pulled an e-suit out of a locker and slipped it on. Gloves, helmet. Then back to the morgue door. He opened it, stepped inside the airlock. The hatch slid shut behind him. He could feel the suit inflate, all those countless chambers expanding, pressurizing as the atmosphere in the airlock was sucked away.

There was another window in the inner hatch looking into
the morgue compartment. Fingers of frost had settled around its
edges. Through his plastic helmet bubble, Tsumada could see the
bodies in there drifting in plastic cocoons. The green light came on,
depressurization complete, and he stepped in.

There was no gravity.

He took a step and bounded two feet into the air, spinning around
like a top, crashing through the body bags which were scattered like
bowling pins. He thumped into the wall, got his bearings, propelled
himself amongst the bags again. They were vacuum sealed, made of
some transparent plastic alloy that was clouded with ice crystals. The
bodies within were just blurry forms, freeze-dried embryos locked in
vinyl placentas.

Tsumada clung to one wall like a spider, watching the bags.

They were tethered to the ceiling above with static lines. They
floated vertically, frozen faces pressed against synthetic shrouds, hands
clutched over bosoms.

Mentally then, he counted them…Zerecki, Kregen, Huckstep,
the Weise-thing. Yes, four of them. Should have been five, but Weise
herself had been burned to ash. Unless that was just a duplicate body
they had burned and her actual body was somewhere else…but did it
honestly matter?

What the hell are you doing in here?

He honestly did not know, yet he did not question his motives. He
had come for a reason and even though his thinking was cloudy now,
the reason had been a valid one. Twenty years in the service made
you careful, made you act instantly on impulse. And your impulses,
sharpened by experience, were invariably right.

Tsumada waited there against the wall.

God, how strangely murky it was in here. Like the corridor, but
worse. The shadows thrown by the floating bags seemed to move of
their own volition. They crept along the walls, bloated and grotesque,
somehow reptilian in their undulations.

Just do what you came to do, get it over with.

Yes, that was what had to be done. Gradually, he let himself drift
upwards to the suspended bags, feeling their mass and motion through
his gloved fingertips.

That sound...it had come from in here. Which meant...which meant that one of them, one of the dead ones, had made it. It made perfect sense, didn't it? Hanging up there like a fly caught in a dark web, he began to root through the bags, the name tags on them. Kregen, Zerecki. Yes, Huckstep...and one with a blank tag.

The Weise-thing.

The suit gloves were not meant for fine manipulation, so it took some doing to unfasten the catch on the body bag, yank the zipper down. Beyond the helmet's plastic bubble, Tsumada's face was pinched and sweaty, his eyes bulging with madness.

Something coiled in his belly.

The Weise-thing was in worse shape than he had imagined. The left side of its face was cadaverous, shrunken, but looked more or less like Weise, but a Weise sculpted from white wax. But the right side... oh my Christ...blasted right down to the charred skull beneath. No eye there, just a blackened cavity, the nose melted into a skeletal draw, teeth jutting like fangs.

But it was the eye on the left side that drew him.

It was wide and shining and very much alive.

Tsumada hovered there as the corpse reached out for him. He did not even flinch as that face—half-flesh and half-skull—swam out at him with a hideous appetite, lips suckering to the bubble of his helmet.

16

Egan had suspected the course events would take.

As the *Taurus* pushed through the cold ether of the Omicron Ceti system making for the outer reaches, he set aside his toothpicks. He had assembled a collection of oak posts leftover from a previous voyage and had sharpened them now into stakes.

He knew how to handle problems like this.

Perhaps the others did not, but he did. Being a student of history, it was the first thing that occurred to him. The posts were about four feet long with a diameter slightly greater than that of a broomstick. A good stout wood that would handle the job expertly.

Gathering his weapons, Egan went vampire hunting.

17

Pach had not slept since any of it began.

Her eyes were veined with red, set in sallow pockets. Her hands shook and she had been hallucinating freely since Weise had burst her skin. She had gone up to the neuro-plex sphere to make a bioscan of the ship…but then had fled in terror. She was a tough, confident woman by anyone's standards, but even she could only take so much. When she heard the voices of Kregen and Zerecki calling to her from the loudspeaker, that was enough.

She had been holed up in her cabin since.

About a half hour ago, the scratching began.

She was certain it existed only in her head. But as it went on and on, sounding like the tines of a fork drawn against the hatch, she began to get angry.

She keyed the door lock, opened it.

Then, with pulser in hand, she waited.

Weise came in, naked and white as cream, save for the right side of her face, neck, and upper torso which had been blasted to the bone. She was a living horror. Her hands were held out before her, fingers scratching the air like bloodless sticks.

"What the hell do you want?" Pach said, her voice breaking into sobs, her heart feeling like a brick in her chest. *"Oh, please, dear God, what do you want?"*

Weise moved forward, her gaping grin seeming to split her face right open. Black, viscid drool hung from her mouth.

"We're all sisters under the skin," she said.

Pach felt the pulser drop from her fingers as she began to scream.

18

Orhane got into auxiliary control, but it took some time.

He had to go up a maintenance shaft and short out the power. When he was done with that, he went into the control room and the first thing he found was Dahl's body. Shriveled, cold, throat punctured by a single wound. He was very dead and had been dead for some time.

Orhane, who had seen his share of corpses, figured Dahl had been dead at least three hours. But he had talked to him through the door less than an hour before.

Dear God, what…what was it that I was talking to?

Frantically, he checked the life support controls. They were still operating. He went over to the com counsel, punched up the ship's loudspeaker.

"Pach? Tsumada?" he cried. "Goddammit, if you're on board, answer me, answer me—"

"They're all gone," a voice behind him said.

Orhane twisted around, his heart lodged in his throat. *Egan.* Captain Egan was standing there. He had a sharpened wooden pole in his hands. He saw Orhane's pulser, but did not seem impressed or intimidated.

"Come with me," was all he would say. "Help me with him."

Together, they carried Dahl's body away.

Orhane had to suppress a mad desire to break out in manic laughter. Egan was armed with pulsers and wooden stakes, a 22nd Century vampire hunter. He was dressed in a freshly-starched uniform, his thinning hair slicked back, his little beard immaculately trimmed. Was there nothing that could move this man?

Down on the lower level, deck #1, which was generally used for storage and maintenance, Egan led him to the morgue. He opened the hatch and they deposited Dahl's body next to Pach's.

"Tsumada?" Orhane asked.

"Already in cold storage."

Orhane could see the other bodies in there, zipped in their bags. A body in an e-suit drifted amongst them. He stared through the frosted uniglass, everything in him melting, running, coagulating in the wrong places. He had always been a man who knew how to keep his head, but right then it felt like a balloon that might float away and pop.

Egan led him out of the airlock.

Once the outer hatch was closed, the airlock depressurized and the inner hatch to the morgue opened. Dahl and Pach floated out into the morgue.

"The Weise-copy is still in the ship," Egan said, almost too calmly, "let's go tend to her."

19

They found her in a storage bin in the galley.

She lay in the cool darkness, jerking slightly as the light hit her. Egan pressed the tip of his stake to her chest. "Did you know," he said, "that the original purpose of the stake through the chest was not so much to puncture the heart, but to pin the offending corpse in its grave so it could not prowl about?"

Orhane, pulser in hand, tried to answer that, but his voice, along with his spit, had simply evaporated. His mouth was filled with dust and it seemed to be trickling down from that wide, bleak emptiness that was his mind.

The Weise-thing appeared oddly synthetic under the unflattering scrutiny of artificial lights. She lay stiffly, arms at her sides, looking strangely like an old-time window dummy, something pressed out of plastic and wax, painted up to represent a woman, but missing the mark by light-years. The left side of her face looked peaceful—lips pressed closed, eye shut; but the right side…the pulser had eaten away the meat and tissue, left a grinning skull in its place.

"I'll pin her," Egan said, "and you burn her. Simple."

But it was not simple.

Orhane expected her to wake at any moment and vomit black goo all over them, but she did nothing. She was a simulacrum, a mannequin. Egan, sucking in a sharp breath, brought the stake down with amazing strength. The tip sank right through the creature's chest like she was made of putty…and suddenly she was writhing and thrashing and that black jelly was filling the bin.

Egan stepped back and Orhane incinerated what was in the bin and most of the bin itself. Within seconds, there was nothing left but ash and soot and clouds of acrid smoke.

"That's how it's done," Egan said, washing his hands at the sink.

20

Egan and Orhane suited up and went into the morgue compartment. They unhooked the body bags from their static lines. It didn't take long. Once that was done, they went through the airlock back into the corridor. Egan then pressurized the morgue compartment and blew the outer hatch in the ship's hull. The bodies were sucked out into space. But the worst thing was that they were alive in there, clawing at the airlock, wanting in.

Orhane saw it and wanted to scream. Because they were out there and he could *feel* them. Feel their cold, alien minds seeking out his own like cancer cells reaching out to healthy ones. They were at the portholes now, pallid, grinning faces watching him, mouthing his name. Pach wanted him to—

"Don't look at them, you fool," Egan said, closing all the portholes.

Then they were gone.

"What now?" Orhane said.

Egan looked at him, shrugged. "Now we wait and see what transpires. Hopefully the infection has been eradicated…but who can say? We just wait…wait and see what happens."

He led them back to the galley. It was important that they eat, he said. Now was not a time for them to become weak from the lack of food. They needed their strength more than ever.

"I'm not hungry," Orhane told him. How in the hell could he have an appetite after what they'd been through?

Egan eyed him sternly. "You'll eat nonetheless, my boy. Consider that an order. We must maintain our vigilance and in order to do that, we must be well nourished." He served him a plate of reconstituted food—meat loaf, potatoes, green beans. "Eat up now. It's the best we can do."

Orhane set his pulser on the table and chewed a rubbery green bean. With closed eyes, it was hard to differentiate between what was on his plate save for the texture. When he looked up, Egan was watching him.

"Are you going to eat, Captain?"

Egan's eyes did not blink. "I supped well earlier. I rarely miss a meal, regardless of the situation." He smiled thinly. "How I wish I could offer you a nice grilled steak, rare. Nothing like red meat to build up the blood."

As Orhane contemplated the significance of that, Egan took his pulser.

"What are you doing?"

"Charging it, my boy. We must be ready at all times."

It took about ten minutes and Orhane waited, staring at the food on his plate, thinking about Egan. He had no relationship with him. Nobody onboard did. The captain was a loner. He was weird. With a trickle of fear in his belly, he wondered if he was something more than that.

Egan gave him his pulser back. "Now, I believe we are ready for the final act."

At that moment, an alarm began to shrill. Both of them knew what it meant—life support had failed. It was the sound no one on the ship ever wanted to hear.

"Quick!" Egan said, pushing him toward the galley door. "Get your suit on! Something's happening here!"

"But you—"

"Don't worry about me, mister! Get your suit on!"

Orhane dashed out into the corridor, the alarm nearly deafening out there. There was an emergency locker at the end. He could already feel the air getting thin and the artificial gravity growing weaker. He had less than two minutes and he knew it.

21

Egan, even in the most desperate of situations, refused to be rattled. He had unfortunately been in this situation before and had survived it with a cool head. So while Orhane dashed away to the emergency locker, he calmly took the access ladder up to the next deck and strolled to his cabin.

By design, auxiliary control, engineering, and the captain's cabin would be the last places to lose life support and pressure. He climbed into his suit which uplinked with the chip in his arm and sealed him inside it, instantly pressurizing.

The question now became *why* were they experiencing a systems failure and why had the neuro-plex not tipped them off to the possibility beforehand? It made no sense. The only possibility, as he saw it, was that someone had activated the command override. The only people who could access that via their chips were the captain, the chief engineer...and the first officer.

Standing there in his suit, contemplating this, Egan felt the gravity cease. He floated gradually upwards. Well now, it seemed too coincidental for all this to be happening at such a time, which meant somebody had rigged it.

That someone, of course, had to be Orhane.

He must have done it before Egan had found him in aux control. It was an access site. Logic would dictate that the first officer was no longer human, that he had engineered this entire scenario so he could feed on Egan.

The captain did not want to believe this—and particularly because Orhane had seemed so human, so fragile and scared and at his wit's end. But, then, as he'd heard, so had Weise.

Chameleons, Egan thought. *That's what these creatures are and what they use as their primary strength. Of course, Orhane had seemed human. It was a feeding mechanism of the vampiric aliens.*

The important thing was that he had gotten away from him. After the alarm began, he knew it had been rigged and Orhane was the only one who could conceivably have done it, so he sent him to the emergency locker while he made his escape.

Egan felt better, more sure of himself. Now that he'd had a few minutes to sort things out, he could move carefully onto the next step: the eradication of the first officer.

22

The lights went out.

The *Taurus* was plunged into the eternal, fathomless blackness of buried coffins and ancient tombs, shrouded in the sort of darkness that exists beyond the realm of the known universe.

It was not by accident.

Orhane did not know much about the aliens, but he was certain they had come from a place like this—a place of perpetual, endless night where light as such did not exist.

Now they had the advantage.

Now they would come for him.

Floating up the corridor in his e-suit, his terror spiked. *Dammit.* Where the hell was Egan? One system after another was failing and the captain was either dead or cowering in his suit somewhere.

Or he was one of them all along.

Now the emergency system kicked in. The corridor strobed with red warning lights. It only made things worse, creating wild blood-colored shadows that jumped and slid around him. He was in danger as he'd never been before. There was only one thing to do and that was to reach aux control or the neuro-plex sphere. From either location, he could sort this out. Maybe get some light and gravity going at the very least.

Like a swimmer in a thrashing blood sea, he pulled himself along the wall, avoiding the drifting debris, everything from dishes and tools to coffee cups and pressure helmets. Things brushed against him, scraping along the outside of his suit. A half-eaten sandwich bumped into his helmet bubble. A drifting bat-like thing spread its wings and he cringed until he realized it was a bra of all things. He giggled madly at the very idea of a bra in the weightlessness.

Pach's, he thought with demented childlike glee. *How long we all fantasized about seeing her out of it and now it's the last thing in the world I would ever want.*

He had to concentrate. He knew *they* were out there and that even now they were seeking him out. They could mess with your head. He knew that very well. He had to keep on guard. The corridor ended and cut to the left. The access hatch that would bring him to the upper decks was just ahead.

In the flashing red lights, he could see something moving in his direction, sort of sliding along, skating, undulating like a paramecium on a microscope slide.

He brought up the pulser.

This wasn't stray debris. It was large and seemed to be growing larger, spreading out. It was a huge shroud-like expanse of glistening black jelly which seemed to be formed of a matrix of shivering eye-like bubbles. It was going to absorb him like an amoeba, fold itself around him and dissolve his suit, vacuum the blood right out of his asphyxiating corpse.

He drifted towards it.

It slithered in his direction.

He blinked and it wasn't jelly but something like a multiplying swarm of termites…dear God, thousands of them winging and flying and breaking free of a central buzzing, writhing mass. Just beneath it, he caught glimpses of Pach's pallid face, mouth yawning open to reveal long scarlet teeth.

As cool sweat flooded his body, plastering his hair to his head, he cried out, *"No! I know what you're doing! You're not real! Not real!"*

It was a much needed, refreshing slap in the face and he now saw what was really down there—a floating plastic mortuary bag. It was torn and frayed, streamers of it drifting around like pseudopods. A billowing vinyl ghost with a creeping shape inside it like a fetus in an amniotic sac. In the flashing red light, it resembled a ruptured bag of blood.

An incapacitating fear held him in an uneasy stasis. He needed to get away from it, but at the same time, his body would not obey. He felt numb and useless as he was drawn slowly, inexorably towards the monstrosity that would leech his life away.

The pulser, a weak voice in the back of his head told him. *Use the fucking pulser.*

The zipper of the bag was opening as if drawn down by an unseen hand. He caught a glimpse of a face like a mask of yellow bone and a single gleaming eye like a black scarab. Now something emerged. It looked to be a hand at first, but now he saw it was some weird, alien appendage, a limb segmented like a worm. There were three gray-black talons at the end of it, chitinous and deadly-looking, and stretched between them, a web of flesh with an eye-like orb at its center.

With a cry inside his helmet, he fired the pulser at the bag. Nothing. The pulser wasn't working. He tried again. Still nothing. He thumbed the reset—a tiny light blinked off and on. Its battery was drained.

Egan…that sonfabitch. He set me up.

The mortuary bag ghosted closer and closer. In his head, he heard a low droning sound. It was machinelike, thrumming inside his skull and he knew it was the horror in the bag trying to make contact with him, trying to open up a pathway. And when it did, it would lull him into some mindless fantasy while it fed on him.

He screamed, going hysterical, fighting and thrashing. The thing was already breaking him with fear.

He had to act, he had to do something—

There. Right there.

The door to Biolab was just down the way. He surged forward, not fighting against zero gravity, but using it, propelling himself away from the wall. He reached the door and the bag was barely ten feet away. He slid through it and closed the hatch.

Now it was outside.

In a few seconds, it would find its way in.

Orhane drifted amongst the lab equipment. There had to be something he could fight it with. In the back of his mind, he knew there was…if only he could think of it.

23

The moment was now, Egan knew. He either took decisive action and took back the ship from the vampires or he surrendered. And he would not do that. The *Taurus* was his ship, his command, his everything. It was his very soul and he refused to surrender it to the undead.

He tried the helmet com again. He was getting nothing but a very active, buzzing sort of static. It could have been simple interference… then again, perhaps it was something his first officer had arranged. But that would end soon.

"Mister Orhane," he said over the com. "I know what you are and I shall destroy you. I am Van Helsing and you are my Dracula."

He didn't know if it was heard or not. But if it was, then Orhane would know that he was proceeding without fear or hesitation. Psychological warfare, nothing more.

Like his first officer, Egan was proceeding up toward aux control and the neuro-plex sphere. There he would take back the ship. If he could reach it in time, he had a plan that even the vampires would not guess at. A very dangerous, yet necessary plan.

Swimming in zero gravity, he nudged floating objects out of his way. As luck would have it, one of them was one of his stakes. He seized it and secured it to the grav belt of the suit.

The access ladder.

He moved up it clumsily in his e-suit, bumping his way up and up until he reached the next deck. As he emerged, he saw movement in the blinking crimson glare of the emergency lights. It was quick, furtive, something sinuous and dead black oozing forth like a ghost from the broken turret of a haunted house. It was there and then it was gone.

Although fear gnawed at his belly, Egan would not let it take control. It was important that he own it rather than the other way around. *Drawing me in, are you? Well then, let us meet on the field of battle.* He moved cautiously down the corridor, the flashing light reflecting off his helmet bubble like fire. Exhibiting a new found grace in his suit, he tracked the shape to the only place it could have gone: the infirmary.

Okay then.

The door slid open and then shut behind him. It was dark in there, a suffocating blackness swallowing him as if he was a mouse sliding down the throat of a snake. His helmet lights panned the room, making long-limbed shadows hop along the walls like monstrous toads. Beads of sweat rolling down his face, an oily stink of fear dripping from his pores, he took it all in the way Van Helsing must have taken in the vaults of Dracula's castle—the banks of med-analyzers, the sterile instrument cases, the steel-faced drug cabinet, the surgical drone hanging from the ceiling like a black ten-legged spider, and, yes, the blood cabinet whose door was still mangled from the Weise-thing wrenching it free with what seemed supernatural strength. All the hema-synth gone now. That which the Weise-thing did not empty, the other creatures had since.

Leeches, Egan thought. *Nothing but disgusting leeches.*

With zero-gravity, the infirmary was like the belly of a sunken ship. But instead of rotting things and silt floating, there were plastic cups, surgical instruments, air hypos and sterile-skin bandages, jars and cotton balls and the drifting sheets from the beds transformed now into eerie ghost shapes.

In the back of his mind, there was a growing droning sort of noise that initially sounded like a distant old-fashioned airplane. But as it rose in volume, he realized it was not his imagination and not something from the ship, which meant it was one of them trying to get into his head. That insectile droning was a voice. An alien voice.

He felt his will weaken.

His insides run hot.

Fight it! Fight it! he told himself.

Now amongst the floating odds and ends, he saw what looked like immense bats flapping in his direction. Hairless, fetal things with puckering, bloodsucking mouths. His eyes burned as if they were full of saltwater. The droning in his head took form, becoming corporeal in his mind. It was a mutiny of licking pink tongues slavering his thoughts and lapping at the walls of his consciousness. He had a perfectly deranged and self-destructive desire to remove his helmet so the bats that circled him like moths around a lamp could fix their hungry mouths to his throat.

He heard his voice make a groaning noise—the sound of agony *and* the sound of pleasure.

He would not allow it.

Aiming the pulser with a shaking hand, he pressed the firing button. One of the bats disintegrated, blazing up into a flaming mass that crashed to the deck like a blazing meteorite. It was purely subjective and he knew it: there was no oxygen for fire and no gravity.

Now his helmet echoed with the whispering voices of Pach and Weise, offering him enticing, forbidding perversions and obscenities if he would only submit.

The bats were gone and he saw a form suspended not ten feet away like a phantom. It was Dahl, but a Dahl sculpted from porcelain-white flesh, his eyes huge and glistening black, his mouth like the sucker of a leech, pulsating open and closed.

It was intended to terrify him and it did. But not so much that he did not fire the pulser at its reality or lack thereof. The blue sword-beam of the weapon sliced Dahl in half like a guillotine blade and he screamed like a witch being burned at the stake. Dirty light and ribbons of wriggling sentient plasma leaked from him, becoming tentacles that reached out for Egan. And then his carcass seemed to turn itself inside-out and black jelly gushed from him in a fluidic protoplasmic mass.

Egan brought his pulser to fire again but a plastic bottle bumped into his viewshield and then a sheet from one of the beds blew in his direction from the motion of the entity.

He fired regardless, a blue pencil-beam of light burning a path through the debris and vaporizing a pseudopod of the alien.

But by then, it was on him.

He screamed in his helmet as he fumbled the pulser and it spun from his hand. The creature opened like a black orchid and he saw its black guts erupt with a pink ectoplasmic mass, a writhing and bloated form of sucking tubes and three-fingered talons that left scratches on his helmet bubble.

I'm seeing it! I'm really seeing it! an elated voice cried out in his mind. *This is it…this is what it really looks like! This is the nature of our beast…*

But there was little to no satisfaction in revelation as the creature seemed to engulf him, winding him up in itself as a spider winds up a fly in silk. Covering him in a webby, viscid mass that crawled all over his suit, seeking a point of entry, wriggling and slithering, an insatiable living hunger that would not be denied. It constricted him like a python, bringing its enormous crushing strength to bear, trying to squeeze him from the pressure suit like toothpaste from a tube. The suit began to overheat as its systems began to fail one after the other. Warnings of imminent catastrophic failure appeared on the inside of the view plate.

Egan wanted to fight, but it was pointless. His limbs were pressed against his body and it was like being encased in a steel cage. The pulsing, hungry mouths of the creature suckered at his helmet bubble, leaving dirty smears and ribbons of slime. He knew very well that they were secreting digestive enzymes that would eat through the suit and lay him bare.

Every inch of the suit was under attack. It was like being submerged in a pool of voracious piranha.

He had bare seconds left.

This was death and there was no escaping it. Being the pragmatic man that he was, he went limp in the suit. Fear was replaced by acceptance and terror by inevitability. Yes, he would die now, but he would observe every moment of it. Not a single nuance would be lost on him.

24

About the time Egan entered the infirmary, Orhane was living out his own little nightmare in Biolab. In the clutter of his racing mind, he knew there was an answer to his dilemma, but he could not think of what it was.

Outside, the alien was scratching at the door to get in. And, he knew, it would. Which meant, he either thought of what that cryptic solution was or he died right here. This ship became his tomb which floated in dead space for an eternity and he never would again see the blue seas of Earth, the rising purple mountains, or green valleys.

No, goddammit! Do not give in! Think! Think! Think!

The *Taurus* was a vacuum now and sound did not carry in a vacuum. It was an immutable law of basic physics, yet through his external mic he could hear the creature clawing to get in. Then he heard a voice: *"Orhane, oh Christ, oh God, please let me in! It's out here! Please don't let it get me!"*

Pach. He knew she was dead. He'd seen her remains in the morgue...yet, she stood outside the door and the desperation in her voice was heartbreaking. He heard the vulnerability in it, the weakness at her core. He knew this was what she really had been all the time—an unsure, sensitive woman in a beautiful form that had gotten her all the wrong kind of attention since she was a teenager. Maybe other women (or men) might see drop-dead good looks as a weapon to use, something to manipulate people with in their innate shallowness... but not Pach. She was uncomfortable with it and he had sensed that numerous times as she overcompensated by being tough and mouthy and superior.

The real Pach was scared.

Self-conscious. Insecure. Even timid by nature.

In death, the creature that had taken her overexposed what she really was—a frightened little girl. And Orhane's soul wept because even though it was a ruse, he recognized the ultimate truth behind Pach because he was exactly the same way. Their eyes had met many times and lingered because they were kindred spirits.

But now she was a monster.

As he thought that, fighting with himself not to open the door, he remembered something Egan had said. *And who is to say that our medieval vampires were not extraterrestrial in origin to begin with?* That was it. That was part of the answer and he knew it. Stop thinking of these creatures as ULFs, as extraterrestrial entities, and start thinking of them as *real* vampires. If Egan was right and Earthly vampires had indeed been alien beings in the first place, then the ancients had destroyed them with what the captain called "traditional methods."

Orhane thought of them now: bits of silly ephemera from movies two centuries old, Halloween stories from when he was a kid, bits and pieces of Stoker's *Dracula* that he'd read in college. Vampires could be killed with religious items. They could be staked. Burned. Decapitated. But there was something else, too.

A puddle of black jelly oozed beneath the door, forming a bulbous blob of midnight that expanded, coalesced, becoming Pach who stood completely naked before him. *The romantic/sexual angle. Remember: they use this purely as a way to get at your blood.* Oh, but God, she made his blood run hot. This was the Pach that lived in his sexual fantasies. The long legs. The smooth golden skin. The beautifully muscular thighs and hairless vulva. The full pointy breasts. And that face…oh, that face: the bee-stung lips and high cheekbones, the sky-blue eyes, and that crop of spiky, lustrous fire-red hair. How many times he had looked at her and thought, *nobody can be that perfect, that flawless, there's gotta be something wrong with her.* But, in the final analysis, there wasn't.

And maybe that was the baggage she carried. The baggage of perfect genes that made her feel small inside, not a human being, but an android, a pinup, a VR woman that lonely, horny men and women alike masturbated to.

All the while, as he thought this, he had been gradually pushing himself away from her, propelling himself backwards and now he bumped into one of the lab tables, the instruments of which floated around him.

As Pach strode forward as if the gravity were perfectly normal, he bounded over the lab table.

A vampire. Fight her like a vampire.

What was that other thing that killed them? It was there in the back of his head. Then he knew: *sunlight.* They could not tolerate sunlight. They would crumble in its rays. Which was fine, but where could he get sunlight?

Attached to a bracket on the wall was a silver cylinder with a fan-shaped cone and a crystalline bulb inside it. A UV light. It was high-intensity. Pach used it for sterilizing specimens, making sure no dangerous microbes were let loose on the ship.

No, it couldn't be that simple.

The real danger in sunlight was the UV radiation that the ozone layer of Earth and hundreds of other planets deflected. There were three types of UV light, he remembered Pach telling him—UVA, UVB, and UVC. The first two were of the sort that penetrated the Earth's atmosphere. In low doses, they gave you a tan, wiped out minor infections, and in higher doses, caused cell damage. The other type, UVC, was deflected. It was considered extreme UV and was a dangerous form of ionizing radiation. That's what the lamp used for sterilizing biological specimens and lab surfaces.

Yet…the Weise-thing and the others had been exposed to UV light in the ship. But, a filtered and harmless sort, not UVC.

Sunlight, sunlight, that's it, that's it!

Now Pach was closing in on him. He had seconds before she took him.

Already her beauty was fading as the true alien beneath was unleashed. Her body became rigid and bony, a grotesque alien skeletal system of rungs and hollows and spoking staffs jutting from underneath the rubbery yellow membrane of flesh. Her face was grinning and cadaverous, lips shriveling back from long, discolored teeth, eyes sunken into black congealed pits. The jelly began to seep from her like blood, sparkling and radiant, sending out coiling tendrils and feelers of the stuff. She burst open and the alien material spurted from her in jets, bits of her human anatomy—stray bones, a lock of red hair, a single blood-infused eyeball swollen to the size of a golf ball— orbited around her pustulant, palpitating mass like moons caught in the orbit of a toxic gas giant.

It moved at him in a rolling tide.

And as it did, it ruptured and the alien entity hid no more. It slithered free of the jelly like a great, squirming nightmare fetus. It was a bloated, pulsating pink sac with dozens and dozens of fleshy, breathing tubes projecting from it like the tentacles of a sea anemone. At the ends of each were slavering, slime-dripping mouths eager to suck him dry. It had three segmented limbs that thrashed in the vacuum, triple-clawed digits slashing and deadly.

As sweat poured from him and urine trickled down his leg, he grabbed the lamp, clicked it on, and turned the wide beam on the alien.

The view plate of his helmet immediately darkened to protect his eyes from the explosion of blinding light. In the dark depths of his mind, he heard Pach scream with agony and the alien make a squealing, trilling noise that erupted with a white-hot intensity. The monstrous wriggling sac not five feet from him went from pink to steel gray, shriveling and melting, its extended feeding tubes withering like tropical flowers in an arctic blast. It folded in on itself. It elongated. It became a sphere of bubbling, liquefying tissue that split open, trying to secrete an envelope of protective jelly that turned to steam as the creature cracked open, peeling and fragmenting. It became a massive, engorged, tumescent ovoid like a gigantic yolk-leaking egg…and then it exploded like a puffball.

The force of the eruption threw Orhane back against the wall. He bounced off of it and was propelled through the vacuum, swimming through the suspended storm of the creature's remains—jelly and streamers of tissue, beads of liquid and albumen-like discharge—and then he was at the door and through it.

The lamp in his hand, a new found confidence filling him, he moved down the corridor and up an access ladder to the next deck. As he emerged, he saw a flash of blue light in the distance.

Only a pulser made that kind of brilliant cobalt light.

The infirmary.

He reached the door and he saw one of the creatures, a throbbing pink mass. He turned the light on it and it died as the Pach-thing had, blackening and breaking apart, finally erupting in a swirling storm of goo.

Egan floated there in his suit.

"The light," he said. "UV light…good thinking."

Together, they moved towards the door. And as they did, Egan, gasping, told him his plan.

25

In the neuro-plex sphere, they overrode the programming that the Dahl-thing had no doubt put into the plex, suspending one system after another. The brain of the ship was the neuro-plex. It ran the *Taurus* as the autonomic nervous system runs the human body. The crew were there to merely to monitor systems. Once it was activated again, it took over, initiating artificial gravity and life support. In fifteen minutes, the ship was once again pressurized.

Egan used his private codes to supersede the plex's safety protocols and laid in a new course.

"Now they'll come for us," he said. "And that's exactly what we want. Hurry. We don't have much time."

Still in their suits, they followed the access ladders to the very top of the ship: the observation deck. It was positioned above the bridge in a huge dome: a wide, spacious area, a place where crew members could be alone and watch the stars, get away from peripherals and interfaces and the constant thrumming of the engines.

Orhane was not crazy about Egan's plan; yet, it made perfect sense. It was dangerous and even reckless. The battery on the UV lamp was at 50% and he knew it wouldn't be enough to destroy the others.

And as Egan had said, "We not only have to fear the crew members the aliens have taken, but the others that have spawned since."

For after all, there had been two of Weise. The original and the duplicate.

As terror gnawed away at Orhane with sharp little teeth, it began. They were outside the OB deck hatch, scratching and clawing to find their way in, calling out in not only the dead voices of Kregan, Huckstep, and Tsumada, but Pack and Dahl as well.

"Don't listen to them," Orhane warned. "They want you to let them in. But they must come to us. We need them all in here at once."

Now they were howling and shrieking, screaming with maniacal frenzy and starvation. They beat on the door violently. It was not a security hatch; it was not designed to withstand such an assault. Already it was groaning with metal fatigue, dents punched into its surface.

"Get ready," Egan said.

Orhane joined him at the other side of the room as the door fell in and the creatures entered the OB deck. Neither man did anything. They just waited for them to get close and away from the door so there could be no escape.

The walking dead came on in a raging, moaning storm-wind of cosmic dust, debris, and plumes of flickering yellow-green mist that filled the room in a cycling tempest. Their uniforms were ragged winding sheets blowing around them in ribbons and tatters. They edged forward with outstretched hands that were white, grasping claws. Grinning red mouths were filled with gray fangs. Black-red eyes peered from pallid faces, glowing like mercury lamps. To the very end, the aliens were the frightful wraiths and revenants that were spawned in the terror-filled catacombs of human minds.

"Hold your ground," Egan said.

The vampires spread out, walking appetites that could never be sated. They would suck each man dry, swim in lagoons of their blood, nourish themselves in dark, rich, red rivers of hemoglobin.

When they were in the center of the room, Egan pressed the button and the dome became transparent, the protective shutters sliding back and revealing the depths of space. Only there were no stars, no constellations, no black endless gulf of the void.

No, there was only the sun.

The immense blazing red-orange eyeball of Omicron Ceti-4, a red giant reaching its final stages of stellar evolution. A raging furnace of hydrogen and fused helium shooting out plumes of radioactive gas and superhot plasma. It filled the observation deck with a flickering luminosity the color of blood and with the shielding of the dome retracted, it flooded the room with high-intensity UVC radiation a hundred times as deadly as Pach's sterilizing lamp.

The effect was instantaneous.

The vampires were caught in its searing rays. The radiation saturation pinned them to the decks like insects speared by hot needles. UVC photons ionized them at a subatomic level, electrons breaking away from atoms as chemical bonds were disrupted. In essence, the very things that held the aliens together were destroyed.

The vampires spasmed and thumped wetly against the deck plating, breaking open with arcs of electrical energy and hissing clouds of phosphorescent gas. They poured out sizzling rivers of black jelly as their pink, sucking anatomies were exposed and incinerated. They screamed. They roared. They shrieked and droned and trilled, decaying, blackening, pissing gray sludge and noxious clouds of steam and smoke. One after the other, they burst into flames, throwing out showers of sparks and burnt remains as they were engulfed in hot blue flames that burned them into flaking heaps of ash.

And then it was over.

Orhane swore under his breath and fell to the floor, hyperventilating, his head spinning.

Egan stepped over to a smoldering heap of ashes that had been Huckstep, kicking it and scattering its carbonized ejecta.

"Now, this day, mister, we reconnect with our ancestors who fought these monsters in crypts and graveyards," he said, seemingly pleased with the idea. "Never did they suspect that the evil they fought had nothing to do with dark witchery and supernatural horror, but was an infestation of extraterrestrial parasites. Amazing, utterly amazing."

Orhane scrambled to his feet. "The ship! Jesus Christ, the ship!"

There was no time to be lost. The *Taurus* was racing toward the furnace of Omicron Ceti-4 at 30% of light velocity and already the plex had activated alarms of imminent destruction as the shielding of the ship began to fail.

A minute later, Egan and Orhane were in the neuro-plex sphere, overriding the captain's suicidal flight path. The ship veered off with less than three minutes to spare, firing off into the black icy depths of space.

26

Three weeks later, they were in the captain's cabin. Egan was content. He had completed the Tower of London. The 11th Century fortress of the British Empire had been skillfully rendered in toothpicks. The captain seemed more pleased by this than he had been by the destruction of the invasive life-form that had infested his ship. He gave Orhane a tour of his masterpiece—the white tower and Waterloo barracks, the royal chapel and Queen's house, the drawbridges and ramparts and rising towers.

"It's all here, mister, including the dungeons," Egan said, glowing with pride.

"Amazing, sir, absolutely amazing."